ECO-FREAKS

ENVIRONMENTALISM IS HAZARDOUS TO YOUR HEALTH!

JOHN BERLAU

NELSON CURRENT

A Subsidiary of Thomas Nelson, Inc.

Published in Nashville, Tennessee, by Nelson Current, a division of a wholly owned subsidiary (Nelson Communications, Inc.) of Thomas Nelson, Inc.

Nelson Current books may be purchased in bulk for educational, business, fundraising, or sales promotional use. For information, please e-mail SpecialMarkets@thomasnelson.com.

Library of Congress Cataloging-in-Publication Data

Berlau, John, 1971-
    Eco-freaks : Environmentalism is Hazardous to Your Health/John Berlau.
        p. cm.
    Includes bibliographical references and index.
    ISBN-13: 978-1-59555-067-5
    ISBN-10: 1-59555-067-4
    1. Environmentalism. 2. Deep ecology. 3. Environmental degradation—Political aspects. I. Title.
    GE195.B468 2006
    363.705—dc22

                                                                    2006029827

Printed in the United States of America
06 07 08 09 10 QW 5 4 3 2 1

Contents

To Manuel S. Nowick, my great-uncle, a great friend,
and a member of the Greatest Generation

I would also like to second a dedication made by the eminent
microbiologist Renè Dubos in his wonderful book,
The Wooing of Earth:

"To the billions of human beings
who, for thousands of years,
have transformed the surface of the Earth
and prepared it for civilization."

1

What I Learned about Environmentalism from Chuck D

Environmentalists have long admitted to using fear to arouse public action. Hollywood global-warming activist Laurie David, wife of *Seinfeld* co-creator and *Curb Your Enthusiasm* star Larry David, recently told the *New York Times* what an effective tool fear can be. A *New York Times* profile of David opened this way:

"'I am terrified,' Laurie David said between bites of her Cobb salad, avocados on the side. 'I'm terrified. I'm terrified. And fear is a great motivator.'"[1]

Like David, I'm also terrified.

You should be too.

But I'm not terrified about global warming or any of the alleged problems with technologies of the last two hundred years, such as the automobile or nuclear power.

Rather, my fear is more basic. What I fear is nature—or rather untrammeled nature, with little intervention by humans. I grew up in Kansas and know how beautiful a prairie sunset, with its reflection on the grass, can be. I often talked to my late grandfather about his memories of rural Colorado. He arrived there as a child from czarist Russia and was put to work on a dairy farm in an area that is now part of suburban Denver. He had some fond memories, even though the work was strenuous and often backbreaking. But my grandfather, and most likely your grandparents and great-grandparents, as well, had no illusions about Mother Nature being a kind force. Neither did people the world over for thousands of years before them. Neither should we.

In fact, our view today of nature as benign "is something of an aberration in human history," writes James Trefil, a professor of physics at

George Mason University in Fairfax, Virginia, and former "Ask Mr. Science" columnist for *USA Weekend* magazine. In his book *Human Nature*, Trefil notes that for most of history, "[a]ny natural event—a flood, a drought, a sudden influx of disease—could (and did) decimate human populations." Back then, Trefil observes, "nature was not a pleasant warm place, but a constant danger, a constant dark force in their lives. Only when nature was tamed and brought under control—in a garden, for example—could it be enjoyed."[2]

Most of those today longing to get back to "nature" have never really had to deal with it. More than nostalgia for old movies and music, the longing to go back to the "good old days" before technology is often felt by the young, rather than those who actually lived through that era. As Trefil writes, "So successful have we been at insulating ourselves from the harmful effects of the natural world that we have largely forgotten that they exist."[3]

And most members of the generations who did have to face more of the "natural world" are not at all like the grumpy old man character on *Saturday Night Live*, saying they had to slog through nature and they "liked it." They are most often grateful for the technologies that made their lives easier. That's why they invented them.

This point is illustrated by an unusual conversation that Ronald Reagan participated in, sometime around 1975. The conversation was with a group of young adults that included some of Reagan's own children, and the topic of discussion was the past. But in defending the past and the present, there seemed to be a reversal of roles.

"Strangely enough it wasn't old Dad who was nostalgic about the good old days and sour about today's world," Reagan later related in a radio commentary. It was the younger generation that was both nostalgic and pessimistic. "They almost seemed resentful toward me because I'd known that other world of yesterday, when life was simple and good with joy on every hand," he said.

So Reagan tried to set them straight about life being "exciting and good today, in truth better in most respects." He told them about walking in the snow to the outhouse in back of his home. And of the swarms of flies that his and the other outhouses—"of which there was one for every home and store and public building"—would bring to town every summer. As for pollution, he educated the young folks about the old coal furnaces that existed before electricity from centralized power plants and gas from pipelines were widespread. "[E]very chimney in town belched black smoke and soot," he recalled. Reagan also could have mentioned that before coal, burning large amounts of wood wasn't exactly good for the air, and it also meant the logging of lots of trees.

Reagan said he hoped the discussion would make his children's generation "feel good about the world they've inherited." At the end of the radio commentary relating the episode, the future president would quote University of Texas chemical engineering professor John J. McKetta as saying, "Perhaps the simple life was not so simple."[4]

If Reagan isn't your political cup of tea, here's what Franklin D. Roosevelt had to say forty years earlier about the "simple life" and unbridled nature. As he was dedicating the Hoover Dam in 1935 (it wasn't officially called Hoover yet, more on this in chapter 6), the father of the modern Democratic Party shed no tears over the loss of the natural Colorado River. On the contrary, FDR hailed the taming of a "turbulent, dangerous river" and bragged about "altering the geography of a whole region." The land along the river that existed before the dam was not, in FDR's view, a natural wonder. To him, it was "cactus-covered waste." And about the pre-dammed river, "Mr. Democrat" said bluntly that "the Colorado added little of value to the region this dam serves."[5]

Any politician talking as negatively about nature today as FDR did then would be dismissed as a shill for big oil!

The Hoover Dam would rise again in a spirited political discussion in the year 2005, thirty years after Reagan's radio commentary and seventy years after FDR's speech. This time the speaker would be a public figure somewhat different from the two presidents: hip-hop mogul

Chuck D. But like Reagan and FDR, he was talking about the need for humans to assert control over the ravages of nature.

It was mid-September, about two weeks after Hurricane Katrina had hit New Orleans. Chuck D and I, from different locations, were guests on Tucker Carlson's MSNBC show, *The Situation*. I was in the green room, listening to the show as I prepared for my own session. Chuck D came on first to talk about the conspiracy theories about levee failures that demagogues like Louis Farrakhan had been promoting. Chuck D was flirting with the theories, and Tucker was grilling him mercilessly. I was half-listening, agreeing 100 percent with Tucker, and thinking, "What nonsense."

Then Chuck D said something that made me do a double take. He told Tucker, "Look, if Hoover Dam could stop the raging Colorado River, I'm pretty sure that they could have come along with a strong enough levee system to stop Lake Pontchartrain."[6] This comment hit me upside the head and rearranged my perspective.

I had done research on how environmentalists had filed lawsuits delaying levee construction, and had written an article about it for *National Review Online*. In fact, that's what I was booked to talk to Tucker about. I had received more e-mails about this issue, including lots of hate mail, than any subject I had written about in the decade I had spent in journalism and public policy.

But Chuck D's remark about the Hoover sent me on a journey. I had never before realized the extent and consequences of what environmentalists had achieved in this country. Their success in stopping technological advances often reduces opportunities for the poor, and their accomplishments also threaten the very health and safety that the green movement claims to be promoting.

Before I heard Chuck D, I had never realized that the Hoover Dam was built to prevent the "raging" Colorado from flooding the region. I thought the Hoover was there just to provide power and water for cities like Las Vegas, and I didn't even know that the Colorado posed that big a danger of flooding. But in my research, I found that Chuck D was indeed correct. The Hoover Dam was primarily built for flood control and navigation, with hydroelectric power as an afterthought. Roosevelt even referred to the Colorado's flood-and-drought cycle in his dedication speech for the dam, noting how every spring, farmers "awaited with dread the coming of a flood."[7]

As you will see in chapter 6, there are prominent environmentalists who propose decommissioning all dams, including the Hoover, to let rivers go back to their natural flows. No way America would ever go for such an absurd idea, right? Don't be so sure. In the 1970s, environmentalists halted the building of the flood barrier that experts believed would have been best at stopping the surge of the Gulf of Mexico from entering Lake Pontchartrain. These giant floodgates were similar to flood protection devices being developed in the Netherlands, a large chunk of which is also below sea level and which is noted for its superior flood protection.

Even with all the incompetence and shenanigans of the levels of government involved, the project was ready to get off the ground and would have been completed were it not for a victorious lawsuit by the Environmental Defense Fund (now Environmental Defense) and the local group, Save Our Wetlands. And since everyone knew—since Hurricane Betsy devastated New Orleans in 1965—that the "big one" would come again, I could understand how it would almost seem like a conspiracy that adequate protection wasn't built there. This doesn't excuse Farrakhan and others who are trying to stir up hate, but it does offer a plausible reason why the conspiracy explanation seems to be so widely believed. And why the environmentalists' role must be pointed out in Katrina histories to show that racism and ill will were not the reasons for the flood-protection delays.

What happened to New Orleans, I began to realize, was the effect of the spread of "eco-imperialism" to the United States. The book *Eco-Imperialism* by Paul Driessen, a scholar at the free-market Atlas Economic Research Foundation, describes how the West's notions of "environmental correctness" cause death and devastation in third world countries that are prevented from developing their public-health systems.

For instance, the DDT bans and foreign-aid restrictions of the United States and Europe have resulted in millions dying in Africa from mosquito-borne malaria. The blocking of dams, which are protested by mostly Western activists, leaves millions without flood protection, electricity, and clean water. Driessen points out that when environmentalist pressure halted the Bujagali dam in Uganda, it left millions without "the 'luxury' of running water, or even safe drinking water."[8]

America, of course, is still mighty prosperous, but environmentalism is putting us on the brink of danger as well. As technology after technology that our grandparents put in place is being banned, and new technologies never even come to market, we risk a public-health disaster. Environmentalists have promoted all sorts of doomsday scenarios about population explosions and massive cancer crises from pesticides that have been shown to be false. But now, because we have done away with so many useful products based on those scares, we are in danger of an old-fashion doomsday returning because we've lost what protected us from the wrath of nature. Indeed, as we will see throughout this book, public health hazards caused by environmental policies are already on the scene.

Ironically, when technologies improved public health and made nature less harsh, these technologies became the new locus of our fears. Political scientist Aaron Wildavsky and anthropologist Mary Douglas write in their book, *Risk and Culture*, that "the rise of alarm over risk to life" occurred "at the same time as health is better than ever before." And many of the technologies that made us safer were turned into "the source of risk."[9]

Former vice president Al Gore, who has ramped up his charges of doomsday from global warming and other alleged environmental dangers, made an interesting comment to *Rolling Stone*. The reason it's interesting is because it's almost exactly the opposite of what's true. When the interviewer asked why people weren't "hearing the message" of global warming's dangers, Gore replied that we may not yet have reached that stage in evolution where we respond quickly to complex scares.

"Our brains are much better at perceiving danger in fangs and claws and spiders and fire," Gore said. "It's more difficult to trigger the alarm parts of the brain—those connected to survival—with grave dangers that can only be perceived through abstract models and complex data."[10]

Today that's almost exactly wrong. Because technology has shielded us from the natural world, we don't perceive simple dangers from nature as easily as our grandparents did. And because of this, we are more prone to believe in complex, speculative scares like global warming than in immediate hazards that are still very dangerous.

There's no better example of this than our modern perceptions of weather. Egged on by Gore and other environmentalists, we increasingly associate any harsh weather event with global warming. In a single *Boston Globe* op-ed published last year just after Hurricane Katrina, author Ross Gelbspan blamed global warming for snow, heat waves, floods, and droughts. As for Katrina, he proclaimed that "its real name is global warming."[11]

I delve into what we should know about the global warming "crisis" in chapters 4 and 6, and I will also refer you to other good sources where you can get the important facts. Let me just state here one of the most important facts. Katrina, by the time it hit landfall, turned out to be an average hurricane rather than a superstorm. It was solely the breech of the levees—again, in large part due to environmentalists nixing stronger protection—that made the storm so destructive. And long before we had cars, electricity, or any of the products that allegedly contribute to global warming, humans knew Mother Nature could be harsh. Any cursory glance of history will give you accounts of dozens of fierce storms, going back thousands of years. Harsh sea storms were part of Homer's ancient Greek tome *The Odyssey*. Here in America, before cars and electricity were used at nearly the volume they are today, storms still caused great amounts of death and destruction. In 1938, an Atlantic hurricane hit New England by surprise with walls of water fifty feet high and winds clocked at 186 miles per hour. The hurricane killed 682 people and seriously injured 1,754.[12]

Similarly, global warming cannot be blamed for the hurricane in 1900 that ravaged Galveston, Texas, and killed as many as ten thousand people. This remains the deadliest natural disaster in American history. Since Galveston residents didn't have global warming to blame back then, they did what they had to do to protect themselves from the next hurricane, whose "real name," to paraphrase Gelbspan, was nature. The town built a seawall, standing seventeen feet high and twenty-seven feet wide. In a hundred years, the wall has never been breached. According to journalist Erik Larson in his definitive book *Isaac's Storm*, it has protected the city from hurricanes nine times, the latest being in 1983.[13]

But today environmentalists have prevented us from using the latest technologies to build strong dams, walls, and gates. Instead, they and their admirers in the media pitch natural solutions like wetlands. Wetlands can be a good thing for other reasons, such as hosting wildlife, but they have never been proven successful as the primary means of flood control. Indeed, as I reveal in chapter 6, the Netherlands took away thousands of acres of wetlands when it built its sophisticated dams that keep the country so well protected from North Atlantic storms.

But lack of flood protection is just one example of where environmentalists, and the policy makers who have followed their prescriptions, have made our country more prone to disasters. Others include the following:

The banning of DDT and other insecticides has left us more vulnerable to insect and tick-borne diseases. West Nile virus and Lyme disease, both of which can have harmful or lethal effects, are on the rise. We need pesticides to control the mosquitoes and ticks that spread them. The pesticide bans may also leave us vulnerable to a host of plagues from bird flu to a bioterrorism-created virus, both of which could be made deadlier by insects spreading the infectious agent.

The ban of asbestos, still ranked by many scientists as the most effective fire retardant, has made American buildings and military ships more prone to deadly fires caused by accidents or terrorist attacks. Lack of asbestos meant a greater number of casualties in both the attacks on the World Trade Center and the fire at The Station nightclub in Rhode Island, as I will detail in the coming pages.

Furthermore, bans on logging in national forests are responsible for the intensity of many of the wildfires that destroy homes, put people in harm's way, and even kill important plants and wildlife.

So that you can think clearly about the future, I first have to take you into the past. I want to bring you on a journey to show you the hazards our grandparents and great-grandparents were faced with—from catching malaria on the battlefield to perishing in a fire when they entered a pre-asbestos school or theater—that explains many of the choices they made. I have constructed this journey through books, old newspaper articles, and interviews with men and women who braved risks and tried to make the world a better place. Our ancestors' decisions weren't always right, and they often corrected themselves when they weren't. But they knew a few things that we don't. And to ensure that the levels of prosperity and public health they created continue and improve, we need to learn a few things that they knew. Namely, that nature is not always our friend. And most importantly, that there's no such thing as a risk-free world.

So—if you're ready—sit back, enjoy the journey, and prepare to laugh, cry, and be frightened of the age-old hazards you should be scared of.

2

Rachel Carson Kills Birds

HOW THE BANNING OF DDT AND OTHER PESTICIDES ENDANGERS HUMANS, WILDLIFE, AND TREES

In town after town in America, the crows fell out of the sky. One by one, they fell in Kansas, Nebraska, even on the White House lawn. Soon the crow population reached its lowest point in fifteen years. Then other birds began to die: condors, eagles, and the endangered peregrine falcon. Some 160 species were affected, according to the US Geological Survey.[1]

Then it spread to horses. And then even dogs. And finally people. What was causing these sudden deaths? Could these be from the effects of industrial chemicals?

Then stately American elm trees began to dwindle. Trees that had been standing for more than one hundred years would rapidly die. Their bark shriveled up, or their branches would simply fall off.

This certainly sounds like the opening scene from Rachel Carson's *Silent Spring*, the "fable for tomorrow," where she painted a hypothetical scenario of animal and human deaths that could arise, she claimed, from the use of the pesticide DDT.

But no, this scenario is all too real, and the acts were committed by nature herself. Insects that are part of natural systems attacked these birds, horses, and people. The mosquitoes spread malaria that killed humans and the West Nile virus that killed birds and other creatures as well. Beetles and gypsy moths clear-cut the trees. But in a sense, humans did have a role, through their lack of action to stop the ravages of nature. And by starting the misinformation campaign that led to the ban of insect-killer DDT, Rachel Carson played a major role in killing these birds, horses, people, and trees too.

HISTORY OF CONFLICT

The history of life on earth is a history of conflict. Not just among humans, but among all living things. Forget about what environmentalists call "harmony in nature." The popular expression used to describe the cutthroat business world is not called the "Law of the Jungle" for nothing.

Every day in the natural world, wolves eat sheep, cattle, and the Alaskan caribou that environmentalists insist must be protected from oil drilling. Cats devour mice and, when they can catch them, juicy birds. Deer gorge on all kinds of plants, as many gardeners and forest stewards know all too well. But plants themselves get into the action, too, by making toxic compounds and molds more potent than many "artificial" pesticides. Celery, for instance, if not given man-made compounds to fight off pests while it is growing, will cook up potent chemical substances called psoralens to do the job. Studies show that these psoralens increase the risk of skin cancer for those who eat celery containing them.[2]

And then there are insects—who prey on us all. Everyone with a dog or cat knows of the enormous discomfort, as well as the long-term health problems, fleas and ticks can cause to their poor pets. In the American South and Southwest, swarms of fire ants have devoured the most beautiful birds.[3]

And no, left to itself, nature does not necessarily achieve a "balance." Most of the world's species have gone extinct, and extinction was the norm before humans even set foot on the planet. Biologist Norman D. Levine has written in the journal *BioScience*, "perhaps 95% of the species that once existed no longer exist."[4]

But one species has emerged that is able to referee this jungle. And that is the species called human. Humans are the only species that restricts its own actions so that other species may live. They strive to conserve and make the best use of natural resources and animal life. With or without laws—in fact laws such as the Endangered Species Act are often counterproductive—they build habitats specifically for other creatures.

What gives them this ability is the human mind, with its virtues of reason and rationality. And deep down, even the most ardent animal rights advocate knows that man ranks above the other creatures. The radical group People for the Ethical Treatment of Animals may have as its mantra, "A rat is a pig is a dog is a boy," but humans are the only group they try to appeal to. They don't try to save sheep, for instance, by forming a picket line in front of a pack of wolves. They know, rightly, that wolves won't likely listen to their shouts and will just see them as more tasty morsels to add to their sheep buffet.

One of the methods humans have developed in order to referee nature to protect themselves, as well as animals and plants, is insecticides. Chemicals, which are often refined forms very similar to substances in plants, are used to kill or repel bugs disturbing everything from trees to people. One of the most effective substances ever made to protect humans, animals, and trees is DDT, the very chemical that Rachel Carson and her followers inveighed against and succeeded in getting banned in most countries across the globe. But this ban is increasingly being seen as the world's loss of a tool to fight horrendous disease. In the past few years, no less than the *New York Times*—in what can be seen as a stunning apology for decades of the establishment press parroting greens' anti-DDT line—declared regarding DDT, "we have forged an instrument of salvation, and we choose to hide it under our robes."[5]

RACHEL CARSON'S DECEPTIONS

Rachel Caron's *Silent Spring* is credited with launching the modern environmental movement. It made a believer of Al Gore, whose apocalyptic rants about the effects of global warming adorn his 1992 book *Earth in the Balance* and many of his recent speeches. In his introduction to the 1994 edition of *Silent Spring*, Gore writes, "Rachel Carson was one of the reasons why I became so conscious of the environment and so involved in environmental issues. Her example inspired me to write *Earth in the Balance*."[6]

The man-against-nature theme of Carson's book resonated, creating a movement. "Without this book, the environmental movement might have been long delayed or never have developed at all," Gore writes.[7]

Then, Gore picked an interesting comparison, Harriet Beecher Stowe's antislavery novel *Uncle Tom's Cabin*. He says, "Both rank among the rare books that have transformed our society."[8] That much is true, but there are important differences. While Stowe's book resulted in giving people their freedom, Carson's tome has resulted in the limiting of freedom and life-saving technologies because of the enslavement of society to the false god of "the natural."

Yet there is another crucial, and even more important, difference. Stowe labeled her book as a novel, but it gave very factual descriptions of the abuses slaves suffered. By contrast, Carson's work is labeled nonfiction, yet it is filled with speculation, distortion to fit the author's purposes, and outright misstatements. And the most notorious and consequential of her fictions concern DDT.

It's true that DDT was relatively new in 1962, and reasonable people could be concerned about possible long-term effects. But Carson manipulated facts about what was known even then. One of Carson's most notorious lies—and yes, this is either an outright lie or extremely willful ignorance—is that DDT was developed in World War II as an "agent of death." She compared it to the development of poison gas.[9] But DDT was specifically developed to fight the insect-borne diseases that were harming US soldiers. The troops then generously shared the powerful new insecticide to save the lives of others in foreign lands, including those ridden with disease from the horrendous conditions at concentration camps during the Holocaust. And nearly everyone DDT touched in World War II came to view DDT as an essential agent of life.

I will describe the development of DDT through several eyes: Joseph Jacobs, scientist; Gloria Lyon, Holocaust victim; Frank Knight, tree lover. All of them will testify to the good that DDT has done. Their stories, along with the tragic events following the DDT ban, will also show the tremendous loss to humans, wildlife, and trees in a world without DDT.

AN AGENT OF LIFE

One of the few factual statements in *Silent Spring* was Carson's assertion that the pesticide "industry was a child of Second World War." She was right about that. But then in describing the development of DDT, Rachel Carson not only managed to mangle science, she also smeared the noble efforts of the American military that was fighting to save the world from the Nazis.

According to Carson's fractured World War II fairy tale, "In the course of developing agents of chemical warfare, some of the chemicals developed in the laboratory were found to be lethal to insects. The discovery did not come by chance: insects were widely used to test chemicals as agents of death for man."[10]

Here is the truth: During World War II, the military never developed insecticides to kill anyone but bugs. DDT and others were specifically developed to save the lives of our troops. The following is what really happened in one of the most valiant achievements of the US military in that war.

It was 1942, and American troops seemed to face an insurmountable problem. America had entered World War II after being attacked at Pearl Harbor the previous year. But although this problem threatened the American ability to win the war, it had nothing to do with the Germans or Japanese. Rather, our troops were being sickened by the thousands from insect-borne diseases.

General Douglas MacArthur expressed alarm. At any given time, two-thirds of his troops in the South Pacific were afflicted with malaria. Even in cases when malaria wasn't life threatening, the fever, chills, headaches, and a weakening of the joints that resulted left the soldiers incapable of fighting in some of the most vital theaters of war. MacArthur and others were also worried about typhus, a deadly disease spread by lice. Today, of course, lice are only associated with mild discomfort and special shampoo. But before DDT, lice, by spreading typhus, had killed millions before and during World War I, and were a threat throughout the war zones as soldiers were placed in close quarters where the disease could spread. It was going to be "a long war," MacArthur said, unless those diseases could be brought under control.[11]

Indeed, throughout history, there had been many "long wars" due in significant part to insects. Author Jared Diamond is right that "germs"—i.e. transmission of diseases—have certainly made a difference in military victories and the "collapse" of nations.[12] (He is not right, however, about most other things, as we will see in upcoming chapters.) Soldiers traditionally fought very close together in the mud and muck of trenches and foxholes, the ideal place for insect-borne diseases to spread. Just after World War I started in 1914, Serbia got a nasty surprise when it captured Austrian prisoners. An epidemic of typhus broke out and killed 150,000 soldiers and civilians in six months. This outbreak gave an advantage to the Central Powers of Germany and Austria, an advantage they kept until the United States entered the war in 1917. Diseases that were probably typhus also killed thousands of soldiers in various global conflicts from the Thirty Years War to the Crimean War.[13] Wrote O.T. Zimmerman and Irvin Lavine, two chemical engineering professors from the University of New Hampshire and University of North Dakota, in 1946, "In all the previous wars of history, the louse [singular for lice] had killed more men than ever died from bullets, swords, or other weapons."[14]

But in World War II, military leaders such as MacArthur had an unyielding faith in American ingenuity. They believed that for the first time, man could conquer not only the traditional enemy but nature's wrath as well. So the army charged an obscure laboratory of the Department of Agriculture in the then sleepy, swampy town of Orlando, Florida, to find a better way to protect US soldiers against insect-borne diseases. In its pre-Disney days, Orlando was the ideal place to test insecticides because it had so many insects. The massive Everglades swamps, which ironically the government is now trying to restore, were similar to tropical regions like the South Pacific and had plenty of mosquitoes and flies of their own. Thousands of chemicals were tested, but one compound won hands down: DDT.

Dichloro-diphenyl-trichloroethane was synthesized in a Swiss lab in the 1870s. But a use for it was never found until the late 1930s, when chemist Paul Muller at the firm JR Geigy (now a part of Ciba Specialty Chemicals) accidentally discovered—after leaving flies in a DDT-laced container overnight—that DDT got rid of insects better than anything. These tests were confirmed by the agricultural lab in the lakes and swamps of Orlando.[15] And the scientists also found that DDT was persistent; one spray would kill and repel insects from a certain area for months. But production—getting a large amount to the troops who needed it—was still a problem.

The government went to the pharmaceutical company Merck, the only company that knew how to mass-produce chloral hydrate, which contained essential ingredients for DDT. Merck gave the assignment to one of its top chemists, Joseph J. Jacobs. In 1943, Jacobs worked day and night to retrofit a fifty-year-old plant to mass-produce DDT to protect the troops. During the final rush to get the shipment out the door, a valve at the bottom of a large vessel was accidentally opened. Jacobs happened to be standing under it and was covered with hot DDT. "When it dried, I had DDT an inch thick all over me," Jacobs recalls in his autobiography *The Anatomy of an Entrepreneur*. "In my hair, in my ears, and in my mouth and nose. I took off my clothes, showered, and scrubbed, but probably ingested more DDT during that one incident than is today considered safe to absorb over many years."[16]

Before we move on to DDT's achievements in World War II, I know many readers are wondering about the fate of Joseph Jacobs. After all, in the years after *Silent Spring*, DDT was called "double death twice." One touch could kill you. And sadly, after being exposed, Jacobs did die—more than sixty years later in 2004, at the tender young age of eighty-eight.[17]

After the war, Jacobs left Merck and formed what is now Jacobs Engineering Group, one of the largest engineering firms in the country. A pioneer among Lebanese Americans, Jacobs also became a noted philanthropist and author. He wrote about everything from science to politics, and is considered to have coined the phrase "Compassionate Conservative," which was the title of his 1996 book. (Radio host Michael Savage also used the phrase early on and claims credit for coining it.) Texas governor George W. Bush would write Jacobs a letter in 1999 about how much he liked the phrase,[18] and Bush would, of course, use the phrase to help win the 2000 presidential election. But Jacobs had friends from across the political spectrum, including the liberal and fellow Lebanese American Casey Kasem, the popular disc jockey.[19]

Jacobs would come to view with alarm the growing status of the environmental movement. In *The Compassionate Conservative* and in a 2000 interview with him that I was privileged to conduct for *Investor's Business Daily*, Jacobs expressed fear that environmentalism would harm innovations that could better society. Until he died, Jacobs considered directing the early production of DDT to be one of his finest achievements.

At Merck, Jacobs was also involved in developing the antibiotic penicillin. He put DDT on the same level as this miracle drug, referring to penicillin as "the other great life-saving chemical that I am proud to have helped bring to market."[20] As shocking as this comparison might sound, Jacobs is far from the only bright person who has made it. The perceptive journalist Malcolm Gladwell, author of the best-selling books *The Tipping Point* and *Blink*, wrote in 2001 in the *New Yorker* that if DDT was still being used to eradicate malaria, it would today be viewed "in the same heroic light as penicillin and the polio vaccine."[21]

But I would modify Gladwell just slightly. Based on what DDT achieved in World War II alone, it should already be viewed in that heroic light.

PRIVATE DDT

Shortly after the army picked up the first shipment of DDT that Jacobs had produced in the Merck lab in New Jersey, Private DDT was called up to report for duty on several battlefields.

In the fall of 1943, American troops established a beachhead in Salerno, at the southern point of Benito Mussolini's fascist Italy. They were advancing up the Italian peninsula when army leaders were warned of trouble. No, it wasn't a strengthened contingent of Italian or German soldiers. It was the beginning of an outbreak of typhus among the population of Naples. The lowly typhus-spreading louse had stopped or delayed military advances in previous wars. And the generals knew that a typhus epidemic had never before been stopped in the dead of winter. Medical professionals had to wait until March or April for the lice to die out.

But the siege of Italy couldn't wait, so Brig. Gen. Leon Fox set up an ambitious program to put to work America's new secret agent of life: DDT.[22] As the soldiers entered Naples, the army also brought gallons and gallons of DDT powder. They spray-dusted the streets, buildings, and even the people. Over one million citizens of Naples were dusted in January of 1944. In places like train stations, US troops sprayed DDT on the people of Naples from their shirt collars down to their shoes. Troops would also spray DDT on themselves in Naples and many other places. By mid-February the typhus epidemic was completely licked, saving not only our troops, but millions of Italian civilians as well. Gladwell writes that the Naples dusting "sav[ed] countless lives,"[23] and even pesticide critic Edmund Russell acknowledges in his book *War and Nature* that this was "the first instance a typhus epidemic was halted in wintertime."[24]

After Naples, DDT was called up again and again to defend the soldiers who were defending freedom. The United States Army Air Force attached tanks of DDT under the wings of B-25s and C-47s, and sprayed Pacific beachheads in advance of America's arrival. When US Marines fell ill from mosquito-borne dengue fever after the 1944 invasion of Saipan, leaders called for a DDT air strike. The dengue was conquered and soon so were the Japanese occupiers at Saipan.[25]

So effective was DDT in the war, that its discoverer, Muller, won the Nobel Prize in 1948. But after the Allies won, there was still one final, vital mission for DDT. The victims of the Holocaust, kept in horrendous conditions in the concentration camps, needed to be liberated from disease after they were liberated from the Nazis.

DDT RESCUES HOLOCAUST SURVIVORS

To understand the epidemic of typhus that struck the Jews in several of the camps, consider the living conditions soldiers and civilians faced during the war and multiply it by one hundred, one thousand, or even one million. There were no bathing facilities and no changes of clothes. The victims were worked to the bone outdoors, weakening their ability to resist insects such as lice. The insects also swarmed on the mass graves, which were in close contact with the living. Then there were the unimaginably cramped conditions. At Bergen-Belsen, six hundred to one thousand victims were crowded into huts that liberating soldiers judged should have held, at most, one hundred.[26]

Thus many who were not shot, beaten to death, or gassed fell victim to the lice. At Bergen-Belsen, typhus is what killed Anne Frank—whose diary would bring home the horrors of the Holocaust—just three weeks before the camp was liberated by the British. When the liberators arrived, the typhus epidemic was so bad that five hundred victims a day were still dying.[27]

Since America had generously shared DDT with its allies, Britain was able to employ it to save the Bergen-Belsen victims. British forces transformed the lavish barracks of Nazi leaders into hospitals, where the survivors of the camp were "shaved, washed, dusted with DDT powder, [and] wrapped in clean blankets," notes Holocaust historian Paul Kemp. It was a difficult task, but DDT once again brought the typhus epidemic under control.[28]

When American soldiers liberated Dachau, they instituted a similar DDT dusting program. Writes Jon Bridgman in the authoritative book *End of the Holocaust*, "Seventy-two hours after the first American troops entered the camp a full-scale DDT dusting program was underway which quickly brought the incipient epidemic under control."[29]

Gloria Hollander Lyon remembers well the DDT spraying she credits with saving her life. A Hungarian Jew, Lyon was sent by the Nazis to seven different concentration camps, including the horrific Auschwitz and the lice-infested Bergen-Belsen. She was rescued from her last camp, Ravensbrück, by the Swedish Red Cross. Then fifteen, she arrived in Sweden on a stretcher, and her hair and body were covered in lice.

At the gymnasium of a Swedish high school, she was given food, a shower, and a new set of clothes. But she was also given something she was not familiar with: a spraying of DDT all over her body. "Everywhere, from head to toe," she recalled in an interview. And the DDT was applied directly to her skin. "We were totally undressed, naked," she said.

Before the "dusting," Lyon recalled, Red Cross officials explained that this was being done to kill the lice before typhus could set in. "They were very open with us, and they had to be, because we were very suspicious of anything," she said. "We didn't trust yet. It had just been a few hours since we were in freedom. But they said they had to kill this vermin, the lice, to keep us healthy."

Lyon described a feeling of relief. The DDT may have stung a little bit, she said, but "we wouldn't complain about a little thing like that. We were survivors." She added, "When I think back, I felt really relieved to know that they were not going to plague me at night."

Now seventy-five, Lyon lives in San Francisco and frequently lectures about the Holocaust. In telling her story, she almost always recounts being sprayed with DDT and how it saved her from the potentially deadly lice. She feels strongly that young people should know that sometimes society and individuals have to take risks to prevent a larger risk. "Every time I talk about it in the schools, the students laugh as if to say, 'If you had only known how harmful that was,'" Lyon said. "I have heard that it is harmful, but at the same time, we have to make choices at times like that. I just felt that they did it for my benefit. Maybe there was nothing else that they could use. Certainly on so many people."[30]

PRECAUTION CAN BE DEADLY

Today's environmentalists wax eloquently about the *Precautionary Principle*. In green manifestos like the Wingspread Consensus, they argue that if there is any doubt about a certain chemical's effects, it should not be introduced. Advocates liken it to the adage "Look before you leap." But, points out science writer Ronald Bailey, the principle goes against another wise adage, "He who hesitates is lost."[31] Imagine if the army had followed the Precautionary Principle of today's advocates. The military and drug companies did do some tests and found that DDT posed no harm to humans, but they could not be certain. But, had DDT not been used in World War II, millions of soldiers, civilians, and Holocaust victims would have died of insect-borne diseases. When talking to students, Gloria Lyon expresses a principle similar to that stated by University of Texas environmental law professor Frank Cross, that in protecting public health, "there is no such thing as a risk-free lunch."[32]

Chemical pioneer Joseph Jacobs was also critical of the Precautionary Principle. He noted that one of the products he helped develop saved many lives, but also "caused quite a few deaths." But this substance was *not* DDT. It was penicillin, which has caused allergic fatalities. No deaths of humans, by contrast, have been linked to DDT. Yet "no one has ever bemoaned the discovery of penicillin or caused it to be banned," Jacobs wrote. "If this had been given the Rachel Carson treatment, think of all the lives which would not have been saved."[33]

And the initial DDT tests have turned out to be right. DDT, used as intended, poses no harm to human health. Even Rachel Carson had to square her apocalyptic warnings with DDT's successful use in World War II. After all, the war had only ended seventeen years before *Silent Spring* was published, and DDT's use in the battlefields would be in many readers' memories. So she conceded in a line that during the war, "so many people came into extremely intimate contact with DDT and suffered no immediate ill effects."[34] But she never conceded that DDT saved lives. And she then tried to explain that DDT would have long-term effects that could not be known.

But now DDT's benefits and risks—or lack of them—are known. And some perceptive journalists, even some who are liberal, are noting them. Alexander Gourevitch, a scribe for the pro-Democrat *American Prospect*, wrote in the liberal opinion magazine *Washington Monthly*, "But when it comes to the kinds of uses once permitted in the United States and abroad, there's simply no solid scientific evidence that exposure to DDT causes cancer or is otherwise harmful to human beings. Not a single study linking DDT exposure to human toxicity has ever been replicated."[35] A 1971 study in particular demonstrated that DDT posed no hazards to people. In that long-term study, volunteers ate thirty-two ounces of DDT for a year and a half. Sixteen years later, they had suffered no increased risk of adverse health effects.[36]

As for DDT's benefits, Malcolm Gladwell stated in the *New Yorker*, "Between 1945 and 1965, DDT saved millions—even tens of millions—of lives around the world, perhaps more than any other man-made drug or chemical before or since."[37]

After the war, DDT was used in a variety of applications, from combating insects that spread devastating diseases such as malaria to fighting pests that devastated crops and plants. Humans were not the only ones to benefit from DDT's use—nor were they the only creatures of nature to suffer when DDT was banned.

RACHEL CARSON, CLEARCUTTER

Very few items fit the cliché "as American as apple pie." But the stately elm tree almost certainly does. These majestic, vase-shaped trees with their canopies of green leaves have symbolized America's can-do spirit. Able to grow more than one hundred feet tall in almost any type of weather and in all regions of the country, they resemble the resilience of the Americans who planted them. Forty years ago in every American city, elms lined the major roads, more than a few of which were named Elm Street. They provided shade to keep the outdoors cooler, and even reduced the need for air conditioning indoors.

But today, there aren't that many elms left in America. In recent decades, more than half of the elms in the United States have been destroyed, and some American towns are now virtually elmless.[38] Is that because of logging or pollution or the catchall global warming that enviros blame nearly everything on? No. It's because of an insect called the elm bark beetle. The beetles eat the bark or twigs of a tree, spreading a fungus. This fungus infects the tree with Dutch elm disease. Named that because it was first diagnosed in Holland, Dutch elm disease causes trees to wilt, curl, and die, either immediately or by slowly wasting away.

Fortunately for the elms, just as the disease started taking its toll, there was a new invention to kill and repel the predatory beetles: DDT. Starting in the late '40s, dedicated foresters and groundskeepers in communities across America began spraying DDT on elms with amazing results. Not only were the trees unharmed by the DDT, but the beetles stopped attacking them nearly so much. It looked like the elms would survive and prosper—thanks to DDT.

"As long as we used it, they did very well," recalled Frank Knight, who has been "tree warden" for the town of Yarmouth, Maine, since

1956.[39] Knight was recently commended as a "champion of trees" in *American Profile*, a national weekend newspaper supplement.[40] Upon taking the job, for which the town of three thousand pays no salary, Knight immediately ordered that the town's seven hundred elm trees be sprayed with DDT before the beetles were able to spread Dutch elm disease any further.

So once a year, the trees were sprayed root and branch with DDT, under Knight's close supervision. "I probably did get some on me," Knight recalled. "I probably inhaled some, but it didn't seem to bother me." Knight then added, "I'm ninety-seven now, so I guess it didn't cut me very short."[41] (Gee, Knight is ninety-seven. Gloria Lyon is seventy-five. And Joseph Jacobs died at eighty-eight. J. Gordon Edwards, an entomologist and Carson critic who would frequently eat a spoonful of DDT during a lecture [I do not recommend this], died at eighty-four in 2004 while climbing the Divide Mountain in California! I'm beginning to wonder if intimate contact with DDT will actually *prolong* your life!)

The spraying worked. Yarmouth only lost one tree while the DDT program was continuing. But then, one spring in the mid-1960s, when Knight was on vacation, an antipesticide activist influenced by Rachel Carson's 1962 book convinced the town council to stop spraying. The next year, the beetles destroyed one hundred elms. "When we didn't spray, we just lost them wholesale," Knight recalled sadly.[42]

DDT SAVES SPOTTED OWL'S HOME— NO THANKS TO ENVIRONMENTALISTS

Other tree species also suffered in the wake of the government's DDT restrictions and eventual ban. In fact, in 1974, a few years after DDT was banned by the Environmental Protection Agency, the US Forest Service begged the EPA for an emergency exemption because tussock moths were devastating the Douglas fir trees in forests of the Pacific Northwest. The moths were eating the trees' needles, stripping the bark, and rapidly killing the trees.

These are the very same trees that environmentalists now insist must not be logged because they are "old-growth" and home to the spotted owls. To protect the trees from logging, enviros have made exaggerated claims that the spotted owl would have nowhere else to live. Yet here nature was threatening these trees with impending doom, and environmentalists were against using the only thing that could save them. Fortunately, the EPA granted the Forest Service a rare exemption, and the Douglas fir was rescued, saving it for future generations—at least until another tussock moth attack.[43] Amazingly, when they speak of it at all, some environmentalists still call this emergency spraying a mistake.[44]

BEETLES REUNITE, EM-BARK ON MAGICAL MYSTERY FUNGUS TOUR; OAK TREES SING, "HELP, WE NEED DDT," TO DEAF EARS

Unfortunately, DDT was not there more recently to save oak trees from the ongoing Sudden Oak Death. Once again beetles fed on bark infected with a new fungus and spread it to other trees through the bark they ate later on. California and Oregon have lost tens of thousands of historic oaks since the 1990s, and the disease and its variations are spreading eastward to an oak tree near you.[45]

As for elms, Yarmouth, Maine's elm population today has dwindled to just fifteen trees, down from seven hundred in the DDT days. And Knight has had to undertake heroic efforts to save even those remaining few from Dutch elm disease. His crew carefully prunes infected branches from "Herbie," a beautiful giant one-hundred-foot elm that has been a resident of Yarmouth for more than 225 years. "We've cut disease out of Herbie about thirteen different years," Knight said. "You got to get that thing out of there quick. The wood in the limb that's diseased has got brown streaks underneath. So you have to cut back until those brown streaks are no longer there. We've done that to trees and been fairly successful." But he is quick to add, "A lot more elms would have lived if they sprayed with DDT."[46]

Indeed, after spraying ceased in other cities, the elm trees were some of the first victims of Rachel Carson's hysteria. According to the *Detroit News*, when the city of Detroit started spraying DDT to combat Dutch elm, it lost a manageable two thousand elm trees a year. But that jumped to ten thousand trees annually in the '60s after Detroit stopped attacking beetles with DDT. Altogether, Detroit lost one hundred thousand trees by 1972, and the state of Michigan has lost 80 percent of its elms.[47] The *Detroit News* also reports that Des Moines and Toledo, Ohio, which ceased spraying DDT early on, lost almost all of their elms within a decade after Dutch elm disease first appeared in the '50s.[48] In 2005, Chicago had to cut down thirty trees in Grant Park, from what is called the nation's largest stand of elms, in order to keep Dutch elm from spreading.[49]

Environmentalist that he is, Al Gore has noticed the beetle infestation. But does he blame it on the ceasing of protective DDT spraying? Yeah, right. No, according to Gore's recent book, *An Inconvenient Truth*, the beetles are attacking trees because of global warming.[50] He never even acknowledges that the very same thing happened fifty years ago before DDT repelled them.

CARSON SAYS, "LET THE ELMS DIE"

And Gore's heroine, Carson, was perfectly willing to let elms die a "natural" death. It can be argued that Carson, who died in 1964, could not foresee many of the disastrous effects to which her book would lead. But in the case of the elms, she made it perfectly clear that she would rather see these majestic trees all vanish rather than let what she regarded as an evil chemical try to save them. "[E]lms, majestic shade trees though they are, are not sacred cows," she opined.[51] She wrote that "many experts believe all efforts to save the elms will in the end be futile."[52]

Ignoring successful ongoing efforts like that of Frank Knight in Yarmouth, she wrote that DDT wouldn't work, using the tortured argument of insect "resistance," which we will examine shortly. She praised Toledo for ceasing to spray DDT in the late '50s, implying that the city could be more successful at preserving elms than those that sprayed.[53] In fact, as the *Detroit News* noted, there are virtually no elms left in Toledo today.[54]

In fact, Carson's solution for the elms would shock many environmentalists today. She advocated cutting down trees that showed any sign of disease. "[N]ot only diseased trees, but all elm wood in which the beetles might breed must be destroyed," the founding mother of modern environmentalism declared.[55]

Now, there is nothing wrong with cutting down trees. As we will see in chapter 5, often it is absolutely necessary so that the whole forest doesn't burn. In a way, Rachel Carson's statements show how far her followers in the environmental movement have veered from common sense. At the same time, there would be no need to cut down many beautiful trees if DDT or other pesticides were used to fend off their insect predators.

DDT SAVES BIRDS

The effort of foresters and tree managers to save elms from insect-borne disease was the activity where Carson leveled her most emotional charge: that DDT was killing the lovely robin. "It would be tragic to lose the elms, but it would be doubly tragic if, in vain efforts to save them, we plunge vast segments of our bird population into the night of extinction," she wrote with alarm.[56] The damage DDT allegedly did to robins and other birds was what galvanized enough of the public to lead to the government's banning of DDT.

And certainly, too much DDT, as with too much of anything, may hurt birds as well as people. But the evidence makes it clear that many other factors were at work in the anecdotes and isolated incidents of bird deaths in supposed connection with DDT spraying. And on balance, DDT probably *increased* the population of many birds by saving them from insect predators.

One of the most prominent of Carson's bird horror stories is that of the dead robins at Michigan State University. The campus began spraying its trees to combat Dutch elm disease in 1954. In the next couple of years, a greater number of dead and dying robins began to appear.

But strong evidence exonerates DDT of these robins' fate. J. Gordon Edwards, who was an avid outdoorsman and professor of entomology—the study of insects—at San Jose State University, found that because of a mercury fungicide to prevent soil fungus, there were high levels of mercury in the ground and in earthworms that robins would eat. The dead robins were never tested for mercury contamination, "even though the symptoms displayed by the dying robins were those attributable to mercury poisoning," Edwards wrote.[57] Furthermore in laboratory experiments, University of Wisconsin researcher Joseph Hickey found he could not make robins die by overdosing them with DDT, because the birds passed the DDT through their digestive tracts and eliminated it in their waste.[58]

Carson also failed to mention that, overall, the robin population was on the rise during the DDT years. The annual Christmas Bird Count of the Audubon Society reported that there were more than twelve times as many robin sightings in 1960 as there were in 1941.[59]

The evidence is also mixed for the claim that followed Carson's book that DDT thinned eggshells. There were some solid studies that found that shell weight decreased up to 20 percent for peregrine falcons, sparrow hawks, and golden eagles. But other studies have found that eggshell thinning of bird species began about fifty years before the introduction of DDT. And as science journalist Ronald Bailey pointed out in *Reason*, "no one has ever identified the physiological mechanism(s) by which [a DDT byproduct] causes eggshell thinning."[60]

And whatever damage DDT might have done to some birds, it more than made up for it by saving them from swirling insects that cause bird, as well as human, diseases. "When marshes were sprayed with DDT to control the mosquitoes, a common result was a population explosion of birds inhabiting the marshes," Edwards wrote. The number of the red-wing blackbirds increased so much that by 1970 it had become a grain-eating pest in the upper Midwest.[61] The role of insect-borne diseases suppressing bird population will come into play later on in this chapter when we discuss the ongoing West Nile virus.

The spraying programs of the 1950s and '60s weren't perfect. DDT would sometimes kill beneficial insects such as the honeybee. But farmers would quickly reduce or shift their spraying when it killed a beneficial bug. As early as 1946, chemists were advising farmers to spray DDT months before the honeybees would come.[62] Local officials, such as Frank Knight of Yarmouth, also minimized their spraying out of respect for their neighbors.

The real problems—minor problems though they were—of excess spraying were the fault of the federal government. In Long Island, airplanes hired by the US Department of Agriculture sprayed trees and everything below, including cars and suburban homes. Although studies have shown there were no long-term health effects to Long Island residents, it did result in inconveniences such as a housewife being drenched.[63] Property rights advocates can certainly sympathize with Carson's statement that "a vast amount of damage can be done when reckless large-scale treatment is substituted for local and moderate control."[64] In a paper for the Property and Environment Research Center, economists Roger Meiners and Andrew Morriss pointed out that while landowners could sue each other when DDT spilled over onto another's property, the government faced no such constraints.[65]

But rather than advocating a halt to federal spraying programs and a transfer of power over pests to states and property owners, environmentalists successfully pushed for the federal government to ban its use. This was the first of many horrific actions stemming from the modern environmental movement, which at bottom is a toxic mixture of pantheism—worshiping nature as a god—with big-government liberalism. Nature worship, rather than the appreciation of nature that we all have, has long existed. But the modern environmentalists, as opposed to previous generations of conservationists, were the first to seek to impose these views on the entire American and world populations. It didn't really matter to many of them what the facts were about DDT. If they could scare enough Americans about it, they could get their hands on the political levers of power. As the chief scientist for the new Environmental Defense Fund (now Environmental Defense), Charles Wurster told the *Seattle Times* in 1969, "If the environmentalists win on DDT, they will achieve a level of authority they never had before. . . . In a sense, much more is at stake than DDT."[66] We should keep this quote in mind today when groups like the very same Environmental Defense talk about how imminent global warming is going to be.

In 1969, the Environmental Defense Fund, the Sierra Club, and the National Audubon Society petitioned the US government to ban DDT. But a hearing was held at the newly formed Environmental Protection Agency that gave the chemical a clean bill of health in 1971. Edmund Sweeney, the judge who presided over the EPA hearings, came to this conclusion after seven months of examination: "DDT is not a carcinogenic, mutagenic or tetragenic hazard to man. The uses under regulations involved here do not have a deleterious effect on freshwater fish, estuarine organisms, wild birds or other wildlife. . . . The evidence in this proceeding supports the conclusion that there is a present need for essential uses of DDT."[67]

But newly elected Richard Nixon, perhaps to soften his image, had promised to ban DDT in 1970.[68] So despite Judge Sweeney's strong statement, and despite support for DDT from the American Medical Association, the National Academy of Sciences, and the US Surgeon General, EPA Administrator William Ruckelshaus, a Nixon appointee, banned it anyway for virtually all uses. Ruckelshaus would later say in a 1979 letter to then president of the American Farm Bureau Federation Allan Grant that "decisions by the government involving the use of toxic substances are poltical with a small 'p.' . . . The ultimate judgment [to ban DDT] remains political."[69] This was the first of many environmental policy actions to have dramatic human costs for public health.

NO MALARIA = MORE PEOPLE = MORE PROBLEMS

Around the same time it emerged victorious on banning DDT, the Environmental Defense Fund suffered an internal schism. It appeared to be over something chief scientist Wurster said, something that made its way into a congressional hearing. EDF cofounder Victor John Yannacone Jr., the attorney who filed successful lawsuits for the group, suddenly quit or was fired, depending on the account.

Yannacone was and remains a committed environmentalist and has never had any regret for his role in the DDT ban. But as reported in a House of Representatives hearing in 1971, Yannacone was incensed by outrageous comments he claimed were made by Dr. Wurster. In a 1970 speech that was excerpted in the hearing, Yannacone claimed that Wurster made the following shocking comments:

In response to a reporter's question as to whether a DDT ban could result in the use of organophosphate pesticides that are more dangerous to farm workers, Wurster allegedly replied, "So what? People are the cause of all the problems. We have too many of them. We need to get rid of some of them and this is as good a way as any."

In response to how Wurster squared human deaths with the loss of some birds, he allegedly said, "It doesn't really make a lot of difference because the organophosphate acts locally and only kills farm workers and most of them are Mexicans and Negroes."

In a letter to the House committee, Wurster denied making the comments. He claimed that Yannacone was fired from the EDF because he had "lost touch with reality."[70] Environmentalist Web sites such as Info-Pollution.com point to that letter to discredit Yannacone in attempts to disprove Wurster's hateful quotes.[71]

But the Web sites *don't* say that Yannacone has plenty of credibility and is now, in fact, viewed as an environmental hero by many in the very same movement. After the dustup with EDF, he went on to win a lawsuit on behalf of veterans exposed to high levels of the herbicide Agent Orange in Vietnam. Retrospective articles on the EDF quote both Yannacone and Wurster remembering the group's founding with fondness, as if no dustup had occurred. But this makes it all the more significant that Yannacone has never taken back his charges against Wurster. In 2006, Yannacone told me, "It was one of the things that led to my parting from the Environmental Defense Fund: their total insensitivity to people who were poorer and less well educated."[72] My attempts to reach Wurster for comment were unsuccessful.

And Wurster's comments, if he did make them, were in line with documented statements and writings around the same time. One of the major problems for some environmentalist leaders was that DDT was working too well at saving lives—and contributing to the dreaded overpopulation. The ban on DDT cannot be understood without looking at the hysteria at the time surrounding the population "crisis." But first, let's catch up with DDT's busy activity after the war of saving human lives across the globe.

MALARIA ALMOST ERADICATED

After the good guys won World War II, public health officials launched a global war on malaria with amazing results from the amazing chemical DDT. In the American South and much of the world, malaria infections were reduced to virtually zero. In the 1950s, the World Health Organization began the Global Malaria Eradication program. The US Congress, with bipartisan backing from those such as Democratic senator and future president John F. Kennedy, approved spending the equivalent of billions of today's dollars to spray DDT around the globe. And even with the usual bureaucratic encumbrances, it was working. As Malcolm Gladwell retrospectively wrote, "The results were dramatic. In Taiwan, much of the Caribbean, the Balkans, parts of northern Africa, the northern region of Australia, and a large swath of the

South Pacific, malaria was eliminated." Before DDT spraying, India suffered seventy-five million malaria infections and eight hundred thousand deaths every year. By the early 1960s, after continued spraying, malaria deaths had dropped to zero.[73]

In 1970, as the DDT ban was being debated, the National Academy of Sciences put forward this official statement: "To only a few chemicals does man owe as great a debt as to DDT. It is estimated that, in little more than two decades, DDT has prevented five hundred million human deaths, due to malaria, that would otherwise have been inevitable."[74]

But what were we to do with so many people? Environmentalists wanted to know. After all, according to some greens, people are a "plague" on the "natural" world. As environmentalist critic Dixy Lee Ray, former governor of Washington and chairman of the Atomic Energy Commission, noted, "If we are to believe the statements of some people, including several well-known biologists, that was just the problem with DDT. It saved human lives."[75] For instance, in justifying withholding money from DDT spraying in the third world, US Agency for International Development (USAID) economist Edwin J. Cohn said in the early 1970s, "Better dead than alive and riotously reproducing."[76]

Population control also appeared to be a big concern for Michael McCloskey, then director of the Sierra Club. McCloskey said in 1971 that "the Sierra Club wants a ban on pesticides, even in countries where DDT has kept malaria under control." He further explained, "By using DDT, we reduce mortality rates in underdeveloped countries without the consideration of how to support the increase in populations."[77] Similarly, Alexander King, co-founder of the doomsaying Club of Rome, also worried about DDT's effectiveness at saving lives. In a memoir published in 1990, King recounts, "In Guyana, within almost two years, it had almost eliminated malaria, but at the same time the birth rate had doubled. So my chief quarrel with DDT in hindsight is that it greatly added to the population problem."[78]

And even today, in the wake of a malaria epidemic in southern

Africa, population control is still a motivation for some environmentalists not to allow DDT's use. Consider this shocking statement on an organ of mainline environmental discussion, the Gristmill blog. In 2005, a blogger who identified himself as Jeff Hoffman, a former organizer for the eco-terrorist group Earth First! and now an environmental attorney, wrote, "Malaria was actually a natural population control, and DDT has caused a massive population explosion in some places where it has eradicated malaria. More fundamentally, why should humans get priority over other forms of life? . . . I don't see any respect for the mosquitos [*sic*] in these posts."[79] Other posters did disagree with Hoffman, yet the Gristmill still allowed him to post after his "final solution" comments.[80]

Of course the guru of the "overpopulation crisis" is Paul Ehrlich, and his best-selling book *The Population Bomb* was published in 1968 as DDT's use was being hotly debated. It's probably no coincidence that Ehrlich is also one of DDT's staunchest opponents. Even after the *New York Times* recently proclaimed the chemical's virtues in fighting malaria, Ehrlich cowrote a letter to the paper in 2005 opposing its use, saying, "there is no safe way to use it," and DDT was not a "cure of malaria."[81] That's like saying hand washing is not a "cure" for germs. I don't think Ehrlich would recommend dirty hands to reduce the population. But then again, given the other ideas he has proffered, maybe he would.

Ehrlich has been criticized for his silly, repeated predictions of mass starvation, to which I refer in chapter 1. But probably more important are the brutal, often very cruel, measures he has proposed to avoid an overpopulation "catastrophe." Ehrlich proposed that, in the United States, "luxury taxes could be placed on layettes, cribs [and] diapers."[82] He flirted with a proposal to require adding contraceptive material to all food items sold in the United States.[83]

But Ehrlich's most drastic—and contemptuous—measures were reserved for the third world. Ehrlich advocated that all men in India who had three or more children be forcibly sterilized![84] And he had nothing but scorn for what he called "the assorted do-gooders who are deeply involved in the apparatus of international food charity."[85] So Ehrlich endorsed the banning of all food aid—from governments and private charities—to undeveloped nations that didn't toe his line on population control![86]

Even though, mercifully, none of these measures were adopted, the DDT ban can in part be attributed to the cruel intentions behind Ehrlich's twisting of facts. Ehrlich's beyond-the-pale solutions didn't get much press, but his doomsaying predictions permeated the press and popular culture. Johnny Carson was a huge admirer and had Ehrlich as a guest several times on *The Tonight Show*. A host of imitating books were spawned by *The Population Bomb*'s success, with charming titles such as *Famine, 1975!*; *Breeding Ourselves to Death*; and *The Hungry Future*.

Policy makers and the public did not have to endorse or even be aware of Ehrlich's malevolent proposals to be swayed by the "over-population" sentiment he created. After all, people could reason, why save third-world people from malaria when they are sure to die of a mass famine by 1980? So the tradeoff that DDT saved lives was effectively neutralized as an argument against its ban.

The ironic and sad part is that when it came to feeding the world, just the opposite of Ehrlich's prediction happened. Ehrlich and other followers of eighteenth-century population doomsayer Thomas Malthus, such as Jared Diamond, always seem to forget the power of the human mind to stimulate food production and create a higher standard of living. As my boss, Competitive Enterprise Institute president Fred Smith, put it, "although individuals do indeed have stomachs, they also have hands and brains."[87] The late economist Julian Simon, who won a bet with Ehrlich about commodity prices, said that the human mind was "the ultimate resource."[88]

One such resource is the mind of Norman Borlaug, the agronomist. In the 1960s, just as Ehrlich was predicting doom and gloom, Borlaug's methods of high-yield farming—using DDT and other pesticides to fight off insects—made countries such as India and Pakistan more abundant in homegrown food than ever before. As author Michael Crichton points out, by 2000, India would become a net exporter of grain.[89] Although Ehrlich was getting all the attention, it was Borlaug who won the Nobel Peace Prize in 1970 for his contributions to dramatically reducing world hunger. In his nineties, Borlaug continues to develop innovative solutions for food production, now with the promise of biotechnology.

But just as the problems of food supply were dramatically improving, Western anti-DDT policies caused malaria to come roaring back in some countries that had almost completely wiped it out. In 1948, Sri Lanka had 2.8 million cases of malaria. By 1963, after years of DDT use, that number had dwindled to 17 cases. But then in 1964, US environmentalists and world health bodies convinced Sri Lankan officials to stop spraying. By 1969, the number of malaria cases had shot back up to pre-DDT levels of 2.5 million.[90] The use of other pesticides has brought malaria down somewhat there, but never again near the 1963 level. Every year, Sri Lanka has had thousands, and in many years, hundreds of thousands, of cases.[91] And many experts propose that the number of cases could shoot back to the millions as an effect of the Indian Ocean tsunami in late 2004 because mosquitoes thrive in water.[92]

Ethiopia has experienced a similar fate. The country started spraying in the 1950s and received assistance from the World Health Organization (WHO) to nearly eradicate malaria from the anopheles mosquitoes. When the program was in full swing, "something like 800 paramedical personnel using as many as 200 vehicles were spraying rural homes with DDT," according to the *Addis Tribune*, an Ethiopian newspaper. But the WHO's Global Malaria Eradication program bowed to anti-DDT sentiment in 1969 and stopped funding countries' use of the chemical. So did other government and private donor agencies. "[I]t is clear that in the absence of international support in the laudable war against the anopheles mosquitoes, Ethiopia was not in a strong position to fight a winning war against the dreadful disease," the

Addis Tribune noted.[93] And the US ban, although not directly prohibiting manufacture for export, also dried up supply.

In 2003 alone, malaria killed between 45,000 and 114,000 Ethiopians, according to the United Nations Children's Fund (UNICEF).[94] One of them was forty-six-year-old Gidyon Mekonen. A businessman living in the capital of Addis Ababa, Gidyon was visiting his rural hometown of Adama (called Nazareth, after the biblical Nazareth, for most of the twentieth century) in 2003. He had come, ironically, for a funeral, when a bite by a malarial mosquito would cause his own death. Gidyon complained of horrendous pains in his stomach and joints, and he was driven back to a hospital in the capital city, but two days later he died in a hospital there.

Gidyon's older brother, Mesfin, who lives in the Washington DC area, couldn't believe how out of control the disease had gotten. Mesfin is the longtime manager of the famous Reliable Source bar at the National Press Club, and he had plenty of connections among journalists and DC power brokers. He wanted to get Gidyon the best drugs and possibly have him sent to a hospital in the United States. But his relatives informed him that the disease had attacked Gidyon so virulently, it was too late.

Mesfin was sad, but also angry, because he knew the disease had once almost been licked through DDT. Choking up, Mesfin said, "If we still had DDT, this wouldn't have happened, I guarantee you."

Mesfin, fifty-four, vividly remembers the spraying and the DDT stations he saw when he was growing up in Adama. When he left in the 1970s, Ethiopia, despite a host of problems, pretty much had malaria eradicated through the routine spraying of DDT. "DDT was very effective for Ethiopia at preventing people from dying," Mesfin recalled. "It worked well, and I didn't see any problems for the land or the farms when I was there."

What also concerns Mesfin is that his family, compared to many in Ethiopia, is relatively affluent. If it killed his brother, he can only imagine what malaria is doing to rural families far away from hospitals and doctors. He is now working with Ethiopian American activists trying to push Western governments to remove the restrictions on making DDT that hit Ethiopians hard. "I strongly believe they should use DDT again," he said. "That's the best way to eradicate malaria from that part of the world. That's what's been effective time and time again."[95]

Mesfin isn't the only one concerned about African issues who is pushing for renewed DDT use. A petition calling for its widespread application to fight malaria was signed by Archbishop Desmond Tutu, longtime fighter of apartheid in South Africa, and Roy Innis, founder of the prestigious US civil rights group the Congress of Racial Equality. It was also signed by hundreds of notables, including many respected doctors and scientists.[96] As the letter stresses, the spraying would only be indoors, not on the outside where it would affect wildlife (if, and a big *if*, it does affect wildlife). But even this limited spraying has been resisted by the United Nations Environment Programme and the bureaucrats at our Agency for International Development. But they are ever-so-gradually allowing some DDT use because as an epidemic, malaria in Africa now kills more than AIDS does. It afflicts five hundred million a year, and kills two million. Based on the number of deaths from the Indian Ocean tsunami, malaria's death toll is equal to six tsunamis per year every year, points out my colleague Angela Logomasini, CEI's director of risk and environmental policy.[97] And malaria is most harmful to pregnant women and children younger than five.

So what do environmentalists who bashed DDT have to say for themselves? What they always say when a problem in the world arises. Incredibly, but predictably, they're putting the blame for the upshot in malaria on—drumroll, please—global warming! In his new book and movie, Al Gore blames warmer temperatures for African malaria heading north to Nairobi, Kenya. Narrating as if the mosquito-borne disease had never before surfaced in that city, Gore says, "Now, with global warming, the mosquitoes are climbing to higher altitudes." Nairobi's outbreak of malaria, according to Gore, shows that global warming is "increasing human vulnerability to new strains of diseases . . . once under control."[98]

Wrong again, Al. According to the World Health Organization, Nairobi experienced malaria epidemics throughout the 1920s, '30s, and '40s.[99] A 1962 report from the East African Institute of Malaria & Vector Borne Diseases noted that "Nairobi has experienced several serious malaria epidemics in the not-so-distant past and a repetition of this calamity seemed almost inevitable." It credited DDT spraying for a malaria epidemic not reoccurring after a flood in 1961.[100] But now, of course, thanks to Al Gore and Rachel Carson, there is little or no DDT used in Nairobi, and—surprise, surprise—malaria is back with a vengeance!

Further throwing cold water on the global warming-malaria association is Gore and other environmentalists' own doomsaying predictions. You know how they keep saying that global warming will cause, among other things, more severe droughts? Well, if that were the case, there would be *less* malaria, because "there would be fewer pools of standing water where mosquitoes could breed," notes my colleague Marlo Lewis, a senior fellow and energy policy expert at the Competitive Enterprise Institute.[101]

For centuries, actually, malaria was a fairly common disease. "In 1940, malaria was the leading cause of sickness and death of humans; and not only in the steamy tropical lands," states Robert S. Desowitz in *The Malaria Capers*, the authoritative history of the disease. "It was a great health problem in Europe, north to Holland."[102] It was also a problem in the United States. During the Civil War, half of the white troops and 80 percent of the black troops of the Union Army came down with malaria every year.[103] Malaria has occurred even as far north as Minnesota. America was somewhat successful in stamping it out through window screens on homes and the draining of swamps. But it took DDT in the 1940s and '50s to nearly eradicate it. One of the first major health applications of DDT was in the Tennessee River valley.

All this history raises an interesting—and scary—question. Could malaria, or other mosquito-borne diseases, make a comeback in the United States? In some ways, we are literally laying the groundwork, or rather the "wet" work, for it to happen.

In addition to not using DDT, we have stopped draining most of our swamps as well as other pools of standing water. These are now artfully called wetlands and are protected from drainage by federal law. In fact, Florida is going forward with elaborate plans to recreate the vast amount of swamps in the Everglades that were so filled with mosquitoes, they served as an ideal testing ground for DDT in World War II. These swamps are no longer in rural areas, but in metropolitan areas like Miami and Orlando. We will have more in chapter 6 about the federal government's running roughshod over property owners in the rush to preserve wetlands, as well as the incredibly broad definition of wetlands that regulators employ. In this environmental quest, one overlooked problem for public health is that while the government bans property owners from filling wetlands in, it can't ban mosquitoes from swimming in them.

An abundance of wetlands, paired with lack of DDT or other pesticides to control insects, could create a "perfect storm" for devastating diseases in the United States. As Dixy Lee Ray, who was also a longtime zoology professor at the University of Washington, warned in the 1990s, "Wetlands preservation, coupled with restrictions on managing marshy areas [through spraying], makes the future for insect-borne diseases either very dismal or very rosy, depending on whether one takes the human or insect point of view."[104]

Of course, unlike Africa, the United States has plenty of window screens and now air conditioning to counter a mosquito attack. Still, Dr. Ray pointed out that by the 1990s there were ten times the number of US cases of malaria than there were in the 1970s, when DDT spraying ceased.[105] In the late 1980s and early 1990s, for instance, there were malaria cases diagnosed in San Diego and the northern Florida Panhandle.[106]

In his brilliant *Politically Incorrect Guide to Science*, essayist Tom

Bethell confidently predicts, "If malaria returns to the United States, you can bet that DDT will return, too—and quickly."[107] I wish I could share his optimism. Unfortunately, green groups' behavior during another mosquito-borne threat casts doubt on their willingness to budge even in a public health epidemic.

Malaria is just one of several deadly diseases that mischievous mosquitoes can spread. And America is experiencing another in the form of the West Nile virus. In 1999, in New York City, sixty-two people were diagnosed with encephalitis, a painful inflammation of the brain. The cause of these encephalitis cases was soon diagnosed as the West Nile virus, which had previously existed primarily in the Middle East. West Nile is spread in humans and animals by a mosquito catching the virus from biting a bird, then spreading an often fatal infection by biting other birds, humans, and, less frequently, a variety of animals such as horses and cats. Seven of the New Yorkers died, and others experienced debilitating pain and suffering, often permanently. And unlike malaria, there is no medicine to cure encephalitis.

RUDY STANDS UP TO THE GREENS

New York's then mayor Rudolph Giuliani displayed the courageous leadership the nation would again observe in the days after the 9/11 attacks. He ordered aggressive, but targeted spraying of pesticides in spots that mosquitoes were most likely to congregate. But environmentalists fought him all the way. They downplayed the very real risk of West Nile—to humans and animals—while hyping the risks of pesticides.

Claims were made that one's chances of winning the lottery were greater than catching West Nile. The New York City-based "No Spray Coalition" claimed (and as of this writing, still claims) on its Web site, "Even if you are bitten by an infected mosquito, your chances of developing illness are roughly one in 300."[108] (If true, this is relatively high compared to other risks, like car accidents.) Incredibly, the Web site even contains information advising people who think they are coming down with West Nile symptoms to *not* see a doctor. "Patients with mild symptoms are likely to recover completely, and do not require any specific medication or laboratory testing," the Web site explains.[109] But the most outrageous statement of all came in 2000 from the New York City Green Party: "These diseases only kill the old and people whose health is already poor."[110]

The No Spray Coalition filed several lawsuits to divert New York City from spraying, forcing the city to divert vital resources that could have been used to further protect public health. Several environmental activists from across the United States, including the national Audubon Society harshly criticized the city's spraying program.[111]

But Rudy Giuliani fought back. The spraying was "perfectly safe" and essential for public health, he told *Newsday*. And he threw this zinger at his critics: "There are some people who are engaged in the business of wanting to frighten people out of their minds."[112] Unfortunately, some wealthy, liberal, suburban New York communities were taken in by the hype. The health commissioner of Nassau County, in the Long Island area, told the press in August of 2001 that he was not spraying because "[w]e believe the risk of infection for . . . residents remains quite low." But, as CEI's Logomasini noted, "Apparently the risk was not low enough for East Meadow residents Adeline Bisignano and Karl Fink. Both became ill with the virus at the end of the same month and died the following November."[113]

Unfortunately for public health, the mosquitoes have taken their show on the road and are wreaking havoc in almost every state. There have been around twenty thousand diagnosed cases and eight hundred deaths. And in answer to the New York Green Party's callous assertion about West Nile "only" killing the elderly and infirm, the virus has struck those from all stages of life, including small children. In 2003, the median age range for West Nile deaths was forty-seven, according to the government's Centers for Disease Control. Tragically, that year the mosquito-borne disease even took the life of a one-month-old infant.[114] And as the summer of 2006 came to a close, the state of Massachusetts and the nation were stunned and saddened when nine-year-old Boston area boy John Fontaine succumbed to Eastern Equine encephalitis, an illness caused by a mosquito-borne virus similar to West Nile.

Still, most enviros say pesticides are the greater danger. The No Spray Coalition is still filing lawsuits and has spread, just as the virus has spread, throughout the country. The No Spray chapter in Nashville, Tennessee, asserts on its Web site, "Mosquitoes are not the problem. West Nile Virus is not the problem. Mass airborne spraying of toxins into our environment is the problem!"[115]

Pretty bold statement. And incredibly, it was still up on the Nashville No Spray's Web site more than a week after the West Nile virus killed a woman in nearby Rutherford County, Tennessee, in August 2006.[116] Now, to recap, thousands have suffered and hundreds have died from West Nile in a period of just six years. How many people have died as a result of the "problem" of pesticide spraying? The answer, from fifty years of careful studies since modern pesticides have been in use, is a big fat *zero*! When used according to instruction, there have been no documented deaths from man-made pesticides.[117]

Their West Nile response shows, more than anything, that environmentalists only apply their Precautionary Principle to wildly hypothetical threats from man-made substances, not to demonstrable threats from "natural" diseases. No matter how much research is done showing pesticides are safe at doses many times greater than the human exposure levels, and despite the fact that the National Academy of Sciences says background human exposure to pesticides is "so low that they are unlikely to pose an appreciable cancer risk" and "below which any significant adverse biologic effect is likely," enviros still say we just don't know all the risks.[118] Yet we also don't know all the risks of West Nile. Could there be an epidemic if it spreads? What about in the marshy state of Louisiana where there are still standing pools of water from Hurricane Katrina? Why not, as a *precaution*, spray any area that could be conducive to mosquitoes carrying the virus? After all, we *do know* that West Nile can be lethal!

WHAT ABOUT THE BIRDS?

According to the US Geological Survey, more than 225 species of birds have been hit by West Nile.[119] And it has killed a member of nearly every type of bird species Rachel Carson claimed was threatened by DDT. At first, West Nile killed a large number of crows. In July 2002, two dead crows showed up on the White House lawn. One tested positive for West Nile; the other was too badly decomposed to be tested. According to CNN, White House employees had to wear special gloves and repellant to reduce the risk of getting infected by mosquitoes restarting the cycle by feeding on the crows.[120]

Then robins, the bird Carson pleaded for as a victim of DDT, began succumbing to West Nile. A dead robin in Jamaica Plain, Massachusetts, was found to have the virus. And a DNA study of the abdomens of three hundred mosquitoes in Connecticut found that 40 percent of the insects had fed on the blood of the robin.[121]

Majestic bald eagles and other big birds don't fare much better against the West Nile-carrying mosquitoes. In 2002, the *Baltimore Sun* noted an "outbreak of neurological illness and death among hundreds—and quite likely thousands—of hawks, eagles, owls and falcons across the Midwest."[122] The *Milwaukee Journal Sentinel* reported that "professionals who rehabilitate injured and sick wild birds say the virus has ripped through wild bird populations like nothing they have ever seen." One of those professionals told the newspaper, "Eagles seem to go down particularly hard when they catch it."[123]

Mosquitoes attacked many more birds on the endangered species list, including the peregrine falcon, another bird that DDT critics claimed was falling victim to the pesticide. In Virginia, three dead peregrines tested positive for West Nile. "We've only got 19 pairs in Virginia," Mitchell Byrd, chairman of the Center for Conservation Biology at the

College of William & Mary, told the Associated Press. "We can't afford to lose very many of them."[124]

These bird losses seem to vindicate the late Gordon Edwards. Recall that he argued that DDT was responsible for a rise in bird populations in the 1960s by controlling mosquitoes that spread bird and human diseases. Now the converse was occurring; lack of mosquito-killing insecticides appeared to be reducing bird populations. Henry Miller, founding director of the Office of Biotechnology of the Food and Drug Administration, says the situation for birds is much more dangerous today because of West Nile than it ever was in the DDT days. "You have a situation where some of these pathogens that could be controlled by DDT are killing birds by the millions," Dr. Miller says in an interview. "And we're talking about birds being killed, as opposed to a decrease in their reproductive range [as was alleged in *Silent Spring* and other anti-DDT tracts]."[125]

DDT: PERSISTENCE PAYS

Ironically, DDT may now be needed to rescue birds, not to mention people, from falling victim to the virus-carrying mosquitoes. Dr. Miller is among more and more prominent scientists who say it's time to bring DDT back to America as well as Africa, because it's the only thing that can break the back of emerging insect-borne diseases. "We use the alternative pesticides to spray, but they're very rapidly degraded and a lot of municipalities are going through their entire pest control budget very rapidly on frequent spraying," says Miller, who is now a research fellow at the Hoover Institution. Miller says DDT should be used to combat West Nile inside homes and "in swampy areas of municipalities and areas outside where mosquitoes are a particular problem, and the threat is high."

What would make DDT so effective for West Nile and other insect-borne diseases, Miller and other scientists say, is the chemical's persistence. "It's a real advantage of DDT that it perseveres, that it persists in the environment for this,"[126] Miller says. Environmentalists have particular scorn for DDT and other chemicals that persist in the environment. Their rationale seems to be: how dare anything be added into Mother Nature's Eden? But as we have seen with the research on DDT, persistent doesn't mean toxic. As with persistence in an individual, persistence in a chemical can be a very good quality. DDT's persistence in the atmosphere is the reason why Frank Knight only needed to spray it on trees once a year to kill and repel the beetles carrying Dutch elm disease. It's also the reason cash-strapped African communities only need to spray it on the walls of huts once a year to keep out the deadly malaria-carrying mosquitoes. Persistence is a major reason why DDT carries so much public health value for the money. It also means less spraying and less chance for worker injury.

DDT opponents have one final trump card they play when forced to defend the ban in the wake of the epidemic of malaria and emerging diseases. They claim that DDT doesn't work that well anyway because insects develop resistance to it. This argument, too, began with Rachel Carson. Tina Rosenberg noted in her insightful *New York Times Magazine* essay that "[i]n her 297 pages, Rachel Carson never mentioned the fact that by the time she was writing, DDT was responsible for saving tens of millions of lives, perhaps hundreds of millions."[127] Carson mentions malaria on only one page, and there, it is in a convoluted attempt to try to debunk DDT's proven effectiveness in wiping out the disease. Carson's argument, echoed by her followers today, such as blogger Tim Lambert,[128] is that if weak bugs are killed off by DDT, superbugs will immediately evolve that will be resistant to anything humans do.

Carson wrote that it was "the advent of DDT and all its many relatives that ushered in the true Age of Resistance."[129] According to Carson, all victories over deadly insect-borne diseases, many of which had happened before she even put pen to paper, were merely "short-lived triumphs that now strongly support the alarming view that the insect enemy has been made actually stronger by our efforts."[130] As evidence of her sweeping assertions, Carson cited the fact that there were mosquito-borne diseases incidences in Greece and the Republic of Trinidad and Tobago after DDT was used.[131] Carson never paused to consider if this could have been due to inexperience in spraying a new chemical, or simply that it might take more than a few years of spraying to eliminate the malaria that had plagued these countries for centuries. Today, thanks in large part to DDT (and the fact that these countries were able to spray extensively before Rachel Carson's hysteria set in), these countries are virtually malaria-free.[132]

Insects can develop resistance, but it's a process that takes place over decades. "The resistance arguments always strike me as silly," Miller says. "It's like worrying about giving antibiotics to somebody who has pneumonia and is in respiratory distress, because in ten years the bugs will be resistant. You don't withhold an important remedy for existing situations in order to forestall resistance." Germs can develop resistance to antibiotics, but we don't stop taking an antibiotic for our ailments, unless there is a more effective one on the market, Miller points out.[133] In fact one of the reasons DDT is so vitally needed in Africa, and possibly America, is because the malaria virus has grown resistant to drugs like chloroquine.

DDT, furthermore, causes less resistance than other pesticides. This is because it doesn't just kill, it repels. "It functions at extremely low levels as a repellant," says Donald Roberts, a professor of tropical medicine at the Defense Department's Uniformed Services University.

Think of DDT as working like an electric fence. If the bugs are stupid enough to stay on the "fence," or surface that DDT is sprayed on, they will very soon die. But the smart ones just fly away after the initial "shock." And because they weren't exposed to DDT for very long, resistance doesn't develop. And whether mosquitoes are killed or repelled, they don't enter homes to spread deadly infectious diseases. One way or another, "it will prevent mosquitoes from entering houses to a significant degree," Roberts says. "The other chemicals do not have that mode of action."[134]

This is why DDT, even while less acutely toxic to bugs than other pesticides, can have a greater impact at reducing disease. In South Africa, for instance, DDT spraying was halted in 1996 after spraying for about fifty years. One of the reasons for this, according to South African economist Richard Tren, cofounder of the group Africa Fighting Malaria, was because environmentalists persuaded authorities to believe that mosquitoes were becoming resistant. But the mosquitoes actually showed more resistance to the alternative, less persistent pesticides. South African malaria cases shot up from six thousand that year to sixty thousand in 2000. DDT spraying resumed in early 2000 in certain areas, and the number of malaria cases fell nearly 80 percent by the end of 2001 and continue to fall.[135]

And it is clear when environmentalists speak about resistance, they are talking out of both sides of their mouths. After all, if insects were resistant to everything humans do, there would be no need to protect them under the Endangered Species Act. Yet most of the species environmentalists have petitioned the government to be listed under that act are, in fact, insects.

And we didn't hear much about resistance when environmentalists were delaying for years the construction of roads, homes, and even a vitally needed earthquake-proof hospital in Southern California because it might harm the habitat of the Delhi Sands flower-loving fly.[136] The Clinton-Gore administration put this creature on the endangered list right after taking office in 1993. The Sierra Club, the Natural Resources Defense Council, and the National Wildlife Federation all wrote statements in support of protecting this precious fly from man's actions.[137] So following environmentalist logic, insects must become resistant to human activity only when environmentalists have no legal way to stop humans from killing them.

Flies, fleas, and ticks are all known spreaders of deadly diseases, and the last few decades of official "protection" of their habitats could lead to reemergence of the horrendous epidemics that we read about in history books. This is yet another reason why, once again, we may need the most effective insect-control device ever invented: DDT.

For instance, over the past twenty years, there have been an estimated two million cases of Lyme disease. The disease can result in serious conditions such as loss of reflexes and facial paralysis, blindness, and pneumonia. Lyme disease is spread by deer ticks, and is one of the increasing number of tick-borne diseases on the upswing. Another is Rocky Mountain spotted fever, which is similar to the typhus spread by lice that was so deadly in World War II. There is no vaccine for Lyme disease or spotted fever. Treatments are available, but are limited in effectiveness for many patients. So health advocates such as the Lyme Disease Foundation are placing a great emphasis on prevention.

Predictably, once again, Al Gore and his acolytes blame global warming for the ticks. Gore asserted in a speech in late 2005 that the "growing range of disease 'vectors' like mosquitoes, ticks, and many other carriers of viruses and bacteria harmful to people" is one of the "symptoms of a deeper crisis: the 'Category 5' collision between our civilization—as we currently pursue it—and the Earth's environment."[138]

Hmmm. Where do I start? Perhaps with the fact that the vast majority of cases of Lyme disease, the most prevalent tick-borne disease, have occurred in the Northeast and upper Midwest, two of the coldest regions of the country. If warming were a major factor, we would expect that most of the cases would occur in the warmest regions and then head north. Furthermore, an examination of the underlying cause shows it's not "our civilization" that's responsible for the increase in cases, but some "back to nature" policies supported by Gore.

Lyme disease is caused primarily by deer ticks, and this is associated with the explosion in America's deer population, which we will explore in chapter 5. As science journalist Ronald Bailey points out on *Reason* magazine's Web site, the Centers for Disease Control attribute much of the spread of Lyme disease to "reforestation."[139] That is the turning of former farmland to forest areas that attract wild animals and are largely unmanaged by humans. Among other things, this "cre-

ated the perfect habitat for burgeoning herds of deer and coinciden-
tally deer ticks which carry the disease," Bailey writes.[140] Again, we'll
learn more about this disastrous policy in chapter 5 (unless a deer just
hit your car and you can't wait. Then you have my permission to skip
there now).

And this is happening at the same time as the elimination of valuable chemicals that could protect people, as well as their beloved dogs
and cats, from these infectious ticks. In 2000, the Environmental
Protection Agency, led by Gore ally Carol Browner, phased out the multipurpose insecticide Dursban, the trade name for the organophosphate
chlorpyrifos. Dursban was sprayed on lawns, gardens, indoors, and
was in dog and cat collars to kill fleas and ticks. It was also used in products to destroy termites and cockroaches. Its effectiveness against
roaches was particularly valuable in the inner city, where roaches are a
trigger for asthma in children. No less than the Occupational Safety and
Health Administration of the Department of Labor had recommended
that employers use Dursban to control ticks and increase safety for
workers in grassy or wooded areas.[141] OSHA was echoing recommendations of the federal Centers for Disease Control.

But despite liberals' professed concern about asthma among inner-
city kids, a group of Northeastern Democratic state attorney
generals—including the ever-present Eliot Spitzer—lobbied the EPA to
ban and retailers to stop selling Dursban.[142] In announcing the phase-
out, Browner asserted, "Now that we have completed the most extensive scientific evaluation ever conducted on the potential health
hazards from a pesticide, it is clear the time has come to take action to
protect our children from exposure to this chemical."[143]

And what was the harm that was demonstrated that justified
Browner's drastic action? According to a *Forbes* magazine editorial,
three studies of humans exposed to Dursban found no harmful effects
even at the highest level of exposure. But one rat study showed reduced
birth weight and greater death rates in rat offspring when pregnant rats
"had massive doses of [Dursban] pumped directly into their stomachs."

With exasperation, Washington University toxicologist Michael Mullins commented to the magazine, "The mothers were all flagrantly poisoned, and it shouldn't surprise anyone that they were less able to nourish their offspring as a result."[144]

In December 2000, as part of the many "midnight regulations" the Clinton-Gore administration rushed through before George W. Bush took office, Browner's EPA phased out another chemical the CDC had recommended to control ticks that spread Lyme disease: Diazinon. Browner announced, "Today's action will significantly eliminate the vast majority of organophosphate insecticide products in and around the home, and by implementing this phaseout, it will help encourage consumers to move to safer pest control practice."[145]

Safer for whom? Certainly safer for the insects. But what about humans? What about preventing asthma and Lyme disease in children? And what about the poor dogs and cats losing a potent weapon against fleas and ticks? The same year Browner was announcing the phaseouts, the National Academy of Sciences concluded that "chemical pesticides should remain part of a larger toolbox of diverse pest-management tactics in the foreseeable future."[146]

UN TREATY THREATENS SOVEREIGNTY AND PUBLIC HEALTH

To the discredit of the succeeding Bush administration, Bush appointees did not reverse the Clinton-Gore phaseout of these valuable, lifesaving chemicals. Bush also has a mixed record on DDT. Early on, after taking heat for not withdrawing from the Kyoto Protocol on global warming in 2001, Bush signed the Global Convention on Persistent Organic Pollutants. This was likely due to the urging of Bush's then EPA head, former New Jersey governor Christie Whitman, a liberal, self-described "Rockefeller Republican." That treaty was put together by the United Nations environment program and would commit the United States and others to stop production of twelve chemicals, including DDT.

There is a small exception allowing that DDT could be used for malaria control, but countries would have to demonstrate that they were trying to phase it out. And it would severely restrict the export of DDT, greatly limiting the supply available for the unexpected public health emergency.

Fortunately, the US Senate hasn't ratified this UN turkey yet, but not because of any particular boldness shown by most Republicans. Rather, Democrats have blocked it because they want the EPA to go beyond the treaty. Hooray for gridlock! But the Democrats' plan does show that there is more than a dime's worth of difference between the two parties, and how the Donkeys have been so thoroughly captured by the Greens. According to CEI's Logomasini, "Democratic law-makers proposed allowing EPA to implement bans—*without any congressional authorization or consent*—when international bureaucrats add them to the Treaty List."[147] Hmmm. If they're going to bypass the Constitution's treaty provisions, why don't they just allow the EPA to ban the Constitution as well? No, scratch that; you never know when a politician will take an absurd suggestion seriously.

US relief agencies are also finally coming around to see DDT's necessity in African programs. Here Bush and Republicans do deserve some credit, according to Africa Fighting Malaria's Richard Tren and others in the malaria fight. Bush's appointees to the United States Agency for International Development have insisted that DDT be used in malaria-fighting efforts because it is the most effective insecticide against mosquitoes. The bureaucrats who resisted—such as the one who fretted to the *New York Times* that it would look bad because of DDT's stigma—have either left or acquiesced, Tren says.[148]

Tren cites specifically the courageous actions of Senators Tom Coburn (R-OK) and Sam Brownback (R-KS) who constantly scrutinized USAID in congressional hearings. Coburn is a fiscal hawk, and Brownback is involved with many international relief efforts, and both wanted to see foreign aid being spent on the most effective public health measures. Thanks to the efforts of the senators and Bush appointees, the agency recently announced that 20 percent of its malaria-fighting budget would be used for indoor residual spraying with DDT. That still leaves almost one hundred million dollars spent on other, less effective treatments, but it's a start.

Today, the biggest threat to effective DDT use to fight malaria, as well as the use of other valuable chemicals, comes from the all-powerful European Union. They are setting up a protocol called REACH (which stands for Registration, Evaluation, and Authorization of Chemicals) that would instill the environmentalists' pet Precautionary Principle into law. And once again it's only precaution against man-made chemicals, not "natural" diseases and threats to public health. All chemicals used in any significant amount, even those that have been around for fifty years, would have to go through an arduous registration process and a battery of duplicative tests. Basically, a chemical would have to prove it wasn't toxic to continue to be manufactured.

According to Tufts University economists, the total cost of REACH over a decade would be $11.5 to $28 billion.[149] The United States would be hit hard because of the chemicals it exports to Europe. But US chemical policy, and the use of chemicals for public health, could be hit in an even more direct way than that. Europe may try to push REACH on the United States and third-world nations through the Organization for Economic Cooperation and Development (OECD).

Although the United States is a member, the Paris-based OECD is dominated by nations of Western, or "Old," Europe. Started in 1960 as a sort of academic organization that published papers and studies, the OECD has in the past decade been increasingly asserting regulatory power over the domestic policies of all the nations of the world. One of its biggest projects has been its initiative against so-called "harmful tax competition," in which it "blacklisted" nations whose tax rates it deemed too low or who it deemed not cooperative enough in sharing private taxpayer information with other governments.

The OECD backed up its "blacklists" with attempts to influence other organizations to slap trade sanctions on countries that don't comply with the OECD's edicts. Dan Mitchell of the Heritage Foundation and Andrew Quinlan of the Center for Freedom and Prosperity—free-market activists who have long followed the OECD's exploits—believe the OECD's real agenda is to protect high-tax and high-regulation European countries from competition from the United States and developing nations. Mitchell says the OECD seeks "to create an OPEC for politicians" by hindering countries from lowering their taxes and regulatory barriers. Mitchell dug up a statement in which one OECD official blatantly said that tax competition "may hamper the application of progressive tax rates and the achievement of redistributive goals."[150]

And now the OECD is branching out into other areas of domestic policy, such as energy use that affects global warming. The chemicals testing framework of the REACH protocol was developed through the OECD, and the organization has endorsed the dubious Precautionary Principle in certain documents.

These European developments should be worrisome. Especially since, according to South Africa's Tren, the EU already "came out with indirect threats" to block trade from countries bringing back DDT to fight malaria. An EU official, according to Tren, specifically expressed concern to Uganda, saying that if DDT were allowed for malaria control, which would be entirely indoors, it could conceivably be used on agriculture. Part of the EU's motivation could be protecting German chemical giant Bayer AG, which makes non-DDT pesticides as well the well-known aspirin, from competition. In an e-mail unearthed by environmental writer Paul Driessen, a Bayer official told malarial scientists that "we fully support [the EU's move] to ban imports of agricultural products from countries using DDT." The official admitted that "DDT use is for us a commercial threat."[151]

Tren and Africa Fighting Malaria cofounder Roger Bate insist there is only one force that can be an effective counterweight to the EU's bad science and parochial interest. That is the United States of America. "Ultimately, it is poor children in Africa that pay for these policy failures based on abused science," Tren and Bate testified to the US Senate Environment and Public Works Committee. "We urge the US government to insist that years of scaremongering and bad science be reversed and to take a strong stance against the EU."[152]

And the stakes are high—for both Africa and America. In this case, Africa's fate is intertwined with our own. Dr. D. Rutledge Taylor, a preventative medicine physician and documentarian in Los Angeles, bluntly points out, "Now, the threatened faces are lighter, whiter."[153] The United States can't afford to *not* have DDT around if and when an emerging insect- or tick-borne disease turns into an epidemic.

Dr. Taylor points out that there is plenty of havoc that insects are wreaking right now in the United States that DDT could assist with. Combing through volumes of research and traveling the world for his forthcoming documentary on DDT *3 Billion and Counting*, Taylor writes that DDT is "the most effective chemical for preventing malaria and a veritable host of other diseases." He then lists the diseases that he believes DDT would be effective at preventing: "West Nile virus, Lyme disease, Rocky Mountain spotted fever, Dengue fever, lice, yellow fever, river blindness, elephantiasis, St. Louis encephalitis virus, typhus, Chengas disease, bubonic plague, Japanese encephalitis, bed bugs, and many others—not to mention many bird and animal diseases."[154]

Many of the health threats Dr. Taylor lists are on the rise in America. We've talked about the tick-borne Lyme disease and Rocky Mountain spotted fever. Here, it must be said, we don't have as much data as with malaria. These diseases were relatively rare before DDT was banned (which may not be a coincidence; DDT may have killed or repelled infectious ticks when it was being sprayed to combat other insects). Ticks are also not in the insect family of species, although there are certainly some similarities.

It is known, however, that DDT is credited with stopping an epidemic of tick-borne encephalitis (TBE) that spread through Russia in the 1950s and '60s. According to Oxford University Zoology professor Sarah Randolph, the Soviets followed with "a period of aggressive control of ticks by DDT spraying, achieving progressive decrease in incidence until the early '70s." Then, unfortunately, in the one instance when the Soviets shouldn't have followed the United States, they stopped spraying DDT. The USSR then experienced the fate of many countries that saw malaria rise when they stopped spraying. According to Randolph, use of DDT "ceased, and by 1990 TBE cases were back to their 1960s level."[155]

Interestingly, after DDT had long been banned for most uses in the United States, a respected science Web site that covers emerging infectious diseases recommended applying DDT to patients suffering from Rocky Mountain spotted fever and the medical staff who were treating them. "The patient and his medical and nursing staff may also need to be treated with malathion or DDT to prevent reinfection," stated guidelines on CBWInfo.com.[156]

But why not apply the Precautionary Principle to disease prevention instead of the disproven harm of DDT? That would lead us to spray DDT, along with other preventive measures, such as bringing back Dursban and diazinon for residential use.

The data is stronger on DDT's effectiveness against flies and fleas. And fleas spread one of the deadliest diseases known to man: bubonic plague. Fleas bite rats, squirrels, and other animals that carry the plagues, and then give it to humans when they bite them. It was this plague, which produces fever with dark swellings of lymph glands, that was probably responsible for wiping out one-quarter of the population of Europe in the Black Death of the fourteenth century. At the turn of the last century, there was a rash of deaths from bubonic plague in San Francisco.

And at the dawn of the new century, it's showing signs of a comeback. In New York City in 2002, bubonic plague was diagnosed in a husband and wife from New Mexico who fell ill. In April 2006, a Los Angeles woman was hospitalized with the illness. This was the first case in the city in twenty years. It caused some concern because the case was not travel-related, as were the previous cases. Health officials believe there may be infected squirrels in the forests and parks around the city.[157]

Since it was introduced in the '40s, DDT has been used successfully against fleas. US troops used it to control fleas in Dakar, Senegal, in World War II. And army biologist Robert Traub noted in 1954 that in the Korean War, fought in a country that had plenty of fleas as well as a history of bubonic plague outbreaks, "[f]leas proved to be a very minor problem . . . no doubt as a result of the liberal use of DDT powder in clothes and bedding."[158]

INSECT CONTROL, THE BIRD FLU,
BIO-TERROR, AND DDT

We shouldn't forget about the common fly's potential for death and destruction. House flies have spread dysentery, typhus, cholera, and even anthrax from viruses and bacteria that they have picked up on their legs and transmitted to food eaten by humans.

If that isn't bad enough, flies just might be a transmitter of bird flu. This connection, as with many facts about the emerging disease that has the possibility of turning into a pandemic, is far from established. But this much we do know: flies near a chicken farm in Kyoto, Japan, were found in tests in 2005 to have been infected with the HN51 bird flu virus. From what we know, flies aren't exposed to humans for a long enough time to transmit the virus, said Hiroshi Takimoto, who heads the office of infectious disease information at Japan's health ministry. Other scientists agree with him. Still, flies spreading the disease among birds remains a concern for Takimoto, as this could help speed the disease's transmission to humans. That's why he said flies should be exterminated near the site of any future outbreak. "As a preventive measure such things [exterminating flies] are probably needed to ensure the safest measures," Takimoto told the Reuters wire service.[159]

DDT has long been used to successfully combat flies. In fact, the mosquito is actually a member of the fly family, or the Diptera order of insects. All this leads into a topic of grave concern: bioterrorism. Particularly since 9/11, there has been a great fear that the next attack could be a bio-terror incident spreading a deadly disease—a large-scale version of the anthrax mailed to Congress and the media.

But most media accounts of how bioterrorism attacks could occur are misleading. In cases such as anthrax and the plague, the depositing of a spore or infected animal within our borders is not enough to cause mass damage. The damage will depend on how much of the bio-terror agents will be spread by insects. That's why we will need to be prepared with adequate stocks of insecticides, including DDT.

But whether a disease outbreak occurs naturally or through a bio-terror agent, the United States must be prepared and have plenty of DDT on hand. Currently, DDT is only produced in two countries: China and India. But when disaster happens, and one hopes it never will, there will not be a DDT fairy to magically whip up this insect-combating substance. Army leaders in World War II realized the only way to ensure a stable supply of DDT for public health emergencies was to allow the product for civilian use. This is why we need to produce and use DDT in the United States—NOW!

The US government should immediately pull out of the disastrous UN treaty on Persistent Organic Pollutants. Then the EPA should reverse its flawed and unscientific DDT ban of 1972. As discussed, DDT can be used in the United States now to combat diseases such as the West Nile virus and Lyme disease. The use of DDT now by state and local governments and by property owners would also prepare people for use of DDT should a public health emergency arise.

At the end of *Silent Spring*, Rachel Carson wrote that there were two roads, and the pesticides road was "deceptively easy," but ends in disaster.[160] As with nearly everything else in the book, once again Rachel Carson was fantastically wrong on both her points.

Using pesticides is not "deceptively easy." What is "deceptively easy" is the cultural and government philosophy that anything man-made is bad, and anything labeled "natural" or "organic" is good. Unfortunately, today this road is even more deceptively simple than when *Silent Spring* was written almost forty-five years ago. We can't imagine the lives of our grandparents and great-grandparents in the days when disease ran rampant. At the turn of the last century, it was still common for a family to lose at least one child.

The United States has traveled far down Rachel Carson's road, almost too far. But it's not too late to make a sharp U-turn and get back on the road of science and reason and technological progress. The public health of the nation demands no less.

3

The Anti-Asbestos Inferno

ASBESTOS BAN SETS BUILDINGS ABLAZE

All Americans remember the horrific attacks of 9/11, when more than three thousand citizens perished after the brutal al Qaeda terrorists crashed jumbo jets into the Pentagon and the two skyscrapers of the World Trade Center. But for those who were there and the families of those who died, it is something they think about every day of their lives. Mentally and physically, they are still living with its consequences.

This is especially true for the New York City firefighters who worked so valiantly to save as many lives as they could when the Twin Towers collapsed—and for the firefighters' families. Among the casualties that awful day were 343 who served in the New York Fire Department. Many firefighters are reporting illnesses such as severe asthma and chronic bronchitis. Questions remain about the exposure to chemicals in the smoke and dust of the debris, and in this case, it's not environmental alarmism. Exposure was at much higher than normal levels. This is a genuine public health concern.

Of all the materials in the towers, the media has latched on to one in particular: asbestos. "NYC under an asbestos cloud," blared a headline in the *Seattle Post-Intelligencer*. This followed a long string of asbestos scare stories that had run in the newspaper and on TV for more than twenty-five years. The claim that one inhalation of asbestos will eventually kill you had been the theme of many alarming stories. Superlawyers such as Peter Angelos, owner of the Baltimore Orioles, have made large parts of their fortunes suing any company remotely connected to asbestos manufacturing on behalf of anyone with the remotest exposure to asbestos.

But in the case of the World Trade Center, as in many others, the greater threat to public health and safety stemmed from a *lack* of asbestos. This is because, in many cases, nothing comes close to asbestos as a fire retardant. And experts are nearly unanimous that the towers fell not from the impact of the planes, but from the ensuing fires that were started by the jet fuel.

The original plans for the World Trade Center called for the interior steel in both towers to be covered with asbestos-based fireproofing material. These plans were cut short in the 1970s due to overblown scares about asbestos risks. Tragically, if the towers had been fully fireproofed with asbestos as planned, experts believe, at a minimum they would not have fallen so fast. As every firefighter knows, time is of the essence in fighting fires. If the towers had stood for four hours, rather than less than two, this would have given the New York Fire Department more time to save lives. It would also have reduced the firefighters' own exposure to the danger and possible long-term health effects of buildings that collapsed so fast.

And, incredibly, if asbestos had been used as planned, there is more than a good chance that the World Trade Center buildings would still be standing tall today in the financial district of lower Manhattan. One person who knows about quality buildings is real estate mogul Donald Trump. Under oath at a hearing of the US Senate in 2005, Trump testified that in the building industry, "a lot of people say that if the World Trade Center had asbestos, it wouldn't have burned down." He continued, "A lot of people in my industry think asbestos is the greatest fireproofing material ever made."[1] Trump's views are similar to those of trained scientists. Says Cornell University professor Rachel Maines, a Ph.D. from the renowned scientific Carnegie-Mellon University who teaches courses on the history of technology, "It seems likely that asbestos would have performed better than what was in those buildings."[2]

Even the evil mastermind of the attacks apparently did not expect the towers to completely collapse. In a videotape the terrorist made that was aired and translated on CNN, Osama bin Laden cited his experience in construction and said, "I was thinking that the fire from the gas in the plane would melt the iron structure of the building and collapse the area where the plane hit and all the floors above it only. This is all that we hoped for." The towers' complete collapse was just an added bonus in al Qaeda's jihad against America.[3]

So, incredibly, had more asbestos been used as a defense against fire, many of the health problems that may have been caused by asbestos and other elements in the debris might have been prevented—not to mention the thousands of lives that could have been saved. This "bonus" for bin Laden of killing thousands more people than expected and toppling the two second-tallest buildings in the United States might never have happened if the government agency building the Twin Towers hadn't hewed to "environmental correctness" and stopped using asbestos.

Let me pause a moment. I know this is a lot for readers to take in. So I'm going to take a brief departure from that awful day of the World Trade Center collapse before I return to this crucial analysis. Before I go any further, let me say there is only one party primarily responsible for the World Trade Center collapse. They are the evildoers in al Qaeda and the terrorist-sponsoring nations that enabled them.

Having said this, though, it is crucial to examine all types of mistakes to minimize the chance that similar tragedies will occur. Building security is an essential part of homeland security. If materials that can make buildings safer—for both terrorist attacks and accidents—are not being used, we need to have a frank discussion of why. And the very complexities of the World Trade Center collapse—the causes of which hinge on the lack of effective fireproofing—are giving rise to conspiracy theories that need to be convincingly corrected.

Before we go back to what went wrong that terrible day five years ago, we should look at the history and the science of the building materials experts say could have made a difference. And those materials happen to be the products of asbestos.

FRED ASTAIRE'S PAEAN TO ASBESTOS

I happen to be a fan of old movies and music. I also like listening to song lyrics as a way to study history, to get clues about what the attitudes were on culture, politics, and science. And there was one line that always struck me in the 1930s gem "I Won't Dance."

First performed by the famous dancing duo Fred Astaire and Ginger Rogers in the 1935 movie *Roberta*, the song has been covered many times, even though the film has been forgotten. A sophisticated song about how dancing leads to temptation and romance, most of the song's lyrics—penned by brilliant tunesmiths Oscar Hammerstein, Dorothy Fields, Otto Harbach, and Jimmy McHugh (the music was written by the great composer Jerome Kern)—are universal and timeless. Indeed, that is why the song is still so popular.

But there is one particular line that would seem very strange to modern audiences. It's when Fred sings to Ginger, "For heaven rest us. I'm not asbestos."

Fred was tipping his top hat to the important role of asbestos in the America of the 1930s. Asbestos was seen as almost superhuman, a miracle substance. And in many ways, it was—and still is. "Hundreds of thousands of people are now alive at least in part because the buildings or other structures in which they lived, went to school, or worked were rendered fire resistive by asbestos," Maines writes in her recent Rutgers University Press book entitled *Asbestos and Fire: Technological Trade-off and the Body at Risk*.[4]

Asbestos' heroic stature came about because of America's experience with a far greater risk—fire. In the nineteenth and early twentieth centuries, it was common for the United States to experience fires with hundreds of casualties in theaters, ships, schools, and office buildings. The infamous 1871 Chicago fire—in which the cause was falsely attributed to a lantern being kicked over by Mrs. O'Leary's cow (the original cause remains a mystery, but the fire was most likely spread by a cyclonic storm)—destroyed thousands of buildings and claimed the lives of two to three hundred people. And in terms of casualties, as we will see, this fire was far from the worst.

Various building materials were used to minimize fires, but all proved to have fatal flaws in some circumstances. As Maines writes, experience "in which granite exposed to high temperature deteriorated and 'melted,' . . . sprinklers proved unsatisfactory, steel supports weakened and collapsed, brick softened, and concrete cracked and spalled, reinforced the growing conviction that buildings and their occupants could not be reliably protected from fire without asbestos."[5]

Asbestos was, "in the decision environment of highly conspicuous fire risk, a building and insulating material that was incombustible, did not spread flame, had low thermal conductivity, and could be retro-fitted to existing structures with well-understood technology," according to Maines.[6] "There is no way to ignite it," she says of asbestos in an interview. "You might as well try to ignite sandstone or granite. It just will not burn. It will at high temperatures break down, but it will never catch fire. There's no other material like it."[7]

No substitute introduced to replace asbestos has ever been shown to hold up as well. Fire testing organizations, including the National Fire Protection Association, Underwriters Laboratory, and the American Society of Testing Materials, have consistently given asbestos materials a zero flame-spread rating, meaning they have no ability to spread flame under any circumstance. By contrast, the widely used asbestos substitute fiberglass has a flame-spread rating of 10 to 20. And fiberglass will also break down at 1,100 degrees Fahrenheit, whereas asbestos will last to 2,100 degrees.[8] And the sheer versatility of asbestos—it will bond with just about anything—is what has made it such an essential material in many applications.

ASBESTOS IS NATURAL AND ENVIRONMENTALLY FRIENDLY

Asbestos is also 100 percent natural. It's mined from six different types of rocks. In fact, asbestos is even found in the state rock of environmentally conscious California—the serpentine.[9] So, just as herbs and Omega 3 from fish are inserted into nutritional supplements, asbestos from the ground was put into ships, buildings, and other things such as brakes in cars. Given the craze for everything that's "natural," perhaps I should have written a book solely about asbestos and entitled it *Natural Fire Retardants They Don't Want You to Know About.* Just like a book with a similar title, it probably would have sold 4.5 million copies!

Asbestos also has a long history of use in various devices. The ancient Greeks used it to make lamps. In fact, *asbestos* is a derivation of a Greek word meaning "unquenchable." Charlemagne, who ruled over much of Europe in the eighth and ninth centuries, would amaze his guests by tossing a tablecloth made of asbestos into a fire and then retrieving it completely intact.[10] Asbestos was also heralded in the ancient writings of Plutarch, Pausanias, and Strabo.[11]

Asbestos is also environmentally friendly in many respects. By trapping heat, asbestos insulation substantially curbs the amount of energy that needs to be used, whether from oil or coal. In 1879, a hospital in Middletown, New York, reported saving two hundred tons of coal annually from the use of asbestos to cover the pipes.[12] "They made a big deal out of using it on ships in World War I, because it saved so much coal," Maines points out. "In World War II, again, energy supplies were strategic material."[13]

And asbestos also helps keep buildings cool in the summer, which is why it is used in roofing in some African countries even today. "It keeps a building cool because the outside heat doesn't pass through the asbestos in the way that it would through metal," Maines says. "It keeps the building warm because the heat from inside the building doesn't pass through the asbestos either. It keeps the heat from passing through a barrier in either direction."[14] Less fuel use, as we are endlessly told by environmentalists today, also means less pollution and less carbon dioxide emitted to contribute to global warming.

Now, just because something is natural or has been used for

thousands of years and promotes energy efficiency doesn't mean it's completely harmless. Bruce Ames, a biochemist at the University of California-Berkeley and recipient of the National Medal of Science, has discovered that 99.99 percent of substances capable of causing cancer in animal tests are natural substances made by plants.

But Ames and other prominent researchers are also quick to point out what has long been a principle of science: the dose makes the poison. The rat tests for natural and synthetic substances, such as pesticides and the sweetener saccharine, feed chemicals to rats at doses thousands of times higher than humans will ever ingest—doses that are, in fact, just short of poisoning the rat.[15]

If you think about this, it's not so foreign a concept that a small amount of a substance can be good for you, while a larger amount can injure or kill you. One or two aspirin will relieve your headache or cold, but if you take a bottle of aspirin, you'll die from an overdose. If you take a daily multivitamin, as I do and as many doctors recommend, look at the natural ingredients on the bottle. As Tom Bethell notes in *The Politically Incorrect Guide to Science*, "One such product lists the following: iodine, phosphorous, magnesium, selenium, zinc, copper, manganese, chromium, molybdenum, potassium, nickel, boron, and vanadium. All of these are toxic substances—at high doses."[16]

As we look at the risks of asbestos versus the risks of not using it, it's important to keep this knowledge about doses and amounts in mind.

AS AMERICAN AS ASBESTOS

In the nineteenth and twentieth centuries, Americans were building the new republic. Although they were busy tending to their farms and their jobs, they were also constantly innovating, building a better life for their children. And they were literally building the better life through the structures they built. Steamboats and then other types of ships made traveling easier than ever before. Big new theaters would open up, making plays and musical revues no longer the privilege of the wealthy few. Education also was no longer the privilege of rich children with private tutors, as parents and communities banded together to build schools.

What all these structures had in common was that they would house large groups of people gathering together. But with these new opportunities for betterment came danger—the specific danger of fire. Not only were there crowds of people, the methods of powering the activities in the structures presented unknown risks. We were just learning about the properties of steam, kerosene, and electricity. Several large-scale tragedies ensued.

But several more were prevented because of the use of asbestos. New ways of refining this old material meant that fire protection, too, was no longer just a privilege of the elite. As legal commentator Walter Olson, a fellow at the Manhattan Institute, has written, "With modern methods of mass production, fireproofing could develop from a luxury for the rich to something the ordinary citizen would come to expect in his schools and gathering places, passenger vessels, and apartment buildings."[17]

FIRE IN A CROWDED THEATER

One of the most famous sayings about the First Amendment is the admonition of Supreme Court justice Oliver Wendell Holmes that freedom of speech does not protect "falsely shouting 'Fire!' in a theater."[18] Today the saying sounds like a colorful analogy, but in 1919, Holmes was not at all imagining a hypothetical situation. In the decades preceding the Holmes's statement, some of the worst tragedies in America had been fires in theaters.

In 1811, the state of Virginia lost its governor, a former congressman, and sixty-six other citizens when a fire broke out in the Richmond Theater. The fire started after a single candle fell off a chandelier and ignited the stage. Six decades later in 1872, 283 people were killed at

Mrs. Conway's Theater in Brooklyn after a light batten set fire to a border curtain.

But the biggest ever US theater fire—in fact the deadliest single-structure building fire in American history—would occur in 1903 at the Iroquois Theatre in Chicago. The fire started during a matinee performance of the play *Mr. Bluebeard* when a border curtain was ignited by an arc lamp. Six hundred three audience members died. As Maines points out, this is more than twice the number of those who perished in the great "O'Leary fire" in the same city three decades earlier, and more than all the US casualties in the Spanish-American war. And 40 percent of the Iroquois casualties were children.[19]

In Richmond, Brooklyn, and Chicago, the culprit was the curtain. A fire could easily incinerate cotton or vegetable fibers, the material of the curtain in the Iroquois theater.[20] There were curtains made of iron, but they were hard to maneuver between scenes in plays—hence the term *iron curtain* to describe the closed society of the Soviet bloc, where the "curtain" never opened to let anyone out.

But there was a new material that was on the horizon in the early twentieth century that made curtains both maneuverable and fireproof. Or rather a new, old material: asbestos. In the 1870s, entrepreneur Henry W. Johns introduced a line of asbestos-containing products including mittens, cloth, paint, cement, roofing material, as well as boiler packing insulation, which would turn out to be very important, as we will see, for schools and ships. Johns' little company would later become the Johns-Manville Corp., one of the nation's biggest asbestos merchants. Many were noticing that in addition to its fire resistance, asbestos had many other practical qualities. As Cassandra Chrones Moore, an adjunct scholar at the Cato Institute and Competitive Enterprise Institute, writes, "Virtually indestructible, asbestos insulates against noise as well as heat, resists friction and chemicals, and can repel water."[21]

These myriad qualities made asbestos ideal to be used as material in a theater curtain. Here was a material that could be easily woven like cotton, yet was more fire-resistant than iron. By 1909, little more than five years after the Iroquois tragedy, almost all of Chicago's theaters had asbestos curtains. City codes and insurance companies began to require that theater curtains be made from asbestos. And according to Maines, theaters showing both movies and plays would also prominently advertise the existence of an asbestos curtain until the '50s.[22]

Asbestos in theaters saved countless lives. "[T]he slaughter of audiences in the live theater ended in the United States with the Iroquois," writes Maines. Never again was there a theater fire with casualties in the triple digits. In most years of the twentieth and twenty-first centuries, there have been only a handful of deaths from theater fires around the world, and in many years there have been zero in America. It is also very fortunate that asbestos made its way into theaters around the same time as motion pictures did. Early film, made from celluloid, was highly flammable, and there were frequent small fires in the projection booths. But the asbestos linings and floors of those booths prevented the fires from spreading, and they were usually quenched with no injuries.[23]

ASBESTOS SAVES OUR CHILDREN FROM FIRE

Theaters weren't the only firetraps in the "good old days." As recently as the late 1950s, fire was a constant threat in American schools. It is ironic that in the past two decades, asbestos has been described in terms such as used in this *USA Today* article describing "a killer in the corridors, gyms, or boiler rooms of 40,000 schools across the USA."[24] Not only, as we will see, is there little danger from the low-level exposure to asbestos in schools, asbestos was installed to prevent a real danger lurking in a school's corridors, gyms, and boiler rooms: the danger of fire.

In 1908, a fire in the boiler room broke out at Lakeview Elementary School in Collinwood, Ohio. It started either from a coal-fired furnace enclosed by wood or a heating pipe that ignited a wooden floor. The school had practiced fire drills to evacuate the school in ten minutes, but on this occasion, writes Maines, "ten minutes was five minutes longer than they had."[25] The wooded walls around the front door were on fire within five minutes. One hundred seventy-two students—children between the ages of six and fifteen—perished in the fire, as did two teachers. "After that, [fire professionals] were determined they were going to get all the schools' boilers, furnaces, and heating pipes all over the country insulated with asbestos," Maines says.[26]

But boilers and furnaces were not the only things that could spread fire in schools. In 1958, a fire, whose cause is still unknown, broke out at a parochial school called Our Lady of the Angels in Chicago. The fire, which some believed to be arson, quickly spread through walls and the ceiling cemented with combustible cellulose fiber. Ninety students and three teachers perished. Two more victims died in hospitals, where there were seventy-seven with serious injuries from the fire.

The images on black-and-white television of firemen carrying out small limp bodies from the school galvanized the nation to make schools more fire-safe. In 1960, the National Academy of Sciences recommended that schools be built with "non-combustible materials such as asbestos-cement board." By 1964, the National Council on Schoolhouse Construction instructed that schools have asbestos in ceilings, in cracks between walls, and in other areas where fires could break out.[27] Schools took the recommendations seriously, and the fire of 1958 marked the last time a large number of children died in an American school fire.

ASBESTOS PROTECTS AMERICAN SHIPS AND TROOPS

It always makes big news when a "direct action" environmental group such as Greenpeace seizes a ship. They offer the explanation that the ship contains asbestos and other substances that they're preventing from being spread. But have you ever thought to ask yourself why ships have asbestos? It isn't because shipmakers were evil. It is because ship fires were a very real danger—so much that the government actually encouraged asbestos on ships as a fire retardant.

We don't usually think of ships catching on fire. After all, they're sailing in the middle of huge bodies of water. But that water often isn't readily available to be scooped up when a blaze begins. In fact, there's the added danger that the water used to fight the fire will sink or capsize the ship.

Ships are at risk because they operate with huge boilers that reach very high temperatures. And, as is the case in schools, boilers are very prone to start fires throughout the structure. And it is difficult to insulate a boiler with fire- and heatproof materials.

"There's not another mineral that you can easily use on a boiler," says Dr. Maines. "Granite doesn't burn, but it's awfully hard to use granite on your boiler. Ceramic has a zero flame-spread rating. But once you've got baked ceramic on your boiler, it's pretty hard to fix your boiler."[28]

After Robert Fulton invented the steamboat, steamer travel took off, but so did fires. More than two hundred steam vessels caught fire and blew up between 1816 and 1846. In the late nineteenth century, ships began to use asbestos for boiler packing.

But with new technologies, new fire hazards were emerging. Maines writes, "When electricity began to be used on ships, partly to reduce the risks of lighting with open flames, it was soon discovered that two hundred miles or so of electrical wiring running through a passenger liner not only created a continuous stem-to-stern source of ignition, but the conduits through which the wiring ran proved ideal for the passage of smoke and flames." A modern ship also carries more fuel, leaving more opportunities for fire to start.[29]

The stress of war compounds this all. There you have an enemy actively trying to set the ship ablaze through weapons like torpedoes. And an aircraft carrier makes an even more attractive target with its planes full of additional fuel and covered with flammable sealants and paint. When the United States entered World War II, fire played a major role in the sinking of its aircraft carriers in 1942, including the USS *Lexington* at the Battle of Coral Sea, the *Yorktown* at Midway, and the *Wasp* at Guadalcanal.[30]

Just as DDT had been called in to protect the troops from the dangers of malaria and typhus, Private Asbestos reported for duty to save thousands of soldiers from ship fires. President Franklin D. Roosevelt had actually called for asbestos fireproofing in all ships even before the war, after 137 people were killed in the 1934 fire of the Morro Castle cruise ship near Asbury Park, New Jersey.[31] By the time the United States entered World War II, the military listed asbestos as a "critical" material for the war.[32] In the shipbuilding spree of 1943 and 1944, in which millions of ships were built, the vessels were fortified with fireproof asbestos in every place they could be. Special types of asbestos were even imported from Africa and Australia for use on US ships. (This fact would become a crucial element in the debate over asbestos risks.)

There were a lot of areas in the ships where asbestos could be installed with relative ease. Remember that asbestos is also waterproof. So the new ships contained asbestos in bulkheads, gaskets, tape and insulation of electrical wiring, and curtains separating the decks. Maines attributes to these asbestos uses, as well as, of course, to the superb performance of our navy men, the amazing fact the no US aircraft carriers were sunk in the war after 1942.

Even a sinking attempt by a Japanese kamikaze, or suicide, pilot ultimately proved unsuccessful thanks to asbestos and the skills and bravery of our sailors. In the early morning of 19 March 1945, the USS *Franklin* aircraft carrier was within fifty miles of Japan, farther than any US sea vessel. But suddenly, a single Japanese kamikaze plane flew into the ship, piercing the cloud cover and dropping two semi-armor-piercing bombs. Fire spread through two decks, knocking out radio communication and making the *Franklin* appear dead in the water. Seven hundred twenty-five men were killed instantly.

But in significant part due to asbestos, more than three thousand of the crew survived and the ship stayed afloat. The large asbestos curtains separating the deck, as well as the ship's other asbestos-based materials, "protected the flight deck forward of the superstructure and the engine area," writes Maines.

There was also great bravery aboard the ship. Wounded crew members were evacuated onto the nearby USS *Santa Fe*. Lieutenant Donald Gary found three hundred men trapped in a mess hall filled with smoke and returned repeatedly to lead them to safety. He also entered an extremely hot boiler room to turn up the steam so the ship would stay afloat. Gary would later receive the Congressional Medal of Honor, as would the ship's chaplain, Father Joseph O'Callahan, who not only administered last rites to the dying but directed the firefighting and rescue parties to the explosive areas of the ship.

Partly towed by the USS *Pittsburgh*, the *Franklin* sailed eventually under its own power across the Pacific to a rebuilt Pearl Harbor. After the ship was cleaned up, the *Franklin* and her crew sailed to a hero's welcome at the New York Naval Shipyard in Brooklyn on 28 April 1945.

When the *Franklin* arrived in New York, the Germans were less than two weeks away from surrendering. Japan would be defeated a few months later with the dropping of the atomic bomb on Hiroshima and Nagasaki. As the crew was sailing from the port where bombing had started the war to America's largest city, probably no one thought that New York itself would be subject to a surprise attack from a suicide plane some fifty-five years later. And they would have been horrified by the thought that both ships and buildings would be subject to less protection than they were in the 1940s. Yet these were the exact circumstances that made 11 September 2001 such a horrendous day.

ASBESTOS ABATEMENT ARMAGEDDON

On the morning of 9/11, Arthur M. Langer was working from home, and home was not far away from the Twin Towers. Dr. Langer, a mineralogy professor at the City University of New York, was catching the news on CNN before he settled into his daily routine. Just after 8:30, Langer looked up at the TV after hearing a report that a plane had crashed into the World Trade Center.

Viewing the damage, Langer was alarmed, but not terrified. He knew from the beginning this was no "accident." All he had to do was look out the window to see it was a beautiful, clear day, which would give excellent visibility to an airline pilot. But Langer was intimately familiar with the way the towers were built and thought that—except in the areas the plane directly hit—an orderly evacuation was possible. After all, one of the buildings had remained intact after a terrorist bomb was set off in 1993, and just a handful of people were killed. And he knew the building was supposed to be protected from fire for at least four hours. Langer recalled: "I looked at that and said to myself, 'Well, they have a couple of hours to get people out. I think we can get through this.'"

Langer remained confident even after the second plane hit the other tower. But within two hours, both buildings had collapsed. Langer had had a sinking feeling. He thought back to a meeting he and his colleagues had with officials overseeing WTC construction more than thirty years earlier. At the meeting, Langer's boss, Irving Selikoff, warned of the newly-found "dangers" of asbestos in office buildings and urged the use of asbestos substitutes for fireproofing and insulation. Selikoff's pleadings were successful. Watching the wreckage on his TV, Langer was suddenly horrified. "I said, 'Gee,' to myself, 'that asbestos substitute has played some role in this rapid collapse.'" A wealth of evidence would prove Langer's hunch correct.

Today, Dr. Langer says of asbestos, "Knowing what I know thirty-six years later, I would have said we need this material. . . . These materials can be used with relatively little risk. The substitutes do not perform as well, and quite frankly, there are ramifications that would lead to end points that are far more serious than the use of the [asbestos-containing] materials, if you want to do a comparative risk calculation."[33]

Four years after the attacks, the National Institute of Standards and Technology (NIST), a division of the US Department of Commerce, would largely confirm Langer's concerns about asbestos substitutes. The NIST report produced some amazing yet definitive conclusions about the causes of the World Trade Center collapse. The conclusions offered both reasons for confidence and cause for alarm. "Even with the airplane impact and jet-fuel-ignited multi-floor fires, which are not normal building fires, the building would likely not have collapsed had it not been for the fireproofing," said Shyam Sunder, who led the investigation.[34]

First, the reasons for confidence. The WTC buildings were strong— strong enough, if not for other factors, to survive Osama's evil plot. The planes hitting the building did not cause the collapse, nor, by itself, did the fire started by the jets' tremendous amount of fuel. Rather, it was the fireproofing, most of which lacked asbestos, that could not protect the building's steel from either the heat or debris. In fact, because of the faulty non-asbestos fireproofing, a normal, accidental office fire may very well have brought the buildings down if Osama hadn't gotten there first.

And this is the reason for alarm. Because of the abandonment and abatement of asbestos fireproofing, America's skyscrapers and thousands of other buildings are at risk from fires caused by either accidents or terrorist plots. Dr. Langer says, "My concern is that there have been buildings constructed across the United States, from New York City to the earthquake zone in California [with asbestos substitutes shown to be inadequate]. This might be a problem for other buildings."[35]

Had the World Trade Center been built just a few years earlier, the whole building would have been fortified with asbestos as planned, and the 9/11 attack wouldn't have been nearly as deadly. Langer's memories and documents uncovered by the NIST report give a bird's-eye view of how the plans to use asbestos in the WTC were abandoned because of sketchy science. Instead, fireproofing substitutes were used that only had minimal amounts of testing. Once again, the environmentalists' Precautionary Principle, by discounting known risks in favor of hypothetical ones, led to thousands of needless deaths.

And the dismal performance, documented in the NIST report, of the asbestos substitutes in protecting the World Trade Center and its inhabitants from raging fire should serve as a warning against the quick use of other "environmentally friendly" replacements for reliable substances that have been subjected to the scare-of-the-month treatment.

WTC WHISTLEBLOWER PREDICTED LACK OF ASBESTOS WOULD TOPPLE BUILDING IN FIRE

The media lionizes those whom it deems whistleblowers. And 9/11 was no exception. Nearly everyone who had warned that airlines were not safe from hijackers or that law enforcement was not doing enough to track terrorists was profiled and celebrated, as most of them should have been. But except for a few commentators such as Steven Milloy, the "junk science" columnist for FoxNews.com, there has been very little coverage about one of 9/11's most important whistleblowers: the late scientist and inventor Herbert Levine.[36]

Although he never envisioned a situation such as the 9/11 attacks, had Levine's words been heeded, much of the ensuing tragedy could have been avoided. Ever since the WTC complex was built in the early 1970s, Levine warned everyone he knew that the buildings were largely unprotected against fire. Harvard physicist Richard Wilson recalls Levine telling him in 1991, "Whenever I pass by there, I worry. If a fire breaks out above the 64th floor, that building will fall down."[37]

Levine knew a thing or two about steel skyscrapers. He had invented the product that made it possible to build them—asbestos-based, spray-on fireproofing. Until the 1940s, most buildings were built with concrete enclosures. New York's Empire State Building was cased in concrete. Yet steel as a building material was both less expensive and stronger. The steel was credited with saving the World Trade Center from falling in the 1993 bombing.[38]

But there was a well-known problem with steel. It would bend or eventually melt in a fire. Then in the late 1940s, Levine invented AsbestoSpray, a spray-on flame retardant made of asbestos that adhered to steel. The World Trade Center's architect, Minoru Yamasaki, counted on using asbestos-based spray when he decided to build the two towers out of steel.

Yamasaki and the builders planned to make the building as safe as a skyscraper could be to protect its inhabitants from all outside hazards. They even foresaw the remote chance that a plane could crash into the building. (A small plane had accidentally flown into the Empire State Building in 1945.) So each tower was built to withstand the impact of a Boeing 707, the largest jet of the day, loaded with fuel.

But as well-planned as the building was, it was still subject to the pressure of any political entity. The World Trade Center's "owner" was the Port Authority, a government agency run by the states of New York and New Jersey. Like all government agencies, this one was easily subject to political pressure, or the scare of the moment. And in 1970, the brand new scare about asbestos would cause the Port Authority to make a fateful decision that thirty years later would cost the lives of thousands of people on 9/11. Herbert Levine's prophecy, unfortunately, would come true.

Deniers of the asbestos factor say that Levine was just angry because his product wasn't used in the buildings.[39] In the early 1970s, Herbert Levine did, indeed, face many competitors using fire retardant spray for buildings. He would have loved to have had his AbestoSpray used in the World Trade Center. However, the Port Authority had chosen another company's product, but originally one that used asbestos. Levine didn't complain then. He only expressed alarm after the Port Authority suddenly stopped asbestos-based spray on the flimsiest of evidence.

SELIKOFF: PHONY MD BECOMES DR. DOOM
FOR WORLD TRADE CENTER

This evidence would come from Irving Selikoff, a "doctor" across town at Brooklyn's Mount Sinai Hospital, who would go on to become the leading asbestos Chicken Little. I call him that as half a compliment. To be a Chicken Little is to be a step above Rachel Carson and other environmentalists who simply cook up scares to fit their own human-bashing worldviews. Rather, a Chicken Little reacts to a genuine hazard—an acorn hitting a chick's head when he walks under a tree—but then goes off half-cocked shouting, "The sky is falling!" before gathering the facts about the limited problem at hand and how to deal with it. Chicken Little would actually have been very helpful to his fellow barnyard animals had he warned them not to walk under this particular tree or to wear a helmet when doing so.

Similarly, Selikoff and his colleagues documented a genuine danger from asbestos (or at least some types of asbestos) to asbestos workers at certain high-exposure levels and under certain conditions. Had he become an advocate for improved safety measures for asbestos workers, such as more comfortable masks and better methods to measure asbestos in dust, he would have done everyone a service. Instead, Selikoff, in a literal sense, fanned the flames that led to the collapse of the WTC and other disasters through his demonization of a lifesaving product. And he made a series of ethical transgressions.

Although people were impressed with Selikoff's supposed sincerity, Selikoff was a very dishonest man. First, "Dr." Selikoff lied about his medical degree: he never actually had one. Born in Brooklyn, Selikoff traveled abroad after getting a Bachelor of Science from Columbia University. He claimed to have gotten an equivalent to an American MD from the "Anderson College of Medicine" at the University of Melbourne in Australia in 1941. But British scholar Peter Bartrip, a fellow at Oxford University's Centre for Socio-Legal Studies, found that there never was an Anderson College of Medicine at that university.

Selikoff did take some medical courses, but was well short of getting a medical degree in any country. If Selikoff's fraud had been known when he was peddling the asbestos scare, "his credibility would almost certainly have been destroyed," Bartrip concludes.[40]

Instead, from one big fraud came several distortions of fact and a manipulation of evidence that would lead to thousands of needless deaths from fire. Selikoff's first study on asbestos came out in the mid-1960s. Using his phony credentials, Selikoff got his studies into the prestigious *New England Journal of Medicine* and *Journal of the American Medical Association*. The studies concluded that workers exposed to asbestos, such as the shipbuilders of World War II, would get lung diseases such as lung cancer or mesothelioma.

High exposure to asbestos had long been thought to be a health risk, and caution had been urged by doctors since the early twentieth century. Selikoff's first studies did document a significant risk among a large number of workers, but there are several qualifications that Selikoff would skip over in public appearances. The first is that many of the men who worked in the World War II shipyards were heavy smokers. And in those days there were not even filtered cigarettes. A later study by Selikoff and a coauthor in the late 1970s found that asbestos workers who smoked more than a pack a day had ten times the death rate from lung cancer than those workers who didn't smoke regularly.[41]

Also important were measures that individual worksites took to reduce worker exposure. This included ventilation, dust measurements, and the availability of oxygen masks. Some companies were slipshod in this regard, but one of the biggest offenders here was the US government, which controlled the shipyards during wartime. In the building spree of World War II, the navy's surgeon general warned about shipbuilders' high exposure to asbestos in locations such as the Naval Shipyard in Brooklyn. Yet the Roosevelt administration vetoed the idea of outside inspectors to monitor health issues at the Naval Yard. Federal judge Jack Weinstein would decades later say, despite ruling against asbestos manufacturers on technical grounds, that there was "no doubt" in his mind "that the government is primarily responsible" for the illness of the war's shipbuilders because it "did not inform workers of the dangers and neglected to make available protective precautions."[42]

Another important factor was the types of asbestos the US government used to build its warships. Recall that special types of asbestos were imported from Australia and Africa. These asbestos are brown and blue and called amphibole. By contrast, 95 percent of asbestos used in United States were white and called chrysotile. But these types of asbestos did not just differ in color. They differed in length, width, and most importantly, the ability to penetrate the lung. Chrysotile fibers are short and thin, whereas amphibole fibers are longer, thinner, and needle-like. As a result, *Science* magazine concluded in the 1990s after a wealth of studies, it is amphibole fibers that "are the major cause of mesothelioma in asbestos workers."[43]

But Selikoff never made a distinction. In fact, he was almost insistent that chrysotile asbestos was the major culprit. "Irving Selikoff was convinced at that time that the health effects he was observing in that group of US insulation workers were related principally to chrysotile, not to the amphibole asbestos," Langer, who worked under him at Mt. Sinai, recalls. Langer adds that now, "[w]ithout reservation, one would conclude that the amphibole asbestos varieties have produced the preponderance of mesothelioma in various workforces."[44] Unfortunately, US government policy and court verdicts followed Selikoff's lead.

The World Trade Center was using only chrysotile asbestos when Selikoff started his first alarmist campaign. In 1969, he jaunted around New York City making outrageous claims that not one man spraying asbestos fibers on the building would be alive in twenty years.[45] In response and because of heightened awareness, the Port Authority measured the dust regularly and provided workers with top-of-the-line dust filter masks.[46]

So Selikoff moved to another claim, one that had no basis but that he and others would employ with numerous successes in scaring the daylights out of Americans from asbestos. That is, that there was no safe threshold for asbestos exposure for anyone with any exposure to asbestos, including employees and residents who had asbestos in fixtures in their offices and homes.

THE FATAL WTC DECISION

There are "potential problems of exposed fireproofing containing asbestos," wrote World Trade Center construction manager Rino M. Monti in a memorandum dated 15 May 1970. The memo is included in the previously mentioned comprehensive report of the Commerce Department's NIST. Monti specifically cites Selikoff raising the alarm over even modest asbestos exposure. "It was maintained by Dr. Selikoff that studies performed by his staff indicated that exposure over a considerable number of years of people sitting in an office, where the return air passed by exposed spray fireproofing containing asbestos, could cause health problems," Monti wrote. Further, Selikoff inserted himself into the process by telling Monti and others that newly developed asbestos substitutes were just as effective at halting fire.[47]

Langer recalls that Selikoff actively pushed asbestos substitutes, vouching for their safety and effectiveness at meetings with officials in charge of WTC construction. "We argued that asbestos in the formulation should be taken out and substitutes should be used," recalls Langer. "There was a concern with how much risk was associated with lower-level exposure."[48]

But seemingly overlooked was a deadly risk: the age-old risk of fire. Once again, the environmentalist Precautionary Principle trumped common sense by placing a higher value on the unknown than on the known hazard. Reading the documents of Monti and other WTC officials in the '70s, one marvels at how they were so willing to accept asbestos replacements that had barely been tested against fire. Monti expressed concern about what he called the "potential problems of exposed fireproofing containing asbestos." There appeared to be much less concern about the actual, demonstrated problem of fire.

Monti found out about asbestos substitutes from mineral wool that were not independently tested and had never been used in commercial buildings. Monti thought it was adequate to order basic tests from Underwriters Laboratory that were completed in less than six months. In his memo, Monti led others to believe tests had been completed when the spraying started. "The fire rating tests . . . had passed all the requirements," he wrote.[49]

But a letter to Monti from Underwriters Laboratory that was also included in the NIST report says something different. It described the tests as only being "approximately 80 percent completed." And it cautioned that "our test results to date are not 100 percent conclusive."[50]

In the end, the building was even less protected with asbestos fireproofing than Herbert Levine thought. According to the NIST report, the asbestos-based spray was only used on the columns up to the thirty-eighth floor of the first tower and none of the second tower.[51]

Monti was entirely willing to accept fire retardants in their testing stages because he didn't know the extent of asbestos risk. But in doing so, he gave short shrift to the known risk of fire. "It was the unknown that drove this," says Langer. "It was really the enforcement of the Precautionary Principle, which at first blush seems reasonable. If you were to make an error in judgment, you would err on the side of safety. Whether you can do that with every substance turned out to be problematic."[52]

Cornell's Dr. Maines puts Monti and the others' judgment in a less charitable light. "Totally irresponsible!" she says. "It's almost as if they didn't even think about that they were using these thousands of people as guinea pigs. 'Oh, we'll just spray on this completely untested fireproofing material, and then we'll see what happens.'"[53]

What happened first was asbestos proving its worth in the skyscraper.

THE FIRST WTC FIRE

"It was like fighting a blowtorch," one firefighter told the *New York Times*.[54] Firefighters had never seen anything like the fire in World Trade Center. It was raging down multiple stories through the elevator and utility shafts. There was fear it would severely damage the building and leave multiple fatalities.

This, however, was not 11 September 2001. It was 13 February 1975. And the fire, despite its intensity—it burned for more than three hours—left no fatalities or structural damage. The fire quickly became forgotten, a footnote to the WTC's history. But it is very important because of one simple fact: the fire occurred from the ninth to nineteenth floors of the first tower, the area below the thirty-eighth floor where asbestos spraying was stopped. Although the initial cause was unknown, the fire started on the eleventh floor. It spread rapidly after igniting on that floor a one-gallon can of old-fashioned copy-machine fluid that was then made from methyl-alcohol, or methanol. Methanol burns much easier and faster than kerosene-based jet fuel. Because of these facts, this fire offers strong evidence of how very different the 2001 WTC fires might have been had asbestos been used as planned.

A 1975 report of the New York Board of Fire Underwriters marveled that the fire was so intense yet stayed in a confined area, doing minimal damage to the rest of the building. In the area where the fire raged, it burned nearly everything in sight. "It completely burned out the telephone panels and wiring in the telephone closets and caused severe damage in eight others," the report found. It even got hot enough to blow out some windows.[55] But, as the *New York Times* reported, "the blaze did not escape from the shaft out into rooms or hallways on the other floors."[56] The asbestos fireproofing on the columns protected these areas.

"The asbestos used to compartmentalize the structure does seem to have performed well, and to have prevented the spread of fire and smoke," says Dr. Maines.[57] A 1975 fire analysis from the engineering firm Skilling, Helle, Christiansen, Robertson noted that the fire, "while reported in the press to have been very hot, did not damage a single primary, fireproofed element."[58]

This analysis then made a haunting prophecy: "It is likely that this fire did not provide the ultimate test of fire-resistivity. More severe fires will likely strike the project." The engineers then added that since in this fire, "only non-essential, non-fireproofed elements of the floor assembly were damaged, some optimism can be expressed." Twenty-five years later, that optimism proved to be tragically misplaced. The fire next time occurred far above the last asbestos-proofed floor. What followed was a deadly demonstration of the dismal performance of asbestos replacements.

THE COLLAPSE: HOW THE LACK OF ASBESTOS MADE IT HAPPEN

Everything about the 9/11 attacks seemed tremendous. Jet planes loaded with fuel are not crashed into tall buildings every day. We will never forget the vivid footage showcasing the horrible sight of smoke from the buildings and the hole that made it look as if the WTC's face had been punched in. Yet to engineers, both the initial building crash and the ensuing fires, in retrospect, seem manageable events by themselves. Planes hit just a few floors, and the fires started by the jet fuel were probably not as hot as other fires, including the 1975 WTC fire.

In both hits on the two buildings, "the aircraft impacts resulted in severe structural damage, including some localized partial collapse, but did not result in the initiation of a global collapse." So found an exhaustive report by the Federal Emergency Management Agency, or FEMA. (FEMA may not be the best agency at disaster assistance, as Hurricane Katrina showed, but its diagnoses of causes of disasters are recognized as first-rate.) The FEMA report noted that despite the damage, "the structure retained sufficient integrity and strength to remain globally stable" for more than an hour.[59]

Similarly, the ten thousand gallons of jet fuel in each aircraft did create some big fireballs on the building's exterior. But "these fireballs did not explode or generate a shock wave," FEMA noted. Therefore, "it is unlikely that the fireballs, being exterior to the buildings, would have resulted in severe structural damage."[60]

And the temperature did not get hot enough to melt the steel. Indeed, the Commerce Department's NIST report would later conclude that the temperature did not even reach the 2,000 degrees Fahrenheit of a normal building fire.[61] The temperatures in both towers never rose beyond a maximum of 1,800 degrees, and was actually much lower than that on the floors not impacted by the airplane.[62] As Massachusetts Institute of Technology professor Thomas Eagar has written, "The temperature of the fire at the WTC fire was not unusual, and it was most definitely not capable of melting steel."[63] Steel doesn't melt until a fire reaches at least 2,750 degrees.[64]

But steel doesn't have to melt to cause structural damage. It can buckle and bend, and it will do this at fires with temperatures as low as 600 degrees—if the fireproofing applied to steel is inadequate. And the tests performed by NIST showed that the non-asbestos fireproofing, added hastily in the early 1970s as insulation on the steel, was inadequate in every way. The NIST report concludes bluntly, "The WTC towers would likely not have collapsed under the combined effects of aircraft impact damage and the extensive, multi-floor fires that were encountered on September 11, 2001, if the thermal insulation had not been widely dislodged."[65]

The Port Authority had apparently not learned much from the excellent performance of asbestos in the 1975 fire. Not only was asbestos not applied to the upper floors and the second tower, much of it was actually removed from the lower floors of the first tower! All of this would contribute to the buckling of the steel on several floors that ultimately led to the WTC's collapse.

There were two ways the fireproofing could have been dislodged from the steel. And under each scenario, the asbestos would almost certainly have performed better and likely saved the building from falling, experts say.

First, some of the non-asbestos fireproofing probably just burned off. It turns out the initial tests the WTC's builders relied on that were 80 percent completed did not paint anything resembling an accurate picture of how the substitutes would perform in the real world. In simulations by NIST, the fireproofing turned out to be far inferior to asbestos in both terms of melting points and the ability to keep heat from spreading.

The fireproofing was attached to a pushrod to simulate the steel columns at the World Trade Center. Temperature was gradually increased. NIST found that "[a]ll of the specimens shrunk during the tests and in all cases lost contact with the pushrod . . . before reaching the maximum test temperature," says the NIST report. And the material shrunk so rapidly at relatively low fire temperatures that NIST cautioned that the huge "specimen mass loss" made some measurements only valid up to 1,100 degrees. In another set of tests, thermal conductivity, the ability of the fireproofing to spread heat to the subject it is insulating, increased dramatically in the substitutes. It doubled when the heat was increased from 75 degrees to just 400 degrees. By the time the temperature reached 1,800 degrees, the thermal conductivity of the fireproofing had risen almost fivefold, spreading heat rapidly to the vulnerable steel.[66]

For mind-boggling reasons, maybe because it was simply no longer available, NIST did not separately test the original asbestos-based fireproofing that had been sprayed up to the thirty-eighth floor. But we know—from more than a century of fire tests—that asbestos almost certainly would have performed better. It has very low thermal conductivity and will not begin to break down or shrink until it hits 2,100 degrees. The NIST study shows those temperatures were never even reached in the WTC fires!

Then there are some essential qualities of fireproofing that weren't even tested for in the early seventies—qualities such as adhesion, which measures whether insulation will stick to a particular surface under stress. Explains Langer, "They were not interested so much in the homogeneity, adhesion quality, and thickness. All of these became important later. As [builders] started to substitute, they said, 'Gee, this stuff's not very good.'"[67]

But just how poorly these substitutes performed was not known until NIST looked at how the building collapsed. Much of the problem with the fireproofing was that it simply dislodged after the aircraft impact before the fire even started. And this was not simply in the areas where the jets hit the buildings and debris flew. The fireproofing also fell off the steel "in a much larger region that was not in the direct path of the debris but was subject to strong vibrations during and after the aircraft impact."[68] And NIST's tests of the fireproofing showed that even weak vibrations would do the terrorists' trick.

NIST found that the asbestos substitutes were characterized by "adhesion failure." When put on a steel plate with the same material and paint as the WTC column, ten out of fifteen samples of the substitute had "zero adhesion strength." The material came unattached when the "plates were examined by applying a small force of hand."[69] Go ahead and read that phrase again, "small force of hand." That's right, the insulation trusted to protect the WTC steel from fire was so weak it could be pulled off easily by someone's f—ing hand!!! (Fill in the blanks to spell whatever adjective you like that starts with *f*, but I have never known a more appropriate time to curse!) "This is the real shocker to me," Maines says. "If you have zero adhesion of your fireproofing materials, you have got no fireproofing at all."[70]

Again, NIST did not see fit to perform this test with the original asbestos-based fireproofing. But, based on decades worth of tests and real-world applications, asbestos scores as high in this category as it does with others. Langer had actually tested the asbestos-based spray made by Herbert Levine at airports in the 1990s. "This stuff was so damn good that this stuff did not release fibers—even with the vibrations from the airplanes and so forth."[71] And remember the USS

Franklin that we discussed before. Asbestos, although not in spray form, certainly adhered to the steel of this aircraft carrier when the ship was hit by a Japanese kamikaze plane.

Yet the kamikaze attack some fifty-five years later hit a target that was much less protected. With little or no effective fireproofing—even in the first tower, the remaining asbestos had been largely removed in the '90s—the WTC was on its way to collapse. Floors sagged and columns weakened as the fireproofing failed and the steel bent out of shape. As described by scientist Art Robinson in the newsletter *Access to Energy*, "Weakened by the heat, the columns buckled. . . . The lower columns were never designed to resist hundreds of thousands of tons of material dropped on them from above."

Robinson concludes that if asbestos had been used as planned, "an estimated 5,000 people would still be alive and the buildings would probably still be standing—with large gashes in their upper floors."[72] Langer and Maines feel less certain about whether the towers would still be standing, but they're confident they would have been standing longer, saving the lives of thousands of the building's occupants and New York City firefighters. Says Langer, "It could have remained standing, it could have partially collapsed in certain places, or it could have survived for a longer period of time. I believe that asbestos would have delayed that outcome and more lives would have been saved."

ASBESTOS ANSWERS WTC CONSPIRACY THEORIES

As we have seen, lack of asbestos played a crucial role in the World Trade Center collapse. The authors of the NIST report, which gives the history of the switch from asbestos and documents the inferior performance of substitutes, presumably know this. Yet they and others in the know just dance around this fact, probably because asbestos is environmentally incorrect. But their obscuring of this—to borrow Al Gore's phrasing—"inconvenient truth" is having many detrimental effects.

First, it is feeding the burgeoning 9/11 conspiracy theory industry.

You'll get several thousand Web sites just by Googling search terms like "September 11 conspiracy." Books and small-scale documentaries like *Loose Change* promote many wild 9/11 claims. However, unlike the totally off-the-wall "no plane" theory about the Pentagon crash, which attracts mostly those who already subscribe to conspiracy theories about wide and varied subjects, the "controlled demolition" theories regarding the WTC have proliferated in substantial part because of the complex factors of the collapse. The most common alternative explanation of the "9/11 Truth" movement is that there were explosives inside the building set to go off after the plane hit. (There are several answers as to who might have been responsible for setting the explosives, depending upon the conspiracy theorist's politics.)

Popular Mechanics magazine expresses dismay that "healthy skepticism, it seems, has curdled into paranoia."[73] But in part, this is because publications like *Popular Mechanics* have obscured the role in the crash of the environmentally correct asbestos substitutes. After all, the 9/11 conspiracy theorists, although wrongheaded in their major thrust, are correct on major points. Neither the planes nor the fires, by themselves, caused the ensuing collapse. And the temperatures were not high enough to melt the steel. The NIST report reiterates these points.

And without the asbestos context, it can be difficult to buy the conclusion that it was a failure of fireproofing, especially with the history of the 1975 fire. Prison Planet, the Web site of populist radio host Alex Jones, seizes on the fact that the first tower survived the 1975 methyl alcohol fire, which burned for more than three hours with no structural damage. But as we have seen, this occurred because those floors were built before the builders stopped spraying with asbestos, and asbestos kept this fire from spreading.

The only way to combat conspiracy theories is to be straight and open with the facts. And the facts are that the government is partly to blame, not for starting the fires, but for pursuing a reckless policy against asbestos that put the concerns of environmental extremists ahead of the safety concerns of cool-headed engineers and scientists like

Herbert Levine. And the NIST report should serve as a warning that other buildings with asbestos substitutes are at risk as well—from both terrorist attacks and accidental fires.

THE ASBESTOS-TRIAL-LAWYER-MEDIA-JUNK-SCIENCE CONFLAGRATION

Over the thirty years from the building of the World Trade Center towers to the collapse that brought them down, asbestos has been removed from more and more buildings. The asbestos scare raged on, even as science was finding that claims of its dangers were massively overblown. Corresponding to this, the old-fashioned risk of fire is on the rise and is beginning to be reflected in fire-death statistics.

First, here's the sobering news the press largely hasn't told you about asbestos exposure for the average American. In 1989, a report in the *New England Journal of Medicine*—the same journal where Selikoff had published his 1965 study on the danger of high-level asbestos exposure to shipyard workers—came to a verdict on low-level exposure to asbestos that has never been effectively challenged. The report's authors, from Yale and the University of Vermont, concluded bluntly, "Recent epidemiological studies of persons with low exposure to asbestos provided little support for the concept that there is an increased risk of lung cancer."

But by this time, it was too late. "The popular media ignored the study," notes science journalist Michael Fumento in the *American Spectator*. Similar conclusions had also been made years earlier by the United Kingdom Advisory Committee on Asbestos, and the Ontario (Canada) Royal Commission on Asbestos that there was close to zero risk for low-level asbestos exposure.[74] To further put the risk in perspective, the Occupational Safety and Health Administration had found that 40 percent of US land area exposed people to natural background levels of asbestos similar to those in buildings.[75]

However, the demonization of the substance had been completed.

As conservative media watchdog Reed Irvine observed in his foreword to journalist Michael Bennett's exposé *The Asbestos Racket*, fear of asbestos had become "a modern example of mass hysteria as irrational as . . . the witch trials . . . alchemists, fortune tellers, and astrologers."[76]

Until his death in 1992, the phony-credentialed Selikoff would grow increasingly militant in his claim that any exposure to asbestos was dangerous, even though the science was proving otherwise. Selikoff was lionized by Paul Brodeur, a writer for the *New Yorker* who would repeat the most outlandish claims about asbestos in his articles and in his 1984 book, *Outrageous Misconduct: The Asbestos Industry on Trial*. Brodeur made similarly wild claims about dangers from power lines and microwaves in books like *The Zapping of America*. These claims have been discredited even in the conventional media outlets. But the asbestos assertions lived on, and unfortunately, greatly influenced American policy and court verdicts.

Environmental and leftist groups such as Greenpeace, the Sierra Club, and the Ralph Nader-founded Public Interest Research Group soon jumped on the anti-asbestos bandwagon. Even though asbestos was a natural substance used for thousands of years, its handy industrial applications let it fit the media's mold of a villainous new element concocted by evil corporations. Selikoff, Brodeur, and other asbestos scaremongers would dismiss anyone who disputed their claims as shills for the asbestos industry. This argument is particularly ironic in light of the fact that the asbestos panic gave rise to industries that continue to thrive today: asbestos lawsuits and asbestos removal.

Selikoff himself made handsome sums performing x-ray examinations for the clients of high-powered trial lawyers. This became important as many attorneys soon moved from representing those shipbuilders and other workers who were genuinely sick to defendants who were sketchy about their asbestos exposure. Since asbestos was everywhere for the fire prevention reasons that we've discussed, virtually anyone could be found to have asbestos fibers in their body if the x-ray probed deep enough. On top of this, as author James Surowiecki, famous for his book *The Wisdom of Crowds*, puts it, "Plaintiffs didn't have to prove such a product had actually caused them harm—the presence of an asbestos-containing product in the workplace was considered enough." A Mississippi jury awarded $25 million each to six plaintiffs who had not spent a cent on medical expenses related to asbestos.[77] The RAND Institute for Civil Justice estimates that 90 percent of current asbestos claims are from plaintiffs whose health and ability to work are unimpaired.[78] Even in cases in which an actual illness is alleged, doctors affiliated with trial lawyers often perform shoddy diagnoses in vans that travel looking for plaintiffs. A recent analysis of x-rays in the journal *Academic Radiology* found that 85 percent of plaintiffs diagnosed with asbestosis showed no signs of the disease.[79]

As a result of what Dr. Maines calls this "asbestos-tort conflagration" (though my heading above describes the players in the conflagration more extensively, in my opinion), every major American asbestos maker has gone bankrupt or dissolved. Manville Corp., formerly the Johns-Manville company that inventor Henry W. Johns built from scratch in the nineteenth century, became the first major firm to declare bankruptcy in 1982 after being hit with thousands of claims. About sixty thousand jobs associated with these companies have been lost in the past decade. Today Manville and the other beleaguered manufacturers exist as "shells with only enough staff to pay out from dwindling resources the claims of creditors, legal settlements and judgments, attorney's fees and, in many cases, the pensions and health insurance plans of their retirees," writes Maines.[80]

Meanwhile, the lawyers have moved on to other pickings. "[A]ny company that had sold a product containing asbestos became a potential target," writes Surowiecki. Forty billion dollars has been paid out so far, and the estimated price tag for all asbestos claims has risen from $100 billion to $200 hundred billion. And about 60 percent of this money has gone to the trial layers, the RAND Institute found. Legal commentator Olson notes that "if a private charity were found to be operating at that sort of overhead, it might get prosecuted for fraud."[81] Some of America's wealthiest attorneys, from Baltimore Orioles owner Angelos to Ron Motley of Charleston, South Carolina, to Dickie Scruggs of Pascagoula, Mississippi, got started on their fortunes by suing asbestos makers.

THE TOLL OF ASBESTOS REMOVAL

Asbestos abatement has become a lucrative business in itself as well. Fifty billion dollars has been spent so far to remove asbestos from buildings. Much of this money has been spent by schools, often at the expense of leaky roofs and broken windows that needed repair.[82]

The schools were prompted to spend this money by an asbestos-spooked Congress, which in 1986 passed the Asbestos Hazard Emergency Response Act, requiring all schools to test for asbestos and develop a management plan for them. The law, signed by President Ronald Reagan (yes, even the great Reagan could be cowed a few times by the eco-freaks), mandated these costly measures on private schools that received no government aid. In 1989, the Catholic schools of Michigan found that complying with these rules would cost them $75 million.[83] To top it off, by moving asbestos around to circulate in the air, abatement often causes greater exposure to the occupants and especially to the workers doing the abatement than just leaving the asbestos in a sealed area.

And then there's the question that hasn't been asked. After all is said and done and the asbestos, at great cost, is removed, America's children are at more risk of fire. Maines says that schools haven't really tried to replace asbestos, which, as discussed previously, would be difficult to do in places like boilers. Instead they are relying on "active" fire protection systems like more alarms and sprinklers. Unfortunately, says Dr. Maines and other experts, that isn't always enough to prevent a tragedy in a fire. "Sometimes all it takes is one thing to go wrong for everything to go wrong," she says.

About a year and a half after the World Trade Center collapse, another fire tragedy that entailed heavy loss of life occurred in West Warwick, Rhode Island. In February 2003, at a concert by a heavy metal band at The Station nightclub, a fire broke out after the band's tour manager lit pyrotechnics that ignited the ceiling. The tour manager, who pled guilty to and is serving a four-year jail sentence for involuntary manslaughter from negligence, didn't know that the ceiling was covered with flammable polyurethane foam insulation to control noise. Flames rushed through the cramped space and formed a wall of fire surrounding 350 panicked clubgoers. One hundred people died, including Great White guitarist Ty Longley, age thirty-one. Almost 200 more were injured.[84]

At first glance, the nightclub fire and Twin Towers' collapse seem to have nothing to do with each other. After all, one was an accident and the other a deliberate terrorist attack. But probing more deeply, both incidents have at least two factors in common. The most important is that both were magnified by the lack of asbestos.

Dr. Maines, in fact, believes there would have been no deaths and probably no fire at The Station if there had been an asbestos ceiling like most nightclubs had some thirty years earlier. This is because asbestos, among its many other virtues, turned out to be great for soundproofing too. "The sparks would have flown up and hit the asbestos and come back down again," she says. "They might have ignited the stage, doing limited damage. But most likely we would never have heard of The Station nightclub."[85]

Commentators have noted several things the nightclub owners could have done better. The Station had no sprinkler system, and most exits weren't visible during the fire. These issues have been raised in lawsuits and criminal charges against the club owners, who have pleaded not guilty to involuntary manslaughter. But Maines argues that even with sprinklers and more clearly marked exit signs, the death toll probably wouldn't have been much lower because of the rate at which the foam burned. "Those people only had two-and-a-half minutes of breathable air after ignition of that ceiling," she points out, citing published reports. "Everybody that got out alive, got out in the first two-and-a-half minutes. Even if there had been sprinklers, they would not have survived. It takes sprinklers longer than two-and-a-half minutes to get going."

The Rhode Island state legislature even acknowledged the great fire-resistant properties of asbestos in a bill it passed after the tragedy. The Comprehensive Fire Safety Act of 2003 specified that almost all "interior finishes" had to be derived from "noncombustible materials." It then defined noncombustible material as being substances that ranked from twenty-five to zero for flame-spread rating, with zero being the least flammable. It then instructed building owners to use a scale "in which asbestos cement board rates zero (0) on the scale, and red oak lumber, one hundred (100)."[86]

Yet isn't there something wrong when a regulation asks that materials aspire to the safety of a certain substance, yet that substance is, for all purposes, illegal to use? This question leads to the second commonality of the WTC collapse and the fire at The Station. They were both tragedies that can be described "low probability-high consequence," to use the blunt terminology of Harvard University physicist Richard Wilson. And "low probability-high consequence" accidents are precisely the kind that terrorists will try to simulate, Wilson argues.

In a speech in 2003 at the Sandia nuclear weapons laboratory in New Mexico, Wilson emphasized that security specialists and all Americans must envision rare, but deadly accidents, because those are precisely the events that terrorists will try to make less rare. "Most terrorist attacks involve deliberately creating a situation that sometimes can occur by accident," Wilson explained. "A terrorist can easily set a fire in a crowded nightclub, just as an airplane can accidentally hit a tall building. The best defense against terrorism is similar to the best defense against accidents."

And one of the best defenses against both, the Harvard physicist suggests, is to once again use asbestos. "Maybe we should return to the asbestos fire curtain," Wilson advised the nuclear specialists at Sandia.[87]

It is also worth noting that nightclubs have long been targets of terrorist attacks in Israel and elsewhere. So, unfortunately, have schools, the places where asbestos has been removed, ironically in the name of children's safety. But so-called active fire protection systems can only do so much to protect clubgoers and kids. It would be fairly easy for terrorists to sabotage a fire alarm or a sprinkler system. But let's see them try to remove asbestos from a ceiling! If a terrorist dared try this, and the asbestos was right in his face, I would only wish asbestos was as lethal as advertised!

ANCHORS AWAY WITH ASBESTOS!

This is why, during the current War on Terror, asbestos is once again a "critical material" as it was in the 1940s and *must* be used in many applications. Its most important application is once again on military ships. A wealth of evidence shows that our navy sailors today are less protected from fire than their grandfathers and great-grandfathers were in World War II.

When the asbestos scare began in the late 1960s, military leaders were resistant to giving up this great fireproofing material. Many of the highest-rank officers had served in World War II twenty years earlier and remembered what a difference asbestos had made on ships like the *Franklin*.[88] But by the 1970s, the pressure from the media, anti-asbestos activists, and politicians had forced even the military to give the material up—in the United States and in Great Britain.

This led to disastrous consequences in the first war since World War I without asbestos—the Falkland Islands War of 1982. Fought between Britain and Argentina over some islands in the South Atlantic Ocean, it was a short war, with Britain emerging as the victor in two months. But the length of time obscured the high casualty rate for a certain type of event—ship fires. Per capita, the British Royal Navy suffered a greater number of burn deaths among its sailors in the Falklands than had occurred during the years of World War II.

Closer to today's headlines, thirty-seven US Navy men were killed in the Persian Gulf in 1987 when a missile launched by Saddam Hussein's Iraq hit the USS *Stark*. The Iraqi government claimed the missile was meant for Iran, whom it was fighting in the Iran-Iraq War, but the navy was rightly skeptical of Hussein, and the jury is still out on Iraq's true intent. Nevertheless, the ship did not sink, but the injuries and deaths were mostly due to burns and smoke inhalation from the big fires the missile caused. And experts say the fires here and around the Falklands would never have spread as rapidly if there were asbestos separating the compartments, as there had been in World War II. According to Professors J. Bernard L. Gee and W. Keith C. Morgan, respectively of Yale University and the University of Western Ontario, "The number of casualties caused by burns in the Royal Navy warships during the Falklands war and on the USS *Stark* when the latter was hit by an Exocet missile in the Persian Gulf, was appreciably greater than expected because of the exclusion of asbestos insulation from these ships."[89]

On the *Stark* and on the British ships in the South Atlantic, there were now bulkheads made of aluminum rather than of steel coated with asbestos. As a result, the melting or burning aluminum created what Maines describes as "a very stubborn type of metal fire" that spreads rapidly and is very difficult to extinguish.[90]

With hostilities brewing with Iraqi insurgents and in Iran, an incident like that of the *Stark* could happen literally tomorrow on the Persian Gulf. And however the American public may feel about a particular war, almost all of us want our troops to be as well protected as they can be. That's why it's time to put asbestos back on our ships—*today*.

If we as a nation have the will to stand up to the asbestos scaremongers and powerful trial lawyers, this should be a fairly simple task to accomplish. The world has no shortage of raw asbestos, and it is still being mined in Canada. (The fact that politically correct Canada, where it seemed that every supporter of John Kerry wanted to take refuge after the 2004 election, still mines asbestos should itself be enough to answer every liberal's objection to using the stuff!) We would of course need tort reform and liability protection for the shipbuilders. It would also be appropriate to levy big fines on the rapacious attorneys and doctors found to have submitted fraudulent diagnoses to courts, and use the proceeds from these fines to help finance the asbestos fortification of our ships!

As the scientific literature has shown, there would be virtually no risk from the low level of exposure to asbestos for the ships' occupants. But could there be risks to the insulation workers who would come into closer contact with asbestos? Yes—just as there are risks to mining coal, from black lung disease and from mine cave-ins, as we saw so vividly in the West Virginia tragedy of early 2006. But America hasn't stopped using this substance. We recognize that coal is essential to our way of life. So, too, is asbestos, unless we want our soldiers and sailors to perish in fires that could have been contained.

As with coal, we should make sure that asbestos workers do their jobs in the safest conditions possible—in ventilated areas, with frequent breaks, and with the most comfortable and effective dust masks. And we should make sure they're fully aware that there are risks to high asbestos exposure. But we should recognize that members of the US armed forces risk their lives every day on the job, and Americans shouldn't hesitate to take on a few more risks as a society if we can lessen the risks of our troops.

After military ships are fortified, Americans should have a long, hard discussion about the most critical buildings and where asbestos is most needed as fireproofing here. To borrow a phrase from the title of an anti-asbestos tome, it's time to put an end to the outrageous misconduct of the asbestos demonizers. And time to start protecting ourselves and our children again from the very real dangers of fire.

4

Smashing the Engine of Public Health

ANTI-AUTO ACTS ENDANGER HEALTH, SAFETY, AND FREEDOM

Efficiency is not a word that is often associated with the city government of New Orleans, either before or after Hurricane Katrina. The Big Easy, as it's called, almost takes a sense of pride in its history of endemic corruption and relaxed attitudes toward public services.

Yet there was one thing the city did do fairly efficiently: public transportation. The New Orleans streetcars, reintroduced to the city in the 1990s at costs of more than $200 million, did run on time, and they were even one of the highlights for tourists. City buses also ran fairly well, although they didn't always keep up with the neighborhood shifts of their riders.

So many New Orleanians opted not to get a car. When Katrina struck, 27 percent of city households did not have automobiles, a much greater number than the nationwide rate of less than 10 percent who are car-less. Many could not afford a car, and others didn't see a need.

After all, with its narrow streets and lack of parking lots, New Orleans wasn't exactly the most car-friendly city. Even when New Orleans received money for elevated freeways, which could be very useful for a city below sea level, anti-highway activists convinced the city and the federal government to scuttle the proposed roads. This wasn't the only time green groups blocked something that was crucial for hurricane safety. As we will see in chapter 6, which explores more fully the dynamics of Katrina, environmentalists repeatedly halted flood-control projects, from floodgates around Lake Pontchartrain to basic repairs of Louisiana's levees.

Before Katrina, New Orleans was actually a shining example for activists pushing the trendy "smart growth" plans designed to discourage automobile use and stop "sprawl." Writes smart growth critic Randal O'Toole, senior economist for the Oregon-based Thoreau Institute, "New Orleans is in many ways a model for smart growth: high densities, low rates of auto ownership, investments in rail transit." But O'Toole observes that when Katrina hit and the levees broke, "[t]his proved to be its downfall."[1]

KATRINA—CAR-LESS AND STRANDED

There have been many theories about why roughly 80 percent of the city had evacuated after warnings of Katrina were forecast on 27 and 28 August 2005, and why the remaining 20 percent were stuck there when the levees failed two days later on 30 August. Poverty, racism, and lack of individual responsibility were among the explanations that various commentators expressed. "The white people got out," declared *New York Times* reporter Jason DeParle in the first sentence of a news analysis in the paper.[2] But so did many blacks. After all, the city is over two-thirds black, and if whites had been the only ones to leave, there would have been at most a 28-percent evacuation rate. Looking at the demographics of who got out and who didn't, one characteristic correlates more closely than anything else—the ownership of a car. And in New Orleans, even the car-lessness rate for white households was, according to the same *Times* article, 15 percent, which was five percentage points higher than the national number.[3]

"White families with cars got out, as did black families," writes O'Toole in the *Seattle Times*. "Families without cars, white and black, for the most part did not."[4] This differs from analyses from some conservative pundits and bloggers that most New Orleanians who stayed were fatalistic or irresponsible. I happen to think in this case that many of my fellow conservatives were blaming the victim. I know, I know. The Left overuses that phrase to absolve people from personal responsibility for just about anything. But being trapped in a storm is different from being dependent on welfare. It happens quickly, and it's largely a function of time, place, and circumstances. If you didn't have a car in New Orleans—especially if you didn't know anyone with a car there—your circumstances were bleak.

First, let's look at the only part of the evacuation that was an unqualified success, the automobile contraflow of the 27th and 28th of August. Louisiana Democratic governor Kathleen Blanco and Mississippi Republican governor Haley Barbour agreed to make all the lanes flow in one direction, doubling the amount of lanes available for escaping the storm's path. Barbour generously facilitated Mississippi's highways for Louisianans' use, even as Mississippians were also trying to flee.[5] Even with obstacles such as New Orleans' narrow roads, in thirty-eight hours, every vehicle got to safe ground in northern Mississippi. This was done in almost half the time the US Army Corps of Engineers had estimated would be needed.[6]

But for those without cars, everything went wrong. According to a poll taken by the Associated Press, a majority of those who stayed behind said they did so, at least in part, because they didn't have a car.[7] Other evidence indicates that many New Orleanians tried to get a vehicle to leave with, but were unsuccessful. John Renne, an assistant professor of transportation at the University of New Orleans, wrote that even on the morning of Saturday the 27th, just after the contraflow was announced, he "called around to find a rental, and sure enough several companies were already sold out." Renne and his wife found a rental, but countless others weren't so lucky. Katrina should serve as a reminder that there is nothing better for homeland security and public health than private ownership of cars.

Writing a week after Katrina, Renne was appalled there were no evacuation procedures for the car-less except for Mayor Ray Nagin's admonition to go to the New Orleans Superdome. "I was astonished that no information was made available to evacuate people without access to a car," he recalled. He found out that Amtrak had stopped service on Saturday just as the contraflow had started.[8] Many have heard about the several buses that were under water because the City of New Orleans had inexplicably parked them on low ground. Historian Douglas Brinkley goes into further detail about the transit mishaps in his book, *The Great Deluge*.

But Renne, now head of the Transportation Equity and Evacuation Planning Project at the University of New Orleans, doesn't advocate that the government make it easier to get cars to keep vulnerable people from being at the mercy of transit bureaucracies. No, like most liberals, his answer is more money for mass transportation. Even after acknowledging in his essay that "the contra-flow highway evacuation plan worked well," he concluded that the Katrina lives in jeopardy were "a result of our extreme dependence on cars."[9]

But how can auto-dependency be the problem when the folks who were "auto-dependent" got out? For the Katrina victims, the suffering was a result of being dependent on public transit. Writes O'Toole, "Katrina proved that the automobile is a liberator. It is those who don't own autos who are dependent—dependent on the competence of government officials, dependent on charity, dependent on complex and sometimes uncaring institutions."[10]

This is not to say that mass transit is not important and that we shouldn't make improvements like, say, keeping emergency buses on high ground away from flooding. But even the best-planned public transportation will never take the place of the flexibility of privately owned automobiles, especially in a disaster. Imagine, for instance, that instead of a hurricane, America's next major disaster is, God forbid, another terrorist attack. If this happens, train and bus stations might have to close because they could be targets. Even if they're closed for only a few hours, without automobiles this could be a big problem.

CARS FOR HOMELAND SECURITY

To further illustrate the importance of automobiles in a crisis, let me recall my own experience on Capitol Hill in Washington DC on the morning of 11 September 2001. When commuting to work from northern Virginia, I do the environmentally correct thing. I ride the DC subway, or Metro, as it's called. Many other DC professionals also commute this way from Virginia and Maryland. I have a car but it's prohibitively expensive to park in DC. Plus I like to read or sleep as I'm coming and going, and these are difficult things to do when you are driving a car.

On the morning of 9/11, I took the Metro Orange Line from Falls Church, Virginia, to the Capitol South stop. At a little after nine, I walked to an outdoor press conference a block away from the Capitol building. At the time I was writing for *Insight* magazine and contributing to its sister publication, the *Washington Times* newspaper. It was there I learned that the two towers of the World Trade Center had been hit. Then House majority whip Tom DeLay was speaking, and as soon as he was through, someone whispered something in his ear. He looked shaken. In a few minutes, a green sport utility vehicle whizzed by and whisked him away. We would soon learn that the Pentagon had just been hit.

The Capitol building was evacuated; we knew it was a likely target. If the building were hit, debris could travel for blocks and blocks. Yet there were still dozens of people in the vicinity. Some, like me, were reporters trying to get a story.[11] But most, such as Hill staffers and lobbyists, simply had no place to go. Metro stations near the Capitol closed for several hours after the attacks. The Amtrak train station a few blocks from the Capitol shut down as well, as it was an obvious terrorist target. A bit after 1:00 p.m., I finally found a Pakistani cab driver who would take me to the *Washington Times* building. I and everyone else who was stranded on Capitol Hill that day literally owe our lives to the brave passengers celebrated in the movie *United 93* who sacrificed their own lives to stop a near-certain crash into the Capitol.

The experience of both Katrina and 9/11 should show the policy makers how important auto-mobility—ownership of and access to cars—is to preventing loss of life in a natural disaster or terrorist attack. Transit can help, but even under the best of circumstances, it is hindered by inherent limitations. And Katrina especially shows that in a disaster, expect that you will be on your own in getting your family to safe ground. Having a roomy car in good condition, or relying on someone who does, should be at the very top of your emergency preparedness list.

Yet cars are nowhere near the top of the list for many in the government or in academia for emergency planning or other areas of policy. In fact, for the past thirty years the dominant federal policy has been, consciously and unconsciously, to discourage use of autos. Many liberals have a visceral dislike of cars, even the ones that are smaller and more fuel-efficient.

Think about this strange disconnect in liberals' dichotomy. Any time the poor lack something, liberals usually say the government should pay for it or force the private sector to pay for it. Subsidize home ownership. Mandate employer-provided health insurance. Guarantee access to the Internet. But when was the last time you heard a liberal say the government should help poor people get cars? They will argue about how the poor suffer from lack of automobiles, but then propose to spend more money expanding transit.

The only exception that I can think of is former Clinton administration adviser Margy Waller. Waller compellingly argued in the liberal *Washington Monthly* that the "federal government should offer tax credits that would lower the cost of commuting to work for low and middle-income employees, and would allow low income workers who can't afford a reliable car to get one." She pointed out that "no amount of money will enable us to use transit to meet the needs of most workers," because of the inherent difficulties of trips to the grocery store and family doctor appointments on a transit system. Transit often takes a good deal longer than a car because one or more transfers are involved to get to a rider's destination of choice. After these exhausting trips, Waller noted, "there isn't much time for anything else—like helping with homework or after-school activities."[12]

I don't completely agree with Waller's prescriptions, particularly her plan to pay for these subsidies by repealing the Bush administration tax cuts, but she has made a valuable contribution to policy debate by recognizing the essential value of cars. Unfortunately, hers is a voice in the wilderness among Democrats wanting to advertise their "green" credentials by pushing policies that punish drivers. In waxing eloquently about the "Two Americas," John Edwards noted that "more than a quarter of the below-poverty level households don't have a vehicle." But the only thing his 2004 Cities Rising plan offered to assist their transportation needs was the expansion of a Federal Transit Administration program giving the poor mass-transit vouchers—nothing to help them acquire a car or pay auto insurance.[13]

For the poor and the rest of Americans, thirty years worth of regulations have forced up the prices of autos and their fuel, greatly limited our choices, and in many instances, even led to a decline in traffic safety. Similarly, roads have not kept pace with the growing number of drivers and the substantial increases in federal and state gasoline taxes. From the 1920s to the 1970s, gasoline taxes operated as a "user fee" almost entirely dedicated to the building and repair of roads. But then gas taxes, at the state and federal level, began to be diverted to transit projects and after that, run-of-the-mill pork projects having little to do with transportation. Between 1970 and 1995, vehicle miles driven skyrocketed by 67 percent, yet miles of roadway only increased .05 percent.[14] Largely because of extensive requirements of environmental impact statements and consideration of every endangered species of bug or rat that might be in their path, such as the Delhi Sands flower-loving fly that was discussed in chapter 2, construction of major roadways have been delayed for more than twenty years. Construction still has not even begun on the Intercounty Connector in the highly populated DC suburbs of Maryland, even though initial plans were approved more than five decades ago!

Politicians and bureaucrats have been influenced by a wide car-hating subculture of social critics and environmentalists. They attack the car not just because of any side effects like pollution, but specifically because they don't like the mobility and autonomy the car provides. Books like *Asphalt Nation* by Jane Holtz Kay and *The Geography of Nowhere* by James Howard Kunstler blame the automobile for fostering social isolation and destroying the nation's sense of community. Air pollution isn't even the main motivation for many environmentalists. Greens want to halt the car to limit travel from spreading the human "footprint" in too many places. Of course they're reluctant to limit *their* travel to environmental conferences at chic resorts. But everyone *else* should stay home!

Clogged traffic is an explicit part of their strategy. The next time you're sitting in traffic, you might want to think about the fact that congestion, in fact, is openly discussed by anti-auto forces as a strategy for getting people out of their cars and inducing them to take transit. Officials of an agency serving the metro area of Portland, Oregon, which has put in place rigid "urban growth boundaries" to halt suburban development and preserve the countryside, say in a planning document that "[c]ongestion signals positive urban development." Earl Blumenauer, a Democratic congressman from the Portland area who pushes federal growth controls, has called for "a more nuanced view of congestion."[15] Blumenauer also told National Public Radio that congestion "means an exciting street life," and "people don't mind going slow."[16] Of course, with congressmen having the ability to be driven places by aides and charter a plane for nearby campaign rallies, this is an easy sentiment to express! One thing the eco-friendly activists don't seem to notice about so-called traffic calming, notes O'Toole, is that "[o]ne important side effect of traffic calming is increased air pollution" in a concentrated area.[17]

Former vice president, senator, and presidential candidate Al Gore, who globe-trots in limousines and jet planes, has long had an animus toward cars—at least those driven by everyone else. More so than in his new book and documentary, *An Inconvenient Truth*, Gore expressed an extreme hatred of the car in his 1992 book, *Earth in the Balance*. He then wrote that the "cumulative impact" of automobiles with fuel-burning engines "is posing a mortal threat to the security of every nation that is more deadly than that of any military enemy we are ever again likely to confront." Gore then proposed, in his words, "the strategic goal of completely eliminating the internal combustion engine over, say, a twenty-five year period."[18]

This statement is simply breathtaking. Keep in mind that an internal combustion engine is any engine that internally burns fuel—whether that fuel is gasoline, ethanol, or biodiesel. The definition would even cover the fuel-burning engine that partly powers the hybrid car. And Gore has never taken back or modified anything he has written in *Earth in the Balance*. When he was running for the 2000 presidential election, he told a reporter, "There is not a single passage in that book that I disagree with, or would change."[19]

Ordinarily, Gore's extreme rantings would not be cause for alarm. But a set of events has come together to put him, to use an ironic metaphor, in the driver's seat of this debate. Gasoline prices have risen rapidly. In part this is due to increased demand for oil from oil-emerging economies like China. But it has also been caused by environmentalists and other interest groups pushing bad policies, such as mandating many different combinations of gasoline and ethanol, enacting rules making it extremely difficult to open new refineries, and putting American oil in the Arctic and the oceans off limits to drilling.

Then there is the threat of global warming that Gore, the media, and others are pushing at a fever pitch. Many reporters have publicly said they won't talk to skeptics, because they proclaim the debate is over.[20] But the debate is actually just beginning, and there are several questions to ask before we go with Gore-like restrictions on automobiles.

CARBON DIOXIDE: PLANT FOOD, NOT A POLLUTANT

The main charge against cars made since the late 1970s is not that they are adding harmful pollution. It's that they are contributing to the buildup of carbon dioxide—a so-called greenhouse gas—in the atmosphere. Yes, the amount of carbon dioxide has increased, but carbon dioxide is not a pollutant like lead. It is a basic element that humans breathe out and plants breathe in.

In fact, cars are emitting carbon dioxide in part as a way of reducing pollutants. Catalytic converters, placed in cars after the mandated pollution reductions from the Clean Air Act of 1970, "oxidize" pollutants such as carbon monoxide and harmful hydrocarbons and transform what comes out of the tailpipe into water and carbon dioxide.[21] Proponents of the Clean Air Act, including many environmentalists now sounding the alarm about carbon dioxide, thought this was great. The liberal senator Edmund Muskie (D-ME), sponsor of the 1970 act, proclaimed proudly that with catalytic converters, cars would now be primarily emitting the same substance that plants breathe.

So it is indeed strange that President Bush would take so much flack from green activists and the media for stating this very same fact in 2001: that carbon dioxide is "not a pollutant."[22] Melissa Carey, a climate policy specialist at Environmental Defense, told Knight Ridder News Service, "Refusing to call greenhouse-gas emissions a pollutant is like refusing to say that smoking causes lung cancer."[23] In a case now pending before the Supreme Court, a group of Northeastern attorney generals, almost all Democrats, is suing the Bush administration to force it to regulate carbon dioxide under the Clean Air Act as a "pollutant."

But when they're not in the midst of heated rhetoric on global warming, environmentalists concede the simple fact that Bush expressed: that emission of CO_2 is not pollution. Bill McKibben, one of the earliest and staunchest alarmists about global warming, wrote in 1998 that carbon dioxide was "not pollution." McKibben then explained, "Carbon *mon*oxide is pollution—it kills you if you breathe enough of it. But carbon *di*oxide, carbon with two oxygen atoms, can't do a blessed thing to you. If you're reading this indoors, you're breathing more CO_2 than you'll ever get outside."[24]

So the real question today is whether the buildup of carbon dioxide will change the earth's climate in harmful ways. Alarmists like McKibben and Gore maintain that global warming is here, it already is harming us, and it will do so even more in the future unless we take drastic measures to reduce the amount of carbon dioxide emissions already harming us. For them, every extreme weather condition, from heat waves to heavy snowfall, confirms their thesis of carbon dioxide causing harmful global climate change. But contrary to what they would like you to believe, the jury is still very much out on all this. And yes, as discussed elsewhere in this book, there were hurricanes, floods, and wildfires long before we ever started driving.

It is beyond the scope of this book to explore all the variances of the global warming debate. To get a fuller picture of what the media isn't telling you, I would recommend *Unstoppable Global Warming: Every 1500 Years* by Dennis Avery and S. Fred Singer and *Meltdown: The Predictable Distortion of Global Warming by Scientists, Politicians, and the Media* by Patrick Michaels. For a brief overview of the issues, I would also recommend my colleague Iain Murray's essay on "What Every Citizen Needs to Know About Global Warming," available on the Competitive Enterprise Institute Web site at http://www.cei.org.

But here are some basic questions. Is the earth warming? Some studies say yes, but remember we have only had precise satellite measurements of surface temperature since the 1960s. The recorded observations before then are of limited accuracy. Thirty years ago, magazines like *Newsweek* had covers promoting an opposite scare: global cooling![25]

Second, if there is global warming, how much of it is a natural phenomenon? Even before cars and electricity came on the scene, the climate was always changing. Hundreds of years ago Greenland was really green, and there was grain farming in Iceland. There has been a documented Medieval Warm Period from the tenth to the fourteenth century followed by a Little Ice Age from 1450 to 1850. Since there were no automobiles back then, scientists such as Sallie Baliunas of the Harvard-Smithsonian Center for Astrophysics attribute this to natural cycles of the sun. Baliunas and other scientists today believe the earth is warming, but maintain it is still primarily caused by natural solar cycles, and that we are still recovering from the Little Ice Age.

Then there is the question of if there is global warming, whether from natural or man-made causes, would it be so bad? Prominent experts believe we could adjust to possible negative effects, and there could be many benefits as well. Many farmers, for instance, would love longer growing seasons for their crops. And there would be fewer people dying in cold spells. "All things being equal, warming is better than cooling," argues atmospheric scientist S. Fred Singer, who formerly taught at the University of Virginia and now runs the Science and Environmental Policy Project.

But the most important question to ask is what would be the consequences of taking steps today to avert a possible crisis tomorrow? If we restrict automobile use and design, the costs would be substantial, not just to the economy, but also to public health. The history of the car and flawed environmental policies demonstrate that the consequences of halting auto-mobility would be dramatic. For ever since the first cars were driven and the first roads were built, the automobile has revved up as an engine of public health.

CARS INCREASE LIFE SPAN, HUMAN HEALTH

The twentieth century witnessed remarkable progress in life expectancy and human health. At the end of the nineteenth century, the average American lived to be less than forty, and it was normal for at least one child in a family to die before adulthood. But at the end of the last century, six years ago, the average life expectancy for Americans was close to eighty, and the death of a child was tragic, but rare. All sorts of measures of human health, including height and access to nutritious food, also improved markedly.[26]

It's safe to say that much of this improvement in public health is due to the car. When we talk about mortality rates and the automobile, we're usually referring to car accidents. It's time now to look at how many premature deaths automobiles have *prevented*. The number is probably in the millions.

First of all, imagine how many more patients would die on their way to the hospital if ambulances were still horse-drawn vehicles and there were no paved roads going to medical centers. Then there is the ability to travel to the doctor of your choice and seek out medical experts. Before autos, health spas and clinics were the province of the wealthy. Only the rich could afford the expensive train tickets and the length of time away from work that those trips would entail.

But when the automobile came around, public-spirited doctors pushed their communities to build the roads that could accommodate patients from further distances. The headquarters of the renowned Mayo Clinic, for instance, sits in Rochester, Minnesota, a rural town in one of the coldest and snowiest parts of the country. Brothers William and Charles Mayo founded the original clinic with a mission to provide the best, most systematic care for patients with difficult medical problems. They wanted to serve everyone they could, but because of travel obstacles, their clients had been limited to locals and very wealthy out-of-towners. So in 1915—a few years after Henry Ford introduced his Model T and began pricing it within the reach of the masses—Dr. William Mayo became the head of the Taxpayers' Good Roads Association of the county. He urged the construction of paved roads "to use every day, rain or shine."[27]

Cars and trucks have also brought constant access to plentiful, healthy food. Trucks can deliver fresh fruits and vegetable from longer distances. And consumers can travel farther to get the food they want. And because of what the car has enabled, there is also more choice and competition among grocers, bringing down food prices.[28]

The car has also had significant environmental, as well as public health, benefits. Widespread use of the car immediately got rid of a rather noxious form of pollution on city streets: the waste of the horses used to pull buggies. In 1900 in New York City, horses emitted one thousand tons of manure and seventy thousand gallons of urine on the streets each day. There was also an average of twenty horse carcasses on the street each day for the city to remove. In London, an analysis of the city's "road mud" in 1886 found it to be 30 percent abraded stone, 10 percent abraded iron (mostly from horseshoes), and 60 percent organic matter and manure.[29]

And this manure didn't just smell bad. Manure is well-known to attract disease-spreading flies, and the burning of horse manure at a Kansas army base may have even played a substantial role in spreading the 1918 flu epidemic that killed millions across the world. In an article in *American Heritage* magazine, historian Joseph Persico writes, "Some nine thousand tons of manure were burned every month at this prairie cavalry post, continuously mantling the area in a malodorous haze."[30] Cars made this public health menace disappear from military bases and city streets almost overnight.

CARS FOR CONSERVATION

Cars even added fuel to the conservation movement. Writes historian James J. Flink, before the automobile, "the average middle-class family could not afford railroad fares to a remote national park." Flink's book *The Automobile Age* is mostly critical of cars, but he admits that they boosted the numbers of lovers of the outdoors. As more people visited parks, they got more public support and funding increased in Congress. Some conservation groups were even created by meetings of motorists. According to Flink, the Save the Redwoods League formed in California at the Pacific Auto Show in 1920.[31]

The anti-dam movement, which I discuss at length in chapter 6, was also jump-started by the car. As Flink writes, "Schemes to build a series of dams on the Yellowstone River in the 1930s and in the Grand Canyon on the Colorado River in the 1960s failed for one significant reason: Congressmen received countless letters from irate constituents who recognized the value of preserving the parks because they had visited them in an automobile."[32] As we will see in the next two chapters, however, the "pristine" wilderness that the first-time motorists and tourists thought they saw had already been altered significantly by human hands for hundreds of years.

Speaking of the outdoors, how many were inspired to visit the Grand Canyon by watching the "Brady Bunch" travel there in their station wagon in the early 1970s? Writing about cars, both pro and con, tends to focus on the individual driver, with issues like speed and flashy design. But from the very beginning, carmakers had the family in mind. The family excursion and longer trips became a valued tradition and inspired innovations like Holiday Inn and other quality roadside motel chains. Automakers also innovated, making cars with more features for the family. Prominent among these was the station wagon, a car perfectly suited to large families and one that could also haul pets, camping gear, and sports equipment such as bats and balls for Little League games.

But watching *The Brady Bunch* today, one is struck by the fact that there is no passenger car of recent years that can fit comfortably a mom, a dad, six children, and a maid for a trip to the Grand Canyon or even a neighborhood jaunt to Chuck E. Cheese. Or one that can, as the Brady wagon did in the Grand Canyon episode, haul camping equipment on its roof and in an attached trailer. And unlike other Brady items such as bell-bottoms and perms for men, the station wagon could actually be practical for the "bunches" of today. If you have a large family, your only option is a minivan or SUV. Ever wondered why the station wagon and other large cars, as opposed to trucks, seemed to vanish? It would be a good documentary.

In fact there is a movie documentary about a car that seemingly disappeared, but it's called *Who Killed the Electric Car?* This film was the talk of the chattering classes in the summer of 2006. Produced by a subsidiary of Sony Pictures, this antiestablishment film pushed a corporate conspiracy theory reminiscent of the classic urban legend about car companies suppressing a super-carburetor.[33] The film centered on a battery-powered car called the EV1 electricity that was produced by General Motors in the late '90s.

But what killed this car is really no mystery. In a free market, the consumer is king. And despite the millions of dollars GM spent promoting the car, only about four thousand drivers bought it. Most consumers did not like the high price of about $30,000 or having to recharge the car every night. And what really killed the vehicle was a fire hazard from the battery that occurred when the car was recharged, a fact widely reported in the press at the time, yet mentioned very little in the film. This could have had severe consequences if GM hadn't recalled and destroyed the models in use. The big, high-voltage batteries needed to power an electric vehicle could also lead to potential safety problems in hybrid cars.[34]

A much more vexing question, then, is who killed the family car? Unlike the GM electric car, large sedans and station wagons were bought by millions of American families who relied on them for safe, roomy, and dependable transportation. And these were cars that also had better safety and environmental features than many vehicles that have taken their place. The answer to what killed the family car is a tragic experiment in mandated fuel efficiency that has led to thousands of lives lost as well. And not having learned from their mistakes, environmentalists—plus some well-meaning folks concerned about dependence on oil from Islamofascist nations in the Middle East—are engaged in a new crusade to extend these deadly policies even further.

THE "FUELISH" QUEST FOR EFFICIENCY

Ever since the car was invented, there has been a quest for efficiency. But there have also always been trade-offs. Making a car more fuel-efficient can reduce safety, performance, and comfort. It can also increase pollution.

According to Dr. Leonard Evans, a former GM research scientist who has been honored by the US Department of Transportation and the American Society of Automotive Engineers for his contributions to auto safety, "Every impediment you put on spent gases by the engine reduces fuel economy."[35] For instance, if a car ran without a muffler, it would use less fuel, but it would certainly increase noise pollution.

In many cases, environmentalists have pushed for changes that actually make cars less fuel-efficient. The catalytic converter reduced pollution, but the trade-off was that it took more gasoline to power both the car and the converter. As noted by the Science and Environmental Policy Project, "The catalytic converter reduces engine efficiency and creates less fuel efficiency than we could achieve without it, but we accept burning more gasoline to get a cleaner exhaust."[36] In this case, many were willing to trade off fuel efficiency for public health benefits. And in this case, unlike other environmental crusades, the public health benefits of cleaner air and less smog were real.

But just as real are the public health benefits allowing drivers to choose cars of adequate weight and size. Size and weight of the automobile are some of the most important determinants of whether drivers and passengers survive an automobile collision. As noted in the *American Journal of Public Health*, "Drivers of larger, heavier cars have lower risks in crashes than drivers of smaller, lighter cars."[37]

Cars that are larger and heavier are also less fuel efficient than smaller and lighter cars. A principle of physics is that it takes more energy to move more mass. And as that famous philosopher of science, Mr. Spock, has told legions of *Star Trek* viewers, "You cannot change the laws of physics."

THE HARD CRASH "CAFE"

The laws of Congress, however, are a science of their own. In 1975, Congress passed a law that didn't change the laws of physics, but gave the properties of physics a more painful and deadly impact for thousands of Americans in car crashes.

The Corporate Average Fuel Economy, or CAFE, standards were passed as part of the Energy Policy and Conservation Act in response to the oil shortages after the Arab oil embargo in the mid-1970s. The shortages were caused primarily by price controls imposed by Richard Nixon in 1971. According to James D. Johnston, a resident fellow at the American Enterprise Institute and a former vice president of government relations at General Motors, President Gerald Ford had seen the error of Nixon's ways and wanted to lift the price controls. Although the Democrats, who then controlled both houses of Congress, may have despised Nixon, they wanted to keep his socialistic policy. So they wrote his price controls into this statute, while at the same time instituting the CAFE standards micromanaging automobile design. Ford signed the bill reluctantly, according to Johnston, because he wanted to make his other vetoes stick.[38]

The law mandated that by 1985 the average fuel economy of all cars sold by a manufacturer in the United States be 27.5 miles per gallon. Congress and environmentalists were not about to grant carmakers any relief from the mandated pollution reduction measures, so they had to live with the catalytic converters as a drag on mileage. The only option carmakers had was to dramatically downsize their fleets. The average weight of cars sold in the United States had decreased by about 700 pounds, from 3,610 pounds in 1978 to 2,921 pounds in the late 1980s.[39] Some of this downsizing could have been due to consumer demand, but a study by researchers from the Harvard Center for Risk Analysis and the politically liberal Brookings Institution estimated that CAFE alone caused carmakers to reduce the average weight of their fleet by 500 pounds.[40]

Automakers achieved CAFE's mandated goals through a series of steps that left families who needed the protection of big cars with less choices and higher costs. To achieve CAFE's average for their fleet, car companies made many tiny cars, sometimes selling them at a loss, according to Johnston, who was then at GM. To make up these costs, the companies then transferred many of their bigger cars to the luxury vehicles division and substantially hiked their prices.

Since family-size station wagons were the biggest of all cars, and their customer base was not that affluent, many models were simply eliminated by the late 1970s. "Detroit could no longer produce [big station wagons] if it also wanted to build large luxury cars," writes Keith Bradsher, former Detroit bureau chief of the *New York Times*. So by the 1980s, Bradsher notes, "Middle-class families were starved for the big, roomy, reliable, sturdy cars they remembered."[41]

Drivers with families were also starved for something else: the safety and protection big cars had given them and their children. By the late 1980s, statistics on CAFE would bear out its deadly impact. The Insurance Institute for Highway Safety, which is funded by car insurance companies that have a direct bottom-line interest in lower numbers of auto deaths and injuries, found that when compared to the size mix of cars on the road in 1975, each one-mile-per-gallon increase in cars from model years 1985 to 1987 was associated with a 3.9 percent increase in the occupant fatality rate. The Insurance Institute's study also found that "during 1989, 425 more people died in crashes of 1988 model-year cars than would have if these cars had the same size mix as the 1975 models."[42] Then in 1989, the study that I previously mentioned by researchers from Harvard and the Brooking Institution, published in the *Journal of Law and Economics*, found that CAFE was responsible for two thousand to four thousand traffic deaths.[43]

Based on this study, the Competitive Enterprise Institute and the free-market Consumer Alert sued the Department of Transportation for not considering safety before it increased the CAFE standard. In 1992, the DC Circuit Court of Appeals sided with CEI and Consumer Alert and forced the government to reconsider the CAFE standard. The court stated bluntly, "Nothing in the record or in NHTSA's analysis appears to undermine the inference that the 27.5 mpg standard kills people."[44]

As the years have gone by, the casualties of CAFE have mounted. In 2002, the National Academy of Sciences calculated that CAFE's mandates caused two thousand additional traffic deaths per year.[45] A *USA Today* analysis of data from the government and the Insurance Institute in 1999 found that since CAFE went into effect in the 1970s, forty-six thousand people were killed in car crashes they likely would have survived had they been traveling in larger, heavier cars.[46]

As the authors of the Harvard-Brookings study note, "the negative relationship between weight and occupant fatality risks is one of the most secure findings in the safety literature."[47] Both the size and weight of a car help to absorb the impacts of a collision. Former Heritage Foundation analyst Charli Coon explains the principle in very simple terms. In a crash, she writes, "[t]he less the car absorbs, the more the people inside the vehicle must absorb."[48]

NADER'S SAFETY HYPOCRISY

Many statements from Ralph Nader do not disagree with the conservative Heritage's arguments that larger cars are safer. Here's what he and colleagues once had to say on the matter: "Small size and light weight impose inherent limitations on the degree of safety that can be built into a vehicle. All known studies relating car size to crash injury conclude that occupants of smaller cars run a higher risk of serious or fatal injury than occupants of larger cars."[49] But this was in 1972, from a report by his Center for Auto Safety, when Nader was crusading against the Volkswagen Beetle. Nader had, in fact, begun his career crusading against another small (for the time) car: the Chevrolet Corvair. But in those days, unlike now, no one was forcing Americans into smaller cars. Drivers had the freedom to weigh the safety risks against factors like style, performance, and yes, fuel economy.

Yet with the advent of CAFE, Nader changed his tune on size and safety. He may not have liked individuals choosing certain small cars, but once Big Government forced reductions in size, he was all for it—

safety be damned. He would even admit to *Woman's Day* in 1989 that "larger cars are safer. There is more bulk to protect the occupant." "But," he quickly added, "they are less fuel efficient."[50] So Nader and his associates like the Center for Auto Safety's Clarence Ditlow, an author of the 1972 report, sacrificed safety on the altar of environmental correctness. Today, ignoring their earlier statements, they say size doesn't matter in safety. But they still seem to grant one exception to their new rule when they scream about small cars being hit by the hated SUVs. More on this later.

Nader and Ditlow seem to be saying that all cars and trucks should be small, so there would be little or no weight differences among colliding vehicles. In testifying before Congress in 2001 in support of a proposal to drastically hike CAFE to forty miles per gallon for the entire fleet of cars and SUVs, Ditlow argued that "the disparity in the weights of vehicles is much more important to occupant safety than the average weight of all vehicles sharing the road." He said that "large cars posed more of a hazard to small cars until they were downsized," and that "large SUVs should go on a diet to lose a similar amount of weight."[51] In other words, Ditlow basically argued that if everyone drove small cars, everything would be fine.

But prominent researchers in the field of auto safety dispute arguments like this for a number of reasons. First, it's not practical. Different-size families will want different-size cars. There will also always be big trucks on the road, and discouraging SUVs may mean even more full-size trucks used for things such as business deliveries. Most importantly, there will still be trees and telephone polls close to the road. Small cars also have much greater risks against stationary objects such as these. And collisions with stationary objects, rather than another vehicle, are actually responsible for the majority of deaths and serious injuries on the highway. This is one of the reasons a report for the Insurance Institute for Highway Safety concludes, "The high risks for occupants in light cars have more to do with the vulnerability of their own vehicles than with the aggressivity of other vehicles."[52]

Similarly John Graham, coauthor of the Harvard-Brookings study that documented CAFE's safety hazards, wrote a letter to Congress in 2000 pointing out that government studies have found that making small cars heavier has seven times the safety benefits of making the SUV vehicle class lighter.[53]

At the end of his congressional testimony, Ditlow also expressed another agenda for CAFE other than conservation: stopping the supposed threat of global warming. He argued that "the desirability of fuel economy" in achieving "a lesser global warming threat—should not be considered antithetical to safety."[54] By this time, the global warming "crisis" had become the newest justification for keeping the deadly CAFE system.

After fuel prices went down in the eighties, thanks to President Ronald Reagan's lifting of oil price controls, the Reagan administration pushed for repealing CAFE. But so-called safety advocates such as Ralph Nader stood foursquare against this. Oil shortages gave way to alleged environmental crises to justify the deadly meddling of this program. As Michelle Malkin, whose expertise and sharp wit extend far beyond border security, wrote in her column in 1996, "CAFE advocates quit riding the tired horse named Energy Crisis and hopped on the back of Global Warming."[55]

In the early 1990s, the Democrat-controlled Senate even tried to hike CAFE by 40 percent, to 38.5 miles per gallon. The bill, sponsored by Gore and Richard Bryan (D-NE), had the support of sixty-eight senators on a procedural vote. Only a concerted effort that included unions, farmers, and others who make or depend on big cars, and a Republican-led filibuster, stopped this effort. Although Republicans unfortunately didn't repeal CAFE when they took over Congress after the 1994 elections, they did freeze the standards at current levels every year of Bill Clinton's tenure to prevent his administration from raising them.

But much of the damage from CAFE had already been done. By 1990, the average car in a model year had the size dimensions of 1970s compact cars such as the Ford Pinto, which had been much maligned by Nader and company in the day.[56]

THE SUV ESCAPE HATCH

Due to their support for CAFE, environmentalists have themselves to blame for the popularity of the SUVs that they so hate. America's moms and dads may not have been familiar with the safety studies, but they knew intuitively that cars were no longer the same vehicles that they could count on to protect their families. So they began flocking first to Jeep Wagoneers, and then to newly made minivans and sport utility vehicles. These were not subject to the same CAFE standards as cars because they are classified as "light trucks." Environmentalists and liberals rail against what they call the "SUV loophole." But, points out my colleague Sam Kazman of the Competitive Enterprise Institute, for parents looking out for the safety of their children, "[i]t's not that SUVs are a loophole; they're an escape hatch from CAFE."[57]

But the fact that Americans would dare try to escape their rules has environmentalists and various other busybodies in a tizzy. SUVs are now the targets of ecoterrorism in parking and dealer lots.[58] And the owners of SUVs are routinely vilified by whiny liberal commentators like Keith Bradsher of the *New York Times*. Bradsher had long written biased stories in the *Times* about the "hidden dangers" of SUVs. In his book *High and Mighty: SUVs—The World's Most Dangerous Vehicles and How They Got That Way*, Bradsher, though often informative, gives up any pretense of being objective and slams into anyone with the temerity to buy an SUV.

SUV owners, Bradsher proclaims, "tend to be people who are insecure and vain. They are frequently nervous about their marriage and uncomfortable about parenthood. . . . Above all, they tend to be self-centered and self-absorbed, with little interest in their neighbors or communities."[59] After making these smears, Bradsher tries to pull back by claiming he is only reporting the results of carmakers' market research. But he never cites the specific data nor tells the reader any of the individual questions and responses. So it's apparent this is pretty much his own spin on parents who may be a bit nostalgic for their single days and simply like the small luxury of some power and style when they're shuttling their kids to school and soccer practice.

Looking at his profile when the book was published, it would be pretty easy to spin Bradsher himself as with some of the same pejoratives he throws at SUV drivers: "self-centered," "self-absorbed," and "uncomfortable about parenthood." After all, he has only one child and, by his own description, spends a good deal of time on the road at elite auto conferences. And it could be seen as pretty "self-centered" of him to, shortly before the book was published, become the *Times* bureau chief in Hong Kong. That kind of move would be disruptive to any family. I'm not saying that Bradsher is a bad husband and father—all families make tough choices. I'm just letting him have a taste of his own judgmental medicine.

Here are some of the real reasons why people buy SUVs:

1. More space for kids means less fighting and a more tranquil car ride.

In an article entitled "Feuding Kids Might Need Hummer to Be Happy," Cincinnati *Enquirer* contributor Patricia Gallagher Newberry describes her "traveling torture chamber" in her modern station wagon and longs for an SUV to reduce the tension. "With less space, segregation is not as easy," she states. Recalling her mother's "behemoth" station wagon, which would have been in the days before CAFE effectively outlawed them, Newberry writes, "I fought with my siblings growing up. But I don't remember going at it in the car. My guess: we weren't on top of one another."[60]

But of course today, the nanny state frowns on children being "on top of one another." This brings us to:

2. Car seats and air bags.

Air bags on the passenger side, another Nader-backed mandate that has had fatal side effects and doesn't deliver nearly the safety benefit as advertised, mean all children must be in back so the air bag doesn't break their necks in a collision.[61] (Hmm, I thought air bags were mandated in part to save children. Nader actually made the case for air bags in the late 1970s by demonstrating one on a three-year-old.[62] It wasn't until the mid-nineties, after a string of child deaths, that it was stressed that kids should always be away from airbags.) And infants and toddlers must be in car seats. And increasingly, states are mandating booster seats for older children close to age ten. Booster seats also don't have the safety benefits they're advertised with, according to the Insurance Institute for Highway Safety.[63] Many child seats take up as much room in a vehicle as an adult passenger. Consequently, writes a poster named Elena on the liberal blog Alas, "a real reason people like SUVs is car seats." Elena writes that today's station wagons (which are downsized because they are part of the auto fleet of CAFE) "don't give you any more seating space than sedans. You cannot fit three car seats in the back seat of most station wagons." She adds, "If you have more than one kid, you can't even fit a dog into most cars."[64]

This bring us to number three, the reason why a famous guy who prides himself on being "politically correct" says he has to have an SUV. The gentleman is Howard Dean, the fiery form presidential candidate and current chairman of the Democratic National Committee.

3. Sports equipment for Little League and soccer.

During his presidential campaign, the environmentalist online magazine *Grist* asked Howard Dean what he drives. Dean answered sheepishly, "Well, I drive an SUV. Naughty, naughty. But I have two children who play hockey and soccer, and there was no way I could do without a seven- or eight-passenger car." He promised his next car would be "an SUV, but it will be a hybrid."[65]

Dean's justification for his "environmentally incorrect" indulgence is not exactly clear. He could mean that he has to take his kids' teammates to and from games and practices. Or it could be that his children have to bring their equipment to the game. It's hard to put hockey sticks in the trunk of any passenger car these days. Or he just could mean that the smell of sweat after a game goes over better in a larger vehicle. Any of these reasons should suffice, if Dean were not going to limit the choices by making SUVs part of the same auto fleet as cars in CAFE, which would mean drastic reductions in weight and size. But he expressed just such a desire in the *Grist* interview and elsewhere.

"SMALLER CARS, SMALLER FAMILIES," ENVIROS DEMAND

If it's hard for Howard Dean to haul two kids around without today's size SUV, imagine what it would be like for larger families. Environmentalists often do not take big families into consideration for one simple reason: they hold them in contempt for contributing to "overpopulation" and want to discourage others from having what they consider to be too many children.

In response to the complaint about car seats on the liberal blog Alas, a poster called M wrote that it was possible to get two kids and one in a booster seat in the back seat of a certain car. But if a person had more kids, that was her own tough luck. "More children than that is ecologically unsound to start with anyway," M writes.[66]

This may be typical of what environmentalists and many liberals believe. CAFE was born in an atmosphere where the leading population control theorists openly advocated punitive measures for large families. As mentioned in chapter 2, population guru Paul Ehrlich recommended "luxury taxes" on cribs and diapers. In his 1968 bestseller *The Population Bomb*, Ehrlich called for making "the plush life," as he called it, "difficult to attain for those with large families." He even pushed boycotts of sponsors of TV shows that featured families with more than two children.[67] Another population control fanatic, economist Kenneth Boulding, said parents should have a government license to have a child. "The right to have children should be a marketable commodity, bought and traded by individuals but absolutely limited by the state, said Boulding."[68]

And population control theory influenced legislation, from the DDT ban, as we have already seen, to reducing child tax credits in the 1970s along the lines that Ehrlich recommended. Ehrlich backed a bill by liberal Republican senator Bob Packwood to reduce the child tax deduction for each additional child and eliminate it entirely after the third. Although legislation was not enacted with such a clear social engineering intent, the tax deduction for kids decreased by an inflation-adjusted 43 percent from the 1960s to the early 1980s, and this was no doubt influenced by arguments about too many births.[69] Several members of Congress, such as Democratic congressmen James Scheuer of New York and Morris Udall of Arizona, sponsored bills that would have made lowering the birthrate an official goal of US policy.

So large families as well as large cars were probably a target of the Democrat-controlled Congress that enacted CAFE in 1975. "Smaller cars, smaller families" had become a rallying cry for some in the environmental movement.[70] Allan Carlson, president of the Howard Center for Family, Religion & Society, sees the population control movement's fingerprints all over fuel economy mandates. "At the expert level, those who saw children as a problem and not a gift linked big cars to large families" and thought that discouraging one would discourage the other, Carlson says.[71]

And today, despite the fact that Ehrlich's predictions of mass famine have been proven spectacularly wrong, and despite the fact that economically there is an underpopulation problem—not enough young workers to support aging boomers—environmental groups are still pushing population control. "It's still very real as a guiding force" for liberals and environmentalists shaping public policy, Carlson says.[72] Enviros don't talk about population control as openly as the 1970s, but they will always believe there are too many humans and too few of other species!

Take the Sierra Club. Carl Pope, the current head of the group, got his start running the Ehrlich-founded Zero Population Growth. On the Sierra Club's Web site today, you can still find a resolution of the organization, last amended in 1995, declaring that "state and federal laws should be changed to encourage small families and discourage large families." And the Sierra Club spells out its definition of "large families": more than two. "[F]amilies should not have more than two natural children," the resolution commands.[73] Meanwhile, the Sierra Club for the past fifteen years has been urging that CAFE standards on cars and SUVs be raised because of the urgency to fight global warming.

Many liberals who are not apocalyptic environmentalists have their own reasons for wanting to keep certain populations down. Feminist scholar Linda Hirshman wants women to only have one baby because she fears if they have more than that they may—*gasp*—not go back to work![74] Many a Democrat also sees today's red state rugrats buckled tightly in their SUVs as tomorrow's Republican voters. All these factors add fuel to the metaphorical SUV fire.

Listen to this entry from a poster on anti-SUV crusader Arianna Huffington's Huffington Post blog site. The target of this lovely post, from an enlightened individual who identifies himself as SBJack, is "sniveling over-privileged children." In all capital letters, he proclaims, "People need to stop breeding." He then channels his anger at kids onto SUVs, criticizing women who he says are "wasting petroleum and increasing pollution driving all over town to take the little ankle-biters are off to soccer in SUVs."[75] He then professed concern that "our resources our dwindling" and "the world has too many mouths to feed already." It used to be said of elitist liberals that they loved humanity but hated people. Today, they still hate people, but the only thing they love is "the earth."

JUST SAY NO TO . . . OIL

Recently, events in the Middle East have caused some new folks to jump on the CAFE bandwagon. Fresh from George W. Bush's proclamation that America was "addicted to oil"—as if there was something unhealthy about the way we get to work, go shopping, and drive kids to soccer practice (as my CEI colleague Myron Ebell points out, Bush might has well have said we're "addicted to prosperity"[76]), Bush's transportation department announced a three-mile-per-gallon increase in the CAFE standard for "light trucks," the class that includes SUVs. This set off a bidding war with Democrats proposing to raise CAFE even higher. By ignoring the safety effects of CAFE, Republicans once again have yielded the moral high ground in arguing against harmful government regulations.

A strategic mistake has also been made by some foreign policy conservatives in allying themselves with environmentalists in supporting subsidies and mandates to sharply reduce "oil dependency." America should indeed have a diverse basket of options for energy. This would include sources that many environmentalists campaign against such as nuclear and hydroelectric power. Even the current "environmentally correct" fuel sources being touted like biodiesel and cellulosic ethanol from switch grass and tree branches could hold promise. (As opposed to corn-based ethanol that even some environmentalists have criticized because some studies show it takes more energy to make than the energy it saves.[77] Ethanol, in general, also raises questions about land use.[78]) But there is no reason for the government, through subsidies and mandates, to discourage the use and exploration of oil if that is currently the most practical and plentiful energy source.

There is an understandable moral objection to buying oil from Islamofascist regimes that have often flirted with terrorists. In allying himself with enviros calling for a massive shift from oil, Center for Security Policy president Frank Gaffney has said, "We are funding terrorism with our petrodollars. . . . We are paying them to kill us."[79] Although Gaffney has not directly called for higher CAFE standards, his statements are used to support the mandates. And in his book *War Footing*, Gaffney has unfortunately even parroted the enviros' misleading arguments that there is no trade-off between safety and reducing the weight of vehicles to achieve fuel efficiency.

But Gaffney has recognized in the past that it is largely futile to affect regime change through economic pressure. He argued—correctly, in my view—that even a near-world blockade of oil from Iraq would not have knocked Saddam Hussein out of power. And with less than a world blockade of oil from the Middle East, there is no way to avoid buying it from them, or (the good news) for them to avoid selling it to us if they get angered by US policy. Oil is fungible and is traded on the world market. If, for whatever reason, trade is blocked from, say, Saudi Arabia to the United States, Saudi Arabia will sell the oil to a third country that the United States will end up buying it from. And the fact that Saddam's evil regime survived twelve years of world oil boycott (that admittedly was breached somewhat by the United Nations' oil-for-food program) bodes ill for the prospect that other regimes will fall even if the United States drastically reduces its oil consumption. The only real way to change terrorist-sponsoring regimes is through military action, finding and funding reform movements, or a combination of the two.

And what Gaffney and other hawks who have joined with enviros seem not to grasp is that if more people die in accidents after being forced into less safe cars through CAFE, the Islamofascists will have indirectly achieved their goals of killing more Americans. Nationally syndicated *Boston Globe* conservative columnist Jeff Jacoby is a strong supporter of the Iraq War and Israel's right to defend herself—in other words, no shrinking violet in the War on Terror. But on CAFE he writes, "Too many Americans have already been sacrificed on the altar of fuel efficiency. It's time for Congress to stop the bloodshed by putting CAFE out of business."[80]

Jacoby and others write that CAFE has failed to reduce dependence on foreign oil. And this is not just because of the "loophole" for SUVs. It's because as cars have gotten more miles to the gallon, their drivers have driven more miles. Drawing from Department of

Transportation data, research scientist Evans, now president of Science Serving Society, notes that from the mid-1940s to the mid-1970s the annual number of miles traveled per vehicle was fairly constant at ten thousand. Then in the late 1970s, right after CAFE went into effect, it increased to twelve thousand. CAFE seemed to be responsible for this increase, says Evans.

Some of this increase has just been because of the reduced cost of driving, as a gallon of gas takes you farther. This does make things like living farther out somewhat more attractive. But as cars have gotten smaller, it has also increased the number of car trips by necessity. When you can't fit all the kids into the station wagon for family outings and long car trips, they will often pile into two cars, using twice as much fuel. If you can't fit all the goods from Costco or Target into your car, you will often make two or three trips to load up on supplies. "Two politically correct vehicles going from A to B will still use more fuel than one politically incorrect vehicle from A to B," Evans says.

MAKING THE SUV RISKIER

This trend will only be exacerbated by higher CAFE standards for SUVs. And the increases will likely create new safety hazards. Critics of SUVs, such as Bradsher of the *New York Times*, like to point out that they have a higher risk for rollover. He points out that "the higher a vehicle's center of gravity was, the more likely it was to flip over in a crash."[81] This is correct, although by Bradsher's own admission later in the book, rollovers are "rare"[82] in comparison to other types of traffic accidents. If there were no CAFE, and families could again choose big station wagons, many might choose them over SUVs for this reason.

But lightening SUVs through CAFE would only serve to increase their unique risks. Brian O'Neill, longtime president of the Insurance Institute for Highway Safety, told me for an article in *Insight* magazine, "The smaller ones are more prone to roll over than the larger ones.

Physics predicts that as you get smaller, you get narrower, and narrower makes [SUVs] more unstable."[83]

Indeed, the rush to make SUVs more fuel efficient already has had tragic consequences. You may have read a few years back about the deaths and injuries that occurred when the treads would separate in the Firestone tires on Ford Explorers. This led to 148 deaths and more than 500 injuries. But what the media didn't tell you is that the quest for fuel economy played a large role in this disaster. Ford for years has been painting itself as a "green" company, as it is doing now with its hybrids. So it decided to reduce the weight of the SUV's tires. According to report by the Nader-founded Public Citizen, a group that strongly supports boosting CAFE, "To improve fuel efficiency, Ford decided to lower the tire's weight." But the report said this is precisely what made the tires less safe. "The tire was lighter, less durable—and therefore less 'robust'— and more susceptible to tread separations," the report concludes.[84]

The author of the report, Ralph Hoar, told me the report should not be taken as broadside against CAFE and said there were other ways to achieve fuel efficiency. "Why would a manufacturer choose an already discredited, proven-unsafe method of achieving fuel economy?" he asked.[85] But CEI's Sam Kazman argues that this proves that under the frenzied atmosphere of CAFE mandates, "[n]o matter what technologies you use, there's a trade-off between safety and fuel economy."[86]

Today, of course, there is much talk of fuel saved from a hybrid, and these cars could one day have the potential to save a substantial amount of fuel to compensate for a vehicle's weight. But today, "weight still matters more than a hybrid engine in determining fuel economy," writes Bradsher.[87] The Ford Escape gets better mileage than other SUVs in part because of its hybrid engine, but mostly because it is the smallest of the small in the SUV fleet—a "compact SUV." And it only seats four passengers and a driver—still not enough for many large families. To top it off, even this vehicle would not survive many of the proposals out there to increase CAFE. A Senate bill sponsored by Dianne Feinstein (D-CA) and liberal Republican Olympia Snowe would raise standards for SUVs to 35 mpg. The Escape gets 31 mpg. So higher CAFE could paradoxically strangle hybrids in their infancy.

DRIVING AND DRILLING TOWARD CONSERVATION

These are tough times for American drivers. Although, when adjusted for inflation, gasoline prices haven't risen nearly as much as prices for other consumer goods over the last twenty years, the suddenness of the sharp price increase has hit many families hard. But we can take heart from this forecast from the secretary of energy: "One thing is for certain: energy prices will continue to rise. We're dealing with a scarce, finite commodity, one that will be running out in a couple of decades."

Why does that quote from such a high official offer any reason for optimism? Because it was actually made by Charles Duncan, the energy secretary for Jimmy Carter, in 1980.[88] One year later, after Reagan decontrolled oil prices, the price of gasoline came crashing down within four months from $1.41 to $0.86 and remained stable for nearly twenty-five years. There are some differences in the situation today, but the most important factor is still the same. The late economist Julian Simon was right. Absent or flawed government policies, and the scarcity of resources is never a problem for very long. As Simon proclaimed in the title of his classic book, the human mind is "the ultimate resource!"

Simon was a guy who put his money where his mouth was. He made a bet with doomsayer Ehrlich that the average price of any six minerals on the open market would go down from 1980 to 1990. And the sporting Simon even let Ehrlich pick the six resources! Ehrlich was sure the population was growing so fast it would exhaust all of them, leading the catastrophic world conditions he was always predicting. But ten years later, the prices of every one of the resources went down. All six fell in inflation-adjusted terms, and some even fell in absolute price.[89]

The reason, according to Simon, that scarcity of a resource is never a long-term problem is three-fold. First is that higher prices induce voluntary conservation. With oil, people will drive less if it's too big a hit on their wallet, even without government measures. Second is that technology develops new ways of finding the resource. The number of known petroleum reserves in the world doubled from 1969 to 1993. And thirty years ago, there was no way to find oil at the bottom of the ocean. The discovery, as this book went to press, of the petroleum pool four miles below the floor of the Gulf of Mexico could be just a hint of the vast, untapped oil reserves waiting for us under the sea.

The third part of Simon's equation is the potential for a replacement for the material's usage. But substitution and exploration go together. For instance, the more uncertainty there is in how much oil reserves we really have, the less likely it is that investments in oil alternatives will be made. And we don't have any idea how much there is until we drill. So locking up large areas of land like the Arctic National Wildlife Refuge (ANWR) does not just keep petroleum prices high. It also, paradoxically, impedes the development of alternatives to gasoline. As my boss and Simon's good friend Fred Smith, president of the Competitive Enterprise Institute, says, "Drilling lowers the risk premium" for developing oil alternatives.

But abundant energy, no matter how clean it is, is actually the last thing the environmental movement wants. Ehrlich puts it this way, "Giving society cheap, abundant energy at this point would be the equivalent of giving an idiot child a machine gun."[90]

Allowing man to move around with ease would ruin the ecosystem, enviros believe. The next chapters will explore the dark view that motivates environmental policies, and the tragic consequences these policies have had for public health and for nature itself.

5

Reagan Was Right: Forests Cause Pollution

FIRES AND ANIMAL ATTACKS IN THE REWILDING OF AMERICA

Every winter, in mountain towns in south and west Texas, residents witness a thick, white haze rising from the plants. The plants emit a substance that looks like a cloud of smoke.

Every year when the plants emit this substance, many of the townsfolk get sick. They sneeze, cough, and get red, watery eyes. Those with asthma have more frequent attacks. Yet these plants stand free to spew their emissions.

Why aren't these plants regulated? Did they get a pass to pollute from former Texas governor George W. Bush? And just what kind of plants are these? Are they auto plants? Power plants?

Actually they're just plain *plants*. Or rather, trees. The hazy clouds residents view in Texas are clouds of pollen from the numerous mountain cedar trees that populate the Southwest. In her book, *What's in the Air?*, Dr. Gillian Shepherd, fellow at the American Academy of Allergy, Asthma, and Immunology and professor of medicine at Cornell University, writes that "mountain cedar pollen causes high incidence of allergies in Texas." She calls cedars "the main culprit of allergies" in the Texas "hill country." Winter is mating season for the cedars, and during this time, "pollen counts are high even miles from the trees," she writes.[1]

Residents of the Southwest are taking action against mountain cedars, whose proper names are Ashe junipers. A Web site has sprung up called PeopleAgainstCedars.com that calls for reducing the number of cedars and for the planting of trees that emit less pollen. The city of Albuquerque, New Mexico, has banned the planting and selling of cedars, slapping a $500 fine on violators.[2]

But mountain cedars, although some of the worst offenders, are not the only allergy-inducing culprits among trees. While most people think of outdoor allergies as coming from low-growing weeds such as ragweed, more research has shown that tree pollen can be an allergen that is much more potent. Shepherd writes that tree pollen can be "fierce when it occurs." During mating season, "even one robust tree could send you reeling when it spews its pollen."[3] Trees are also more prone to induce allergic conjunctivitis, which causes itchy and watery eyes and sometimes more serious eye conditions like corneal ulcers and cataracts, according to Shepherd.[4]

REAGAN'S WISDOM VINDICATED:
TREES ARE A BIG PART OF POLLUTION

Their allergy effects are just one piece of a growing amount of evidence that the noble tree is not entirely benign. Our ancestors, of course, have known for hundreds of years that trees can emit some pretty powerful substances. The blue-gray haze that surrounds the Great Smoky Mountains in North Carolina and Tennessee was there long before cars or electricity. It comes from the more than 150 types of trees there.

But for decades, it has been taboo to even question the value of a standing tree. It is considered, even by some of his supporters, a gaffe for Ronald Reagan to have said in 1980 as a presidential candidate that trees are a significant factor in pollution. In the 1980 campaign, protesters would mock Reagan by dressing up as trees and holding signs saying, "Chop me down before I kill again."[5] The liberal media pooh-poohed his arguments for years. Just after Reagan left office in 1989, NBC's Andrea Mitchell regaled the audience at an environmental conference in Washington with this statement: "For eight years I covered the Reagan White House, which concluded that acid rain was really caused by killer trees."[6]

Yet, as with his prescience on both the evil and weakness of the

Soviet empire, Reagan's assertion about trees' substantial contribution to pollution has also been vindicated by greater knowledge and the test of time. Further, the recent release of his handwritten radio speeches from the 1970s, in the books *Reagan in His Own Hand* and *Reagan's Path to Victory*, reveal that Reagan was far more of a reader and thinker than even his closest allies realized. In discussing science policy, Reagan cited Nobel Prize-winner Norman Borlaug, whose methods of high-yield farming made India and other developing countries to grow an abundant supply of food. In his discussion of the characteristics of pollution, Reagan cited lesser known but respected scientists like John J. McKetta, a professor of chemical engineering at the University of Texas, and William Pecora, the director of the US Geological Survey from 1965 to 1971.[7] To serious scientists now looking at overall emissions, Reagan's belief stands closer to the mark than the "educated" opinions of elites like Mitchell.

First, let's have some context about what Reagan actually said and his views about nature. Contrary to urban myth, Reagan never asserted that "trees cause pollution." He genuinely loved the outdoors, and some of his favorite moments were spent riding horses and working on his ranch northwest of Santa Barbara. In fact, he was so gentle a lover of nature that he couldn't even bear to see a rattlesnake killed. Literally. As documented by biographer Lou Cannon and others, when an infestation of rattlesnakes was discovered on the ranch, rather than ordering them killed, Reagan requested they be transported to a spot in the forest.[8] Reagan's ranch, by the way, is now open to the public, and if you want to visit there, go to http://www.reaganranch.org.

But Reagan also knew of nature's harshness and was grateful for the technology humans had invented. As noted in chapter 1, he had no desire to go back to the outhouses of the "good old days" of his youth. And though he was awed by majestic trees such as California's redwoods—he would often refer to them as "cathedral-like groves"—he realized there was a limit to how many could be or should be preserved. Another widely spread Reagan misquotation is that he supposedly told a timber association in his 1966 campaign for governor of California, "If you've seen one redwood, you've seen them all."[9] But what he actually said, as Cannon has documented, was this: "[W]e've got to recognize that where the preservation of a natural resource like the redwoods is concerned, that there is a common-sense limit. I mean if you've looked at 100,000 acres or so of trees—you know, a tree is a tree, how many more do you need to look at?"[10]

The latter part of the statement could be considered blunt, but Reagan's other speeches and writing proved how knowledgeable and farsighted he was on forestry policy. He noted that the state of California had protected for decades nearly two hundred thousand acres of the state's oldest and tallest redwoods—what he called the "superlatives." But adding to that tens of thousands of acres of mostly younger trees that would be off-limits to logging was troublesome to Reagan for many reasons. He was disturbed about the thousands of loggers whose jobs would be put at risk, but he also noted in his radio speeches of the 1970s that timber companies practiced "sustained yield" forestry, "cutting no faster than replacement growth."[11]

Reagan was concerned that if no trees were cut, the density of the forests would create its own ecological problems. In a cabinet meeting when he was governor in 1967, Reagan asked, "Has anybody ever asked the Sierra Club if they think that these trees will grow forever?"[12] Reagan's question would prove to be a prescient one, as three decades later wildfires would rage in California and other states. Forests that had become dense through logging bans would catch fire and burn for thousands of acres, killing wildlife and harming humans. We will discuss this later in the chapter.

Getting back to air pollution, what Reagan said was that we need careful study before putting costly regulations on cars or factories that could decrease our standard of living, because these rules may not even have the environmental results anticipated. This is because the effects of human activity are often small potatoes compared to the mighty forces of nature. Reagan then said, "Approximately 80 percent of our air pollution stems from hydrocarbons released by vegetation." He made similar statements that simply referred to technical facts about nature's chemical elements.

Even astute observers at the time knew Reagan was right that natural forces had some impact on pollution. The late syndicated columnist Warren T. Brookes wrote that "Reagan's assertion that smog was caused in some measure by 'gases from trees and vegetation' was no joke."[13]

Specifically regarding Reagan's reference to hydrocarbons, a key ingredient of smog, it had long been known that they are produced by trees as well as cars. But scientists had "assumed that in cities, cars and trucks generated much more hydrocarbon pollution than trees," observed the Boston Globe.[14] But something was wrong with this picture. Because of the catalytic converter, as discussed in the last chapter, hydrocarbons and other pollutants had been eliminated from the tailpipe output of cars made since 1975. Yet smog did not decrease in some cities such as Atlanta.

Atlanta has long been full of gas-spewing Georgia pines. So in 1988, Georgia Institute of Technology William Chameides published research in Science magazine that vindicated Reagan on the particulars as well as the general point of his argument. Arriving at his conclusion with sophisticated measurements of satellite data, Chameides told the Boston Globe that trees emit quantities of hydrocarbons "as large as, if not larger than" those from cars.[15]

Chameides argued that the Environmental Protection Agency just wasn't adequately measuring the hydrocarbons from trees. A year later, the EPA took Chameides up on his challenge and agreed with him. Reporting on the EPA's conclusion, even Newsweek was forced to concede (though they don't seem to have done so since) that Reagan "had the right idea" that "trees are major sources of hydrocarbons."[16]

And the studies just keep rolling in from the most prestigious institutions all over the world validating Reagan's thesis that all kinds of trees play a big role in polluting the atmosphere. "Trees cause pollution after all—Reagan vindicated" was the headline of an article on the Web site of the Geological Society of London. The story was about studies from Australia's national science agency, the Commonwealth Scientific and Industrial Research Organization, which found that eucalypts were contributing heavily to smog in Australia. "These volatile chemicals add to the petrochemical smog in the same way as emissions from human sources—there is no discrimination," said Aussie research scientist Peter Nelson.[17]

The studies were, in fact, showing that nature's contribution of hydrocarbons was even greater than Reagan's estimate of 80 percent. The Associated Press stated in 2003, "The world's trees, shrubs and other plants do produce massive amounts of hydrocarbons—nine times as much as do automobiles by some count." The wire service added that "significant numbers of trees of the wrong type, much like a traffic jam of SUVs, can exacerbate" ground-level ozone, the major form of smog.[18]

Then in late 2004, a few months after Reagan passed away, the mother of all studies linking trees to pollution was published. Led by Princeton University postdoctoral fellow Drew Purves and in collaboration with other scientists from Princeton and Harvard, the study published in *Global Change Biology* found that natural production of the hydrocarbons isoprene and monoterpene climbed by 17 percent from the 1980s to the 1990s. This increase was equal to three times the reduction of these emissions from industry and cars during the same period. In the words of *New Scientist* magazine, "The revelation challenges the notion that planting trees is a good way to clean up the atmosphere."[19]

IGNORING THE FOREST FOR THE CARS

Reagan may be smiling in his grave about being vindicated on natural sources of pollution, but he would be disappointed that these new revelations have done so little to change environmental policy. Even those who acknowledge that trees contribute so much more hydrocarbons than originally thought still maintain that trees are untouchable in pollution policy.

In fact, some EPA bureaucrats have actually used this fact as a justification for even more regulation of cars and factories! According to the *San Jose Mercury News*, "EPA spokesman Al Zemsky in San Francisco said the results could mean that regulators have to lean harder on artificial pollution sources." Zemsky told the paper, "This is not an effort to support defoliation of the rainforest." Instead of increasing emission standards to account for trees, there now has to be even further restrictions on man-made sources to meet the legal limits, environmentalists have argued when they are forced to acknowledge the facts.[20]

And despite this new knowledge of trees' contribution, emission limits in the Clinton-Gore administration were lowered even further—to a background level that in many cities could be almost entirely accounted for from natural sources. Says Joel Schwartz, visiting fellow at the American Enterprise Institute who formerly served on the California Inspection & Maintenance Review Committee, "It's possible that, even eliminating all human emissions, you could still not reach this standard in some places."[21]

Yet if a city exceeded these limits, no matter what the contributions of trees and vegetation were, they would still have had to take drastic action that could have included measures limiting driving and banning backyard barbecues and lawn mowers. Clinton's own Council of Economic Advisers estimated that the rules could cost $60 billion a year.[22] Even some Democrats opposed these rules, arguing they would threaten jobs of blue-collar workers. Here's what Rep. John Murtha (D-PA), who is now a hero to the Left for his opposition to the Iraq War, had to say about the Clinton-Gore emission reduction plans in 1997: "We just don't think this proposal is appropriate because we see no scientific evidence that this will improve things much."[23]

Murtha wasn't the only one to question the science behind this drastic reduction in man-made emissions. Investigative journalist James Bovard, who writes on policy issues in prominent publications from *Playboy* to *Reader's Digest*, found, "[s]urprisingly, the new regs were expected—even by the EPA's own Clean Air Science Advisory Committee—to have little or no health benefit."[24] The American Enterprise Institute's Schwartz notes that increases in asthma cases do not seem to be closely linked with air pollution. As emissions from major industrial pollutants have gone down in the United States over the last thirty years, asthma incidences have doubled. "Every kind of air pollution that we measure has been dropping, at the same time asthma has been rising," says Schwartz.[25] The Clinton-Gore regulations went too far even for the federal Circuit Court of Appeals in Washington DC. That court ruled that EPA's actions constituted "an unconstitutional delegation of legislative power" because the EPA "lack[ed] any determinate criterion for drawing lines."[26]

Because of court challenges, the rule was delayed until Bush took office. The Supreme Court partially reversed the Circuit Court ruling, and the Bush administration largely kept the emission reductions, influenced by liberal Republican Christie Whitman, who was then serving as his EPA head. Bush did, however, offer states more time and flexibility to meet these standards through policies such as his Clear Skies Initiative. But even these modest measures to ease the impact of Clinton-Gore standards—standards that Democrats like John Murtha had called too stringent a few years back—sent enviros and much of the media into a tailspin.

Bush has been repeatedly called the "Dirty Air" president. To some, the air will never be clean enough. Employing a tactic repeatedly and often successfully used by her and her husband to promote their agenda, Senator Hillary Rodham Clinton invoked "the children" in promoting her Clean Power Act. Pumping in a New York community paper called the *Staten Island Advance* for her bill that would "dramatically reduce emissions from power plants," Clinton acknowledged that there had already been substantial reductions in industrial pollutants.

Nevertheless, she complained, "There's little doubt that in certain areas, the air our children are breathing is not pollution-free."[27]

But going back to the latest research, if Senator Clinton really wanted zero pollution in the air, she'd have to cut down a hell of a lot of trees! "Pollution-free," of course, is an impossible standard that we should not try to attain. To make the air completely sterile, we would have to stop all manufacturing, planting, and breathing. But to the extent there are pollution problems, the Princeton study shows that the share of hydrocarbon emissions from trees is on the increase as man-made sources have gone down. Perhaps we need to take up the suggestion, sarcastic though it was, of the anti-Reagan protesters who dressed as trees: "Chop me down before I kill again."

TOO MANY TREES

A Princeton summary of the study states that "[w]hile clean-air laws have reduced the level of man-made [hydrocarbons], the tree-produced varieties have increased dramatically in some parts of the country." Princeton's Drew Purves, the lead author, says trees must be considered part of the equation in pollution policy. "If we don't understand what's going on with biogenic [plant sources of pollutants], we are not going to be able to weigh different air-quality strategies properly," he contends. "It's a big enough part of the puzzle that it really needs to go in there with the rest." The Princeton summary notes "land use changes that have altered the mix of trees in the landscape" and concludes that "something as seemingly benign as planting a forest can have a substantial impact."[28]

And over the past thirty years, we have certainly planted, and let grow, many forests and many more trees. And the trees are more densely packed than ever before. One of the biggest land use changes that the study refers to as altering "the mix of trees in the landscape" is a phenomenon called reforestation.

No, I didn't mistakenly spell that last word with an *r* instead of a *d.* You've heard of the supposed environmental problems of *deforestation*. But in the America of the last thirty years, the main trend in land use has been *reforestation*. And it is having negative impacts not just on pollution and allergies, but on the health and well-being of humans, wildlife, and plant species themselves.

If you follow the news, or maybe just watch events in your neighborhood, you probably have noticed that suburb and city dwellers have had a lot more confrontations with what used to be called "the wild." There are, of course, the wildfires and attacks from animals such as grizzlies and cougars that we used to only see on TV shows like *Wild Kingdom.*

But virtually every news account of these incidents—such as when a deer accident kills a passenger or a forest fire reaches residences—spreads a dangerous myth. That is these accidents are occurring because humans are moving out closer to the wilderness and should expect to be inconvenienced more by forest fires and forest animals. In truth, our laws and policy makers, influenced by environmentalists, have been moving the "wild lands" closer to us.

A COYOTE IN THE BIG APPLE

First, let's test the theory that human-wild animal interactions are mainly because of suburban sprawl. In the spring of 2006, a coyote was spotted in New York's Central Park and sent fear through joggers, families, and tourists. The critter was eventually hit with a tranquilizer dart and died on his way to a wildlife rehabilitation center. While he was loose in the park, people were warned to keep their pets close to them on leashes. This is far from the only instance of coyotes getting close to the Big Apple. In nearby suburban Westchester County, beginning in the 1990s, there have been several instances of family dogs being snatched by coyotes.[29]

Now, Central Park is hardly a new development. It was built almost 150 years ago. And Westchester County has been suburban for close to 100 years. So why haven't coyotes been visiting the New York area all this time? The answer is that New York and other states have never had, in the past 100 years, as much uninhabited, open land as they do now. John Jahoda, a professor of biological sciences at Bridgewater State College in Massachusetts, writes that coyotes may have emerged "from remote wilderness areas after the reforestation of the eastern states." He notes that "[i]n the far northern parts of New England a number of species of large mammals are making comebacks."[30]

There has never been a better time for forests and wildlife, and this is, ironically, due to many things environmentalists hate. There are more forests because, thanks to some "environmentally incorrect" innovations, we no longer have such desperate needs for the trees or the land. Oil, natural gas, and coal mean we can heat our homes without chopping down a forest for wood. The advent of high-yield farming through chemical insecticides, as Hudson Institute research fellow Dennis Avery points out in his brilliant book *Saving the Planet with Pesticides and Plastic*, has meant that less acres are needed for agriculture to feed a growing population. These acres can go back to the forest, and that is exactly what has been happening.

Contrary to everything you've heard from the media, most of the farmland has not gone to new suburban homes and shopping malls. Analyzing US Department of Agriculture data from the late 1940s to the 1990s, Reason Public Policy Institute researcher Samuel Staley has found that only 26 percent of former farmland has become urbanized. The rest, Staley writes, has been "converted to pasture, forest, parks, and recreational uses, not residential housing or commercial development."[31]

And much of the old farmland has become new forest land, particularly in the Northeast. The Washington-based research organization Resources for the Future estimated the percent of New Hampshire land that consists of forests has risen from 50 percent in the 1880s to 86 percent in the 1980s. The share of forested land over the same period in Connecticut, Massachusetts, and Rhode Island zoomed from 35 percent to 59 percent.[32] There are now 622 million acres of forest-land in the continental United States, about one-third of the country's landmass.[33]

Trees have been praised to no end, and I'll be the first to give them their due. They're beautiful, provide shade, and are great for children and animals to climb. They also serve as "carbon sinks," absorbing human-emitted carbon dioxide that may contribute to global warming, although there is still much to learn about whether carbon causes warming and the precise role of certain trees in absorbing it.[34] And no one can be against a substantial green landscape.

But there's something lurking in these new deep woods that spells trouble. Or rather something that's not lurking: human management. Since the 1960s, the ideology of forest management has been to let "nature" manage the land. The landscape of the countryside has changed. It used to be that trees lined rural areas with farms and fields between them, in a landscape that was referred to as "checkerboard." Forests had roads for logging or roads for drivers to view them. National parks had quite a few food stands, lodging facilities, and souvenir shops.

Now, there are miles and miles of expanses of nothing but trees. There is a vast amount of public land, but the trees there are increasingly not being harvested for public use. Instead, dense stands of trees form until the oldest ones wither and die. This new landscape, and the policy behind it, is having adverse impacts on humans, wild animals, and the health of the forests themselves.

A HUMANLESS "WILDERNESS" THAT NEVER EXISTED

In 1964, President Lyndon B. Johnson signed the Wilderness Act. In the making for many years, never had such a concerted human effort taken place to declare the impotence of humans. The law directed the federal government to designate portions of federal land as wilderness, which it defined as "an area where the earth and its community of life are untrammeled by man, where man himself is a visitor who does not remain."

Originally nine million acres were designated "wilderness." Now there are 106 million acres the government maintains (or is it *unmaintains*, since maintenance implies man's work?). But more than just preventing new development is involved. The Forest Service has to actively remake the land as it was believed to be more than one hundred years ago. Describing the Frank Church–River of No Return Wilderness in Idaho, *Discover* magazine's Jeff Wheelwright notes, "If I'd arrived a century ago, miners and ranchers would have been pecking and nibbling at the basins and ridges. Central Idaho's forest is wilder now than it was in 1900 or 1940."[35]

On other federal land, the policy is to remove the "human footprint" as much as possible. No management necessary. Just let the animals fend for themselves and don't stop the trees from growing, dying, and decomposing on their own time.

The goal is ostensibly to preserve the "pristine" land as Americans had discovered it. But since the arrival of the Indians, the landscape of America has always been shaped by human hands. The Native Americans did a great deal to shape their surrounding. In fact, it has been argued by academics, including some who are staunch Leftists, that the term *wilderness* is ethnocentric in that it doesn't recognize the Indians' achievements in shaping the land they lived on. The wilderness concept erases "the indigenous inhabitants from the landscape as you and your group socially construct them" and "makes it easier to dispossess and delete them," contends Jay Baird Callicott, a professor of philosophy at the University of North Texas. And he notes the conclusion of recent scholars that "the ecological impact of Native Americans, over the 13,000 years or more since America was originally discovered, . . . has probably far exceeded the ecological impact of the rediscovery and resettlement" by Europeans.[36]

NATIVE AMERICANS: THE FIRST CLEARCUTTERS

Indeed, with the tools they had, Native Americans attempted to conquer nature with the best of them. The Indians, for instance, were often unsentimental about trees. If trees got in the way of attracting a buffalo or other prey they hunted, the tribe would burn them to the ground. Notes nature historian and philosopher Alston Chase in his critically acclaimed book *Playing God in Yellowstone*, "it was not the primeval forest that impressed the first Europeans about America, but the absence of trees." By the time the Europeans arrived, the American landscape had already been substantially altered, Chase notes, and the Indians had blazed vast treeless expanses. "Using fires, the Indians virtually alone created the great prairies of the Midwest," he writes.[37]

It was the European settlers who would add many of the now-historic trees to the landscape, by planting oaks and elms throughout the country. This was largely because, as Chase writes, "[i]n a market economy where lumber was inventory and housing an industry, trees had value and were to be preserved."[38]

Around the 1890s, when the first preservationists were making noises, the Indians were seen as an obstacle to maintaining a pristine wilderness. Sierra Club founder John Muir, who is still widely honored in environmentalist circles, wrote in 1894 that the Indians of the Yosemite Valley in California were "mostly ugly, and some of them altogether hideous." They "seemed to have no right place in the landscape," he would fume, and they disrupted his "solemn calm." Historians Matthew Klingle and Joseph E. Taylor write in the online environmental magazine *Grist* that Muir's "view was widely shared among preservationists" and led to the expelling of Indians from national parks "to uphold the wilderness ideal."[39]

Yet the Sierra Club Web site still devotes several pages of its site to honoring its racist founder! "John Muir is as relevant today as he was over 100 years ago," the Sierra site says.[40] And, indeed, Muir is relevant today. He demonstrates the exclusionary and elitist philosophical roots of the Sierra Club and so many other eco-groups.

THEODORE ROOSEVELT VS. TODAY'S ENVIRONMENTALISTS

The Sierra Club engages in a lot of revisionist history. Just as it white-washes the beliefs of its founder John Muir, it illegitimately claims the mantle of a towering figure of that time: Theodore Roosevelt. The Sierra Club, like a lot of enviro groups, invokes the legacy of Theodore Roosevelt specifically to browbeat Republicans into following today's green agenda. This tactic too often works on moderate Republican lawmakers, particularly those from the Northeast. And the irony is Theodore Roosevelt would be against what many of today's so-called conservationists are for.

In the Bush-bashing book *Strategic Ignorance*, Sierra Club executive director Carl Pope charges that George W. Bush has launched "a conscious attempt to return America to the status quo before Theodore Roosevelt challenged the robber barons and made conservation a national commitment."[41] But to the extent Bush's policies open up federal land for the use and enjoyment of all the public—unfortunately, Bush isn't doing nearly as much in this regard as the Sierra Club claims he is—he is fulfilling Teddy Roosevelt's legacy. And it's the Sierra Club and like-minded groups who are dismantling it.

Theodore Roosevelt loved the outdoors and hated the waste of nature's resources. But unlike John Muir and today's environmentalists, Roosevelt was a true conservationist, rather than a preservationist. He did not want a permanent, unchanging "wilderness." He was an avid hunter and fisher, and he wanted to make sure the national parks could be enjoyed by all Americans, so he pushed the building of access roads that would be anathema to environmentalists today. And he wanted multiple-use forests, in which there would be scenic beauty *and* the harvesting of trees and extraction of minerals.

A Conservation Conference Roosevelt convened in 1908 summed up his philosophy on public lands: "We look upon these resources as a heritage to be made use of in establishing and promoting the comfort, prosperity, and happiness of the American people, but not to be wasted, deteriorated, or needlessly destroyed."[42] Roosevelt's chief of the US Forest Service, Gifford Pinchot, left no doubt where he stood as to what forests were for. Pinchot was praised in the Sierra Club book along with Roosevelt, but for some reason, they don't bother to note his statement on forest policy. Pinchot said, "The object of our forest policy is not to preserve the forests because they are beautiful . . . or because they are refuges for the wild creatures of the wilderness . . . but the making of prosperous homes. Every other consideration comes as secondary."[43]

If any politician or bureaucrat made that statement today, the Sierra Club would attack him or her as a pillager of the earth. Even Pope and his coauthor, *Sierra* magazine senior editor Paul Rauber, do concede in one quick sentence a shift in the environmental movement away from Roosevelt's vision and toward "the preservation of natural values for their own sake."[44]

I am a conservationist in the vein of Theodore Roosevelt and Gifford Pinchot. I disagree with them about government ownership of the land—where it is always subject to political pressures and there is a monopoly on land-use practices. (And that governing policy has now been so hijacked by radical preservationist enviros that Roosevelt and Pinchot are probably rolling over in their graves.) But I think as long as the government is the owner, the land should be used in ways to benefit all the people, not just elitist backpackers.

One issue on which I think Roosevelt would certainly disagree with the Sierra Club and side with Bush is on Bush's reversal of President Bill Clinton's plan to make 58.5 million acres of national forest—a humongous expanse twice the size of the geographical area of Ohio—permanently roadless. This was one of the Clinton administration's "midnight regulations" issued just before he left office in 2001. In 2003, a federal judge ruled that Clinton's "mad dash" (in the judge's words) to rush through this regulation violated the procedures established by Congress for issuing these types of rules.[45] Rather than issue a new "roadless" rule, the Bush administration set up a process by which governors could tell the US Forest Service which patches of forest in their states should be off limits to roads.

Enviros threw a hissy fit that revealed their addiction to federal power. How dare Bush let state governors decide what's best for forests in their states! The Natural Resources Defense Council called the abandoning of Clinton's "roadless" mandate the Bush administration's "most aggressive assault yet on America's last wild forestlands."[46]

But since they have to deal with the states, enviros are once again calling on Theodore Roosevelt to the rescue. Former President Clinton specifically invoked him to attack Bush's new plans after Clinton's old rule was invalidated. Saying in the *Los Angeles Times* that he "worked hard" to follow Roosevelt's example of conserving forest resources, Clinton accused Bush of going back on a policy that would protect a "fragile and priceless gift to all Americans."[47] Clinton used similar language when he announced the rule at the end of his presidency in early 2001. At a news conference at the National Arboretum in Washington, President Clinton said, "Not everyone can travel to the great palaces of the world, but everyone can enjoy the majesty of our great forests."[48]

But if Clinton's rule had gone through, many people would have been forever shut out of enjoying an area that's nearly one-third of the nation's forests. Not every lover of nature can make that long hike. As the group Montanans for Multiple Use noted, the roadless rule "would have locked out the very young, the elderly, and the handicapped."[49] Such a rule that would prevent so many from enjoying America's forests likely would have never passed muster with Clinton's supposed hero, old Teddy Roosevelt!

The roadless rule, however, was only the Clinton-Gore administration's last salvo in a war on loggers and sawmills it fought hand in glove with the environmental movement. The casualties of that war turned out to be not just workers, but forests and wildlife itself. In the late 1980s and early 1990s, enviros cooked up a scheme to prevent nearly any tree from being cut down in the Pacific Northwest. The tall, mature trees included the Douglas fir, which, if you recall from chapter 2, was saved from a tussock moth infestation by an emergency use of the very DDT that's so hated by environmentalists. But now, enviros wanted to banish the human element from those forests for good, and they found just the weapon to do it: the so-called northern spotted owl as an endangered species.

In truth, the owls didn't need the mature, or "old-growth," forests of the Pacific Northwest as habitat, and they were suspect as a species. The "northern" isn't that much different from other spotted owls, and the Fish and Wildlife Service rejected the petition of the Ancient Forest Alliance—which included the Sierra Club and the Wilderness Society—to have it listed as an endangered species. Then skilled public relations-savvy enviros ginned up a flurry of media on the poor spotted owl and how he would suffer without millions of acres of old-growth forest.

The campaign, writes author Bonner Cohen in his book *The Green Wave* for the Capital Research Center, "was brilliantly orchestrated and thoroughly dishonest." Cohen quotes Andy Stahl, an attorney with the Sierra Club Legal Defense Fund, as saying at a conference that "the spotted owl is the wildlife species of choice to act as a surrogate for old growth protection. And I've often thought that thank goodness the spotted owl evolved in the Northwest, for if it hadn't, we'd have to genetically engineer it."[50]

Federal judges sided with the enviros and halted hundreds of timber sales in 1989. The FWS was forced to reverse itself and list the northern spotted owl as a "threatened species." From 1988 to 1993, timber harvest in the national forests of the Pacific Northwest fell by 80 percent. Nineteen million acres of forest was now off limits.[51]

Flush with success, enviros moved south. This time a group called the Center for Biological Diversity sued on behalf of the Mexican spotted owl, as well as thirty-nine other species, in New Mexico, Arizona, and Colorado. A judge in 1995 ordered the FWS to set aside habitat for the owls.

In both cases, after it came into power in 1993, the Clinton administration happily obliged and gave the enviros more than they asked for, at substantial cost to those working in the logging and sawmill industry. The Clinton FWS set aside 4.6 million acres of forest as "critical habitat" for the owls in the southwestern states and kept millions of acres off-limits in the Pacific Northwest too.

The human consequences were grave. Three thousand timber-related jobs were lost in Arizona and New Mexico.[52] In the Pacific Northwest during the 1990s, at least 130,000 jobs were lost in the timber regions, according to a congressional committee. About nine hundred sawmills, pulp mills, and paper mills closed. "Many of these were family businesses, and the effect on small communities was severe," reports Kimberley Strassel in the *Wall Street Journal*. "Divorce rates shot up; men committed suicide."[53] Yet, Cohen notes, nowhere on the Web sites of these groups, which claim to promote human as well as wildlife health, "is there any mention, much less expression of regret, about the human costs" of their actions.[54]

But timber workers weren't the only ones who paid dearly for this policy. Wildlife lost much from the fires that resulted as the forests grew thick from lack of logging, as did property owners in the vicinity. The final nail in the coffin was when the Clinton administration severely restricted even the clearing of salvage timber—trees destroyed by fire, insects, or storms. These vulnerable trees are the ones that are the most likely to ignite a fire throughout the woods.

The new policy of logging bans for millions of acres was in direct contradiction to the sustained yield of harvesting of US forests that went back to Pinchot and Theodore Roosevelt. This policy had conservation benefits for the forests as well. In addition to providing Americans with jobs and wood products, this pattern of logging and replanting made the forests less dense and less prone to big fires. As

Cohen observes, "The periodic clear-cutting of trees that had been the norm before the spotted owl imbroglio had reduced the danger of catastrophic wildfires by creating open spaces in the thick forests."[55]

But from 1989, when the anti-logging lawsuits were starting, to 1999, the timber harvesting in national forests fell from twelve billion board feet a year to three billion.[56] The forests became a tinderbox, and when nature hit them with wildfires, she did not do so in an environmentally correct way. The fires have burned thousands of trees, caused air pollution, and greatly harmed the soil. And, oh yes, according to the Congress's Government Accountability Office, they reduced the population of several endangered or threatened species, including bald eagles in Colorado and the red-cockaded woodpecker in Louisiana.[57]

HEALTHY FORESTS: BUSH TRUTH-SPEAK

So given this impact on nature and wildlife of fires caused by so many trees, have environmental groups rethought at all their opposition to logging? Not one bit. When the Bush administration Forest Service started allowing timber companies to do more forest thinning, enviros started suing like, well, wildfire!

In 2002, the Forest Service reported that of 326 cases of planned cuts of excess small trees since 2001, nearly half had been delayed by lawsuits. And the *Arizona Republic* found that the 2002 Rodeo-Chedisky wildfire, the arson-induced conflagration that burned across 7.2 million acres in Arizona and cost over $1 billion to put out, might have been far less severe if not for a lawsuit by the Center for Biological Diversity. The lawsuit blocked the thinning of trees in many areas of the forest that would become part of the fire's path.

Writing on the legal morass, respected wildfire historian John N. Maclean concludes in his book, *Fire and Ashes*, "[T]here are so many laws, so many ways to intervene, so many groups pulling in radically different directions that it is not inappropriate to draw a metaphorical comparison between the legal state of affairs in managing forests and the buildup of fuels in those same wildlands—a little thinning would help both situations."[58]

But when Bush provided a little legal thinning by signing the Healthy Forests Restoration Act, the media followed the environmentalist drumbeat in a primeval scream. Based on Bush's earlier Healthy Forests Initiative, the law, passed in 2003 with the support of a significant number of rural Democrats, limits lawsuits and reduces some of the red tape blocking the necessary thinning of forests to reduce the intensity of fires. It has lots of environmental safeguards and doesn't even touch some big parts of federal landscape, such as the previously discussed "wilderness areas." Yet observers such as talk show host Bill Maher and *Vanity Fair* editor Graydon Carter, both of whose forestry expertise consists largely of seeing the forest out of the airplane window when jetting from coast to coast, cite this law as a prominent example of supposed Bush doublespeak to subterfuge his efforts at raping and pillaging the earth.

SIERRA CLUB: JUST BURN THE TREES

If they don't want any logging, what are environmentalists' solutions to big forest fires that threaten both humans and wildlife? It's a more "natural" method of getting rid of trees called controlled burning. "The solution," the Sierra Club's Pope and Rauber say, is "to restore fire to the landscape: to allow low-intensity natural fires to burn, to set controlled burns in other situations, and to accept that some forest types, like lodgepole and jack-pine, were fated by ecological design for big, intense, 'stand replacement' fires."[59]

It is indeed true that the Forest Service for most of the twentieth century did go overboard in extinguishing every small fire, which led to an overgrowth of trees and vegetation. But a controlled burn today in most areas of forests is just not feasible. As Robert H. Nelson, a professor in the School of Public Affairs at the University of Maryland (and an adjunct scholar at the Competitive Enterprise Institute), writes of controlled burning in the *Washington Post*, "The weather has to be just right; the total costs of planning and controlling prescribes fires would run to many billions of dollars; and the fires often create air pollution problems."[60]

Then there is also the fact that with our forests so dense, a controlled burn could quickly turn into an *uncontrolled* burn. Fires are often hard to stop once they start. This is in fact what happened in 2000 when a prescribed burn conducted by the Forest Service in New Mexico escaped its parameters, burned for forty-eight thousand acres, and came dangerously close to the Los Alamos nuclear weapons facility. The remnants of another controlled burn ignited a smaller wildfire (about ten thousand acres) near Los Angeles in February 2006.

Yet the Sierra Club and others want a program of *only* controlled burns as a way to control wildfires. Forget about the losses in fire of human lives and property for a minute, as I'm sure many environmental groups have. This policy of zero-cut, as some call it, in national forests poses a severe threat to the fauna and wildlife they claim to care so much about. Why do they advocate it, then? Bonner Cohen has an interesting perspective:

> Some might find it odd that those who feel called upon to "saving the planet" lack even a basic understanding of what fuels a gigantic wildfire, and of how a wildfire behaves once it has been ignited. Yet the ignorance of how the natural world works is largely willful. Modern environmentalism has given green activists unprecedented power to lord over the fate of much of the countryside. And this power takes precedence over all other considerations, including the well-being of the environment.[61]

TREES VS. DEER VS. PEOPLE:
HOW ENVIROS CREATED THE DEER PROBLEM

In the East and the West, in red states and blue, in the country, the suburbs, and increasingly, the city, there is a growing threat to the safety and the environment. We see this threat in our backyards and run into it (all too often, literally) on the roads. It does tremendous damage to vegetation in gardens and in parks. It can defoliate young trees. It spreads diseases that are sometimes debilitating. It's several hundred pounds of sheer weight on the landscape.

It is the deer. Deer is a word that can be singular or plural, and right now deer are very plural. "Today's U.S. deer population has rebounded to equal the herd roaming the country when the Pilgrims first dropped anchor in the 1600s," writes journalist Cathy Nikkel at AutoMedia.com.[62] Around the turn of the century, there were only about five hundred thousand whitetail deer in the United States. Today, there are now more than thirty million whitetails here, and their encounters with people are often not pleasant, for the deer or the human.

Deer are a major cause of car accidents. The Insurance Information Institute estimates that there are 500,000 deer-auto collisions each year. A Utah State University study found that deer-vehicle collisions injured 29,000 and killed 211 people a year. As Nikkel points out, collisions with deer "kill more people in the United States than do all commercial airlines, train and bus accidents combined in a typical year."[63]

Then they interface with humans by spreading Lyme disease, which is carried by deer-borne ticks. Lyme disease has been reported in forty-three states and can, if not diagnosed early, leave devastating effects like arthritis and neurological disorders. The specter of Lyme disease is also worsening because, as discussed in chapter 2, some of the most effective pesticides to kill ticks in gardens and homes have been banned due to environmental crusades that greatly exaggerated the risks of the pesticides.

Deer, of course, can also devastate gardens and landscaping in parks. In Cincinnati recently, a deer charged into a downtown hotel. Communities are increasingly seeing them as a nuisance and debating ways to reduce their population.

Lawmakers in northeastern states, which have experienced some of the biggest deer explosions, are rethinking their policies and allowing more hunting. Also being discussed are longstanding prohibitions, both legal and cultural (people are still saddened by the fate of Bambi's mother), against hunting does as well as bucks. On more suburban land where the sounds of bullets might be disturbing, homeowners associations have agreed to let archers kill deer through bow hunts.

The Humane Society and other animal rights groups stand adamantly against these measures, and propose the new innovation of "deer contraceptives," which involves shooting does with an injection of a contraceptive using a dart gun. But it isn't all that easy to get deer to practice "safe sex." As Dr. James Swan, contributor to ESPNOutdoors.com, wrote in *National Review Online*, University of Georgia conservation research shows that the costs of contraceptives "quickly skyrocket," and "contraceptives have never been proven to be effective for wild, free-ranging herds."[64]

Environmentalists and others are also pushing strongly the idea of bringing back natural predators. More wolves, bears, bobcats, cougars, and coyotes! While this shouldn't be dismissed out of hand and could be tried in controlled circumstances, some caution is in order. There could be, needless to say, some serious safety implications in nearby neighborhoods for small children and pets.

ALASKA: ENVIROS HAND OVER CARIBOU TO WOLVES

Wildlife and the balance of nature, too, may be affected in unpredictable ways. In Alaska, where environmentalists won't let oil be drilled in any small part of the Arctic National Wildlife Refuge because it could possibly limit habitat for the caribou, many caribou herds are being dramatically reduced by wolves. Yet environmental groups such as Defenders of Wildlife and others who oppose ANWR drilling also staunchly oppose Alaska's aerial wolf hunts, even though state conservation managers say it's the only way to reduce the threat to the caribou. A Defenders of Wildlife spokeswoman has the gall and bad taste to even refer to the wolf hunts as a "genocide."[65] It appears to be just fine with enviros if caribou are decimated *naturally*!

And the deer crisis itself is greatly exacerbated by a misguided environmental priority: the preservation, at all costs, of old-growth forests. Even with the deer population as high as it is, there is one way to dramatically reduce deadly deer-human interfaces as well as conflict with other wildlife. This solution could be stated in five simple words: Chop down the big trees! For the sake of deer, of course.

Parroting environmentalists, the media will often talk about the "urban-wildland interface" in reporting deer incidents. But this interface is not as it seems. As we have seen earlier in this chapter, humans are not really moving in on deer habitat. In fact we have created it through "open space" and forestry as we abandoned farming. Now, deer have plenty of places with trees in which to romp, roll, and reproduce. But because these places are populated with big "old-growth" trees that environmentalists have insisted, in the East and the West, can't be cut down, there isn't that much food for deer in the habitats. This creates the "perfect deer storm."

At first, as farms returned to forest, the fragmented landscape, as in suburbia today, was good for wildlife, and deer proliferated," writes Dr. James R. Dunn, geologist and environmental consultant, in a paper for the Property and Environment Research Center. "However, as the forests matured, the food available for deer began to drop off." In discussing the East Coast's Appalachian chain that stretches from Maine through Alabama and Georgia, Dunn notes, "The almost unbroken forest is beautiful to see and experience, but it is not prime wildlife habitat."[66]

The Native Americans knew all too well that trees were not always good for wildlife. That's why, as Alston Chase and others have documented, they clear-cut trees with fire to cultivate game.

OLD GROWTH FORESTS STARVE DEER

In the case of deer, big trees block much of the sunlight needed to grow vegetation suitable for deer. The *New York Times* quotes a biologist at the National Zoo in Washington DC as saying that "deer are an edge species," meaning they need the "edge" that allows sunlight in.[67] Right now, many forests have lost that "edge." And forget about getting food from many of the trees. The giant, old-growth trees that environmentalists love have leaves that are often out of reach for the deer. Deer have many special talents, but tree climbing isn't one of them!

The case of the white cedar forest in Michigan is illustrative. In *Deer & Deer Hunting* magazine (a great source since, as Teddy Roosevelt showed, some of the best conservationists are hunters, because they want to ensure there is a good stock of game), research editor John J. Ozoga writes that many of the cedars "have grown out of the deer's reach." The trees "still provide favorable winter shelter for deer, but very little food." And he notes, "Therein lies the problem. As important as these 'Green Barns' may be for wintering whitetails, they have no food in them, and they are slowly deteriorating."

That, in a nutshell, captures much of the deer problem. Deer have comfortable living quarters, but—because of the big old trees—they have to go out to eat. Hence, their journeys to the nearby suburbs where they crash into cars and, if they make it, decimate gardens. Ozoga even worries about a crash in Michigan's deer population if the winter is too cold. "[H]uge starvation losses occur when deer are locked in a yard by bad weather," he writes.[68]

Of course, there is a relatively simple solution for deer and humans in many of these cases. Log, log, and log some more! Then vegetation would sprout from the sunlight, and deer could also feed on the newer, smaller trees planted in the old trees' places. In an article in *Deer & Deer Hunting* entitled "Don't Curse the Lumberjacks!" respected outdoor writer Joel Fawcett states, "I'd bet at least 75 percent of the November whitetails I've shot were taken from old logging roads."[69] Similarly, deer and other wildlife also frolic and thrive in the clear-cut areas of private tree farms.[70]

So if we cut down some big trees, deer would have an abundance of food in forests and not as many would run across highways and tramp through gardens. But that will not happen until we get a change in current environmental policy, and for that to happen, we need more citizens standing up to environmental groups' demands. And we better do so quickly. The anti-logging train is moving east.

ENVIROS PUSH FOR ZERO-CUT AMERICA

Fresh from their victory at shutting down sawmills, putting thousands out of work and making forests more fire-prone in the Southwest and Pacific Northwest, tree-huggers have moved to the Midwest and East Coast with the same song-and-dance routine about old-growth forests.

Old-growth is a catchy term. It sounds sort of like an ancient forest. As Bonner Cohen notes, "In the hands of skilled PR people, old growth quickly became 'ancient,' inspiring even more reverence and awe in a public largely unfamiliar with the intricacies of forestry."[71]

In the new battles, just about any mature tree that's say, twenty-five years old, can be placed off limits to logging. And enviros have already won quite a few victories. In Michigan, for instance, there is moratorium on white cedar harvesting on state and federal forestland, which, as *Deer & Deer Hunting*'s Ozoga notes, is highly detrimental to the deer. Activists have also succeeded in shutting down a large portion of the timber harvesting in Pennsylvania's Allegheny National Forest, and are looking to eliminate logging completely. And this forest would hardly qualify as ancient. It's been reforested only for a few decades. In his book, *The Agony of an American Wilderness,* journalist Samuel MacDonald notes that when he was growing up near there in the 1970s, the forest was so new it was called the "Allegheny Brush Heap."[72]

There are still fights in every region of the country about even the essential thinning of diseased and dying trees prone to set the forest and possibly the surrounding area on fire. The climate isn't as hot up north, but there were some severe forest fires in Oregon in 1994. The same thing could happen in the Northeast if the same policies are followed.

Even in private forests, activists are trying to shut down harvesting of old-growth trees. They stage tree sit-ins and sometime resort to more violent methods. The group Earth First! for decades has placed metal spikes in groves of trees, although they claim that they warn logging companies after they've done that. As we will see in chapter 7, eco-terrorism is dramatically on the rise.

So unless the government changes its land policy and starts cracking down on eco-terrorism, all of America's forests could become denser, more prone to fire, and less friendly to humans and much of wildlife. What kind of biodiversity is that?!

Trees do have special spiritual meaning beyond their utility to many sects. But, as University of Maryland economist Robert H. Nelson argues, we need to treat pantheism and transcendentalism as the religions they are.[73] If we are not allowed to put crosses or Stars of David on public land, we certainly shouldn't be preserving old trees solely for the sake of what amounts to another religion.

Environmentalists should be free to harvest or not harvest trees any way they want on their own private land. And ultimately, we need to privatize some of the one-third of land owned by the federal government. Even if we didn't have the radical land unmanagement policies dominating federal land management, it's bad to have any one philosophy governing so much land area. Like everything else, innovation in forestry for humans and wildlife comes from a free market with diverse ownership.

But as long as we have so much public land, we must not abandon Theodore Roosevelt's vision of "multiple use." If we turn federal forests into nothing more than tree sanctuaries, humans, deer, and many other creatures will suffer.

And the only ones who will prosper will be power-hungry green activists lording over people and animals while hugging their old, dying trees.

6

Hurricane Katrina: Blame It on Dam Environmentalists

OR, RATHER, ANTI-DAM ENVIRONMENTALISTS

W hen Congress was writing its environmental laws, it forgot to subject to its jurisdiction one very important entity: nature. While humans are now shackled with mandates, fines, and sometimes jail time for activities that could potentially affect the habitat of any species from the kangaroo rat and the Delhi Sands flower-loving fly, to various flora and fauna, nature can throw plants, animals, and people around with impunity.

Hurricane Katrina was a textbook demonstration that nature doesn't really care about what we call ecology. In addition to the nearly two thousand lives that it took and the homes and buildings it destroyed, Katrina also did a good bit of damage to the region's plants and animals. Here are some highlights of a report from the US Congressional Research Service entitled *The Impact of Hurricane Katrina on Biological Resources.*

"The storm surge and strong winds from Hurricane Katrina altered several barrier islands off the coast of Louisiana," the report reads. Land was "significantly altered by the hurricane and permanent habitat loss may have occurred." The hurricane "altered habitat for at least three endangered or threatened species, including the endangered Alabama beach mouse, Kemp's Ridley sea turtle and some species of wading bird."

And when the levees were breached in New Orleans, wildlife refuges near the city, such as Bayou Savage, were filled with floodwater, endangering the animals.[1] We heard stories of many of the heroic efforts people made to save their pets, and the heartbreaking stories of dogs and cats left behind.

A hazardous mix of chemicals was also stirred up in the flood. The *Washington Post* described "dank and putrid floodwaters" as being "poisoned with gasoline, industrial chemicals and other contaminants."[2] While some initial claims of severe health hazards from "toxic gumbo" were overstated, it would have been no doubt better for both human and animal health if humans could have stopped some of nature's wrath.[3]

GORE CONCEDES THAT HURRICANE FREQUENCY IS NOT AFFECTED BY GLOBAL WARMING

Of course, to hear many tell it, hurricanes such as Katrina weren't nature's doing, but that of humans instead, because of our contribution to global warming. Al Gore's movie and book *An Inconvenient Truth* are filled with images of Katrina, and portray the future of our world under "climate change" if we don't make drastic changes to our lifestyle. We also heard a lot from the media about the high number of hurricanes in 2005, along with implications that there was a connection with global warming.

But even Gore concedes that global warming has nothing to do with the *number* of hurricanes in a given season. Scientists are virtually unanimous that oceans go through cycles in which hurricanes are frequent, followed by periods of relative calm. In a long speech to the Sierra Club just after Katrina hit, Gore said, "Yes, it is true that there is a multi-decadal cycle, 20 to 40 years that profoundly affects the number of hurricanes that come in any single season."[4]

Two thousand five was a record year for hurricanes—but not by much. According to the National Oceanic and Atmospheric Administration, the government agency that monitors and forecasts ocean storms, there were fifteen Atlantic Ocean hurricanes in 2005. That might seem like a high number, but it is actually only three more than the previous record of twelve in 1969. Similarly, in 2005, there were twenty-eight Atlantic tropical storms with wind speeds of more than thirty-nine miles per hour. For a point of reference, in 1933, there were twenty-one recorded tropical storms.[5] And it's highly possible that in 1933, without the help of satellites or other advanced equipment of today, those folks measuring storms back then may have missed a few that occurred near an uninhabited area.

What Gore does argue is that global warming has increased the intensity of storms. "Warmer oceans make the average hurricane stronger . . . thus magnifying its destructive power," Gore said at the Sierra Club summit.[6] Some scientists agree that global warming is increasing hurricane intensity. But this, even if it's true, doesn't answer the question posed in chapter 4 of whether global warming itself is mostly a cycle of nature. Even the hurricane intensity theory is disputed by some of the nation's and the world's most prominent weather scientists.

Dr. William Gray is professor emeritus of atmospheric science and head of the Tropical Meteorology Project at Colorado State University. He created the annual seasonal hurricane forecast for the Atlantic Ocean and has been conducting them since 1983. In 2005, he testified before a US Senate committee that "[t]here is no significant correlation between global warming and global hurricane activity." Gray believes there is global warming, but maintains that the effects of its changes to air in the upper atmosphere cancel out those of warmer water, leading to no increase in the average intensity of hurricanes.[7]

KATRINA WHOOPED BY WILMA AND RITA

Nevertheless, 2005 was a significant season. After all, it had a Category 5 storm that ranked as the most intense Atlantic hurricane on record. What was the name of that storm? If you said, "Katrina," you would be wrong. That title belongs to Hurricane Wilma.

You may remember Wilma. She gave parts of Florida a pretty good pounding. There were twenty-one deaths in Florida and eighteen in Haiti and Jamaica. But Wilma didn't inflict nearly as much damage as weaker hurricanes before her. While the name Katrina will be forever etched in our minds because of the tragedy in New Orleans, Wilma will soon go back to being Fred's wife on *The Flintstones* in our collective memory.

Hurricane Rita was also pretty intense. She was also a Category 5 storm and the fourth most intense in history, causing the evacuation of Texas and the Louisiana Gulf Coast.

But Katrina was different. Or rather, she was similar to the intensity of most hurricanes. As an article in *Popular Mechanics* notes, "Though many accounts portray Katrina as a storm of unprecedented magnitude, it was in fact a large, but otherwise typical, hurricane." By the time it reached landfall in New Orleans, Katrina was a mid-level Category 3 storm. In fact, according to this article, "winds in the city barely reached hurricane strength."[8]

Yet this didn't and still doesn't stop a lot of global warming alarmists from capitalizing on Katrina. Ross Gelbspan, one of the strongest "climate change" alarmists, proclaimed in the *Boston Globe* just after the storm hit New Orleans, "The hurricane that struck Louisiana yesterday was nicknamed Katrina by the National Weather Service. Its real name is global warming."[9]

Similarly, in an e-mail to supporters, Hillary Rodham Clinton claimed that "more violent storms like Katrina" was one of the "results" of the Bush administration's leaving "no major environmental law untouched in their push to deregulate."[10]

Perhaps Hillary needs to read the prominent science magazine *Discover*. If she looked in the January 2006 issue, she would find this interesting passage: "If Bill Clinton had submitted the Kyoto treaty to the US Senate, which had then ratified it, and if Ralph Nader had been elected president in 2000 and, with a large Green majority in both houses, had forced the United States to meet its targets for emission reductions in a way that even the European Union is falling far short of doing today, it still would not have made the slightest difference to New Orleans on August 29, 2005."[11]

Al Gore is more careful but still deceptive. He doesn't make any comments directly attributing Katrina to global warming. But his film, book, and speeches still skillfully use the images of that storm to link the tragic scenes we watched on television to this alleged scourge.

The use of Katrina images to promote environmentalism are not just misleading but tragically ironic. For it was Al Gore's friends in the environmental movement who bear a large part of the blame for making Katrina the tragedy it was. Because of environmental restrictions, state and local officials in charge of flood control were thwarted from building the structures that would have best protected New Orleans from storm surges and hurricanes. Furthermore, the Clinton-Gore administration massively shifted the federal agency in charge of flood control into "ecologically correct" projects such as restoring ecosystems.

KATRINA: GREEN POLICIES CULMINATE IN DISASTER

In late summer 2005, we all watched the tragedy of people losing their homes and being trapped in the New Orleans Superdome. Blunders were made by the government at all levels. But in my judgment, the New Orleans evacuation itself was not a failure. As discussed in chapter 4, 80 percent of the city's inhabitants escaped the city before the levees breached in a well-run exodus of traffic conducted by Louisiana and Mississippi. The rest of the city was evacuated six days after the levees breached. Politicians put aside their bickering, at least for the evacuation, and the US troops and National Guard acted with great bravery and effectiveness.

Of all the disaster preparation policies and strategies discussed for all types of emergency situations, there is one policy that saves more lives than any other: disaster prevention. Whether it is a terrorist attack or a natural event, a disaster is never going to be pretty. People will be scurrying to get out, transportation options will be limited, and lines of communication will be stressed and/or disrupted. And no matter how much advance planning is done, there are always unforeseen circumstances. The best policy is, if at all possible, simply to minimize the chances of a disaster occurring in the first place. That means things like:

- Spraying mosquito-infested areas with DDT before an epidemic of malaria or West Nile virus occurs, so that there isn't a scurry for a limited supply of vaccines or drugs (if effective drugs are even available)

- Fireproofing ships and buildings with asbestos so they won't burn as easily from accidental or deliberately set fires

- Cutting down a substantial amount of trees in forests to make sure all the trees don't burn when the forest is too dense and firefighters are possibly overwhelmed

- In the case of flood control, it means building adequate structures like levees, dams, walls, and/or gates to block rivers from carrying storm water into cities.

MY CHEVY TO THE LEVEE, BUT THE LEVEES MUST DIE, GREENS SING . . .

Employees of the federal government were caught saying some rather stupid things in the wake of Katrina, both publicly and in e-mails that were made public. President Bush told *Good Morning America* several days after the storm hit, "I don't think anybody anticipated the breach of the levees." For this ignorant statement, Bush took some well-deserved hits.

Under-funding of flood control became an issue as well. Newly-elected Illinois senator Barack Obama, a rising star of the Democratic Party, accused Republicans of practicing a "Social Darwinism—every man or woman for him or herself" philosophy to "encourage everyone to go buy their own health care, to buy their own retirement security . . . their own roads, their own levees."[12] The media even cited budget requests from years past where the Bush administration seemed to give short-shrift to the Mississippi River's levees.

CLINTON INTERIOR SECRETARY: LEVEES ARE UNNATURAL!

And how about this outrageous statement about levees from a top federal official? "Instead of simply replacing the ruptured and damaged levees, I suggested, why not remove the levees, allowing the rivers to move naturally in their floodplains." Wow! What short-sighted and incompetent Bush administration official said that? None. That was Bruce Babbitt, the former Democratic governor of Arizona and secretary of the Interior for President Bill Clinton.[13]

In his book, *Cities in the Wilderness*, with a publication date on Amazon.com listed as 26 August, just days before Katrina hit landfall, Babbitt was describing much of the Clinton administration's new direction on flood-control policy. It was a philosophy that frowned on man-made structures such as, in Babbitt's words, "artificial levees" that were "imprisoning the rivers."[14] Instead, this policy advocated for letting the natural rivers flow. "Free our rivers to save our souls," Babbitt would later say.[15]

We will disclose more of Babbitt's utterly stunning views about waterworks in a moment.

And we will also look at the role of the administrations of both Clinton and George W. Bush in the failed flood control system that ultimately led to the New Orleans tragedy. But let's start from the beginning.

The philosophy that Obama should be blaming for Katrina is not laissez faire capitalism or downsizing of government. Republicans in recent years haven't come close to adhering to those visions anyway. The philosophy that Obama and everyone else should be holding accountable for the destruction of Katrina is modern environmentalism, the tenets of which are enshrined in a series of federal laws that put "ecosystems" and every species of bug or rat above essential economic activity and even human life.

THE "GREEN" FEDERAL MONSTER
THAT SANK NEW ORLEANS

I will now say something that a lot of my fellow conservatives are going to disagree with. The failure of flood control—everything that happened up to the moment the levees in New Orleans breached—was more than 90 percent the fault of the federal government.

Yes, evacuation after a disaster is primarily the responsibility of state and local government. In that regard, it is my opinion that the governments of Louisiana and New Orleans were more to blame than the feds.

But as for maintaining and building levees and other structures to prevent and mitigate citywide flooding—that responsibility rests almost exclusively with the federal governments, as it has for almost one hundred years. I love to hear accounts of the local levee boards' wasteful spending, such as the widely reported $2.5 million for a Mardi Gras fountain, as much as the next conservative. And some of them did shirk their jobs at inspecting the levees for maintenance problems. But these boards had almost nothing to do with the design and construction of the levee system. By law, the feds took over this job around the 1920s.

The federal government was charged with the construction of flood control devices to mitigate nature's wrath over broad regional areas. This doesn't mean that the federal government should have this responsibility—although as far back as the 1824 case *Gibbons v. Ogden*, the Supreme Court has ruled that facilitating navigation of waterways that connect through several states was one of the federal government's "interstate commerce" Constitutional powers, and I could argue that federal involvement here is a lot more legitimate than many of the other things the feds have constructed, such as the Department of Education.[16]

But by law, as long as the federal government has this power, states and private entities are largely prevented from erecting structures that would compete with the federal jurisdiction. So although it is the duty of the federal government to provide the best flood protection it can for large areas, for nearly forty years the federal government has shirked this duty by handcuffing itself with costly and unreasonable environmental demands.

In New Orleans, these forty years are the exact amount of time between when Hurricane Betsy caused devastation in 1965 to when Katrina wiped out the city in 2005. Right after Betsy, there was a consensus that something beyond levees must be constructed to withstand nature's wrath on the Crescent City. With the backing of Louisiana's congressional delegation and the levee board of New Orleans, both of which were almost exclusively of Democratic persuasion, the US Army Corps of Engineers proposed large steel and concrete gates—to be built primarily in the water—to block storm surge.

The structures would have operated like the "sea gates" then being built in the Netherlands, which are also below sea level, to protect cities from North Sea Storms. (A little later, we will discuss how the Dutch have achieved excellent flood protection.) Under the Corps of Engineers' plan, the gates would be activated during hurricanes to close two natural channels, called the Rigolets and the Chef Menteur, which connect the Gulf of Mexico to Lake Pontchartrain. The purpose of the project, according to Joe Towers, who served as counsel for the New Orleans district of the Corps from 1965 to 1996, was "to prevent hurricane force winds from driving storm surges into the lake and then blowing them south and into the city of New Orleans."[17] After Katrina hit, Towers told the *Los Angeles Times*, "If we had built the barriers, New Orleans would not be flooded."[18]

An oft-quoted media hurricane expert, whose advocacy of wetlands is praised by environmentalists, agrees with Towers' assessment. In his book about Katrina called *The Storm*, Louisiana State University Hurricane Center cofounder Ivor van Heerden writes, "These floodgates at the Rigolets and Chef Menteur entrances to the lake have always been considered the ultimate protection for the city. If the water cannot get into the lake from the Gulf of Mexico in the first place, it cannot then be pushed over the levees by the north wind."[19]

By 1977, the Corps was on track to build the gates, having submitted an environmental impact statement that met the approval of the newly formed Environmental Protection Agency. But a new law called the National Environmental Policy Act (NEPA) allowed any aggrieved citizen to sue to stop a government project if he or she thought it would be bad for the environment. If a judge agreed with the citizen, the project would be halted, even if it had received the approval of environmental regulators and was needed to save lives.

That's exactly what happened in 1977 when the Environmental Defense Fund (now Environmental Defense)—the same bunch whose lawsuit influenced the DDT ban that has resulted in millions of deaths from malaria (see chapter 2)—and the Louisiana group Save Our Wetlands used NEPA to stop the construction of the flood-protection gates. Their lawsuit contended that the gates would harm populations of certain fish species by limiting their mating grounds. The Corps countered that the gates wouldn't harm the species that much, because the gates were only closed during the big storms. (In fact, many fish populations thrive around the Netherlands' gates.) On its Web site today, Save Our Wetlands barely mentions the fish as an issue in the suit and simply brags that the lawsuit saved the area's wetlands.[20] This omission implicitly concedes the Corps' point that the fish wouldn't have been affected very much.

But the group was nevertheless able to convince Judge Charles Schwartz to issue an injunction, despite the fact that US attorney Gerald Gallinghouse told him a delay could kill thousands of New Orleanians in a hurricane.[21] In what author Michael Tremoglie would call on the conservative opinion site FrontPageMag.com—just after Katrina— "one of the most ironic pronouncements of all time," Schwartz wrote, "it is the opinion of the Court that the plaintiffs herein have demonstrated that they, and in fact all persons in this area, will be irreparably harmed if the barrier project based upon the August, 1974 FEIS [federal environmental impact statement] is allowed to continue."[22] Instead, what happened was that "all persons in this area" were "irreparably harmed" (if not "irreparably" killed!) because the judge and the enviro groups did not allow the project to continue.

When facts about enviro lawsuits against hurricane protection were revealed in Tremoglie's article and in my story that ran the same day on *National Review Online*, green and liberal groups responded in two ways.[23] Some groups, such as Save Our Wetlands and some entity called the Center for Progressive Reform, maintained that the gates wouldn't have made any difference in Katrina.[24] This conclusion was unfortunately endorsed in a report by Congress's Government Accountability Office, which usually performs good audits of government waste but has little expertise in the science of hurricanes.

Experts in the field believe resoundingly that the gates would have spared New Orleans the wrath of Katrina, which, as noted above, turned out to be a Category 3 hurricane by the time it hit New Orleans. Johannes Westerink, a professor of civil engineering at the University of Notre Dame, says that a computer simulation of Katrina shows that the gates would have been an "effective barrier" against the surge. "It would have stopped that," he told the *Los Angeles Times*.[25]

Or listen to Louisiana State's van Heerden, who is often in alliance with enviros. In *The Storm*, he writes that while he regrets that "the shelved barrier plan became an issue in the campaign of various right-wing commentators to hammer environmental organizations at every opportunity," there is no question that "[t]hese floodgates *must* be built."[26]

The second response to the articles was to say that all the Corps of Engineers needed to do was to conduct another environmental impact study, as the judge required. The Sierra Club said in a press release, "The Corps has never bothered to do the work despite having nearly 30 years to do so."[27] Actually, it's not uncommon for dams or roads to take around thirty years to build, largely because of environmental studies being conducted to make sure the project doesn't limit the spawning ground of any threatened species.

The Intercounty Connector, a highway extension desperately needed to relieve traffic in the highly populated DC suburbs of Maryland, had its environmental impact statement produced in 1983. (The road was actually approved by the DC area's Capital Planning Commission more than fifty years ago!) But because of roadblocks and opposition put in place by enviros such as the Sierra Club, the road, supported by Maryland's Republicans and Democrats, has been subject to study after study and hasn't seen a foot of construction as of this writing. The building, finally green-lighted by the feds after the Bush administration fast-tracked the road as a priority (that is, if you can call it "fast-tracking" twenty-three years after the first environmental report), is scheduled to begin in the fall of 2006, and the road should be completed by 2010. That is, if there isn't another delay.

The Sierra Club's response regarding New Orleans that the Corps had thirty years to complete the study also overlooks the fact that the Corps did not have a crystal ball telling them when the next big storm would hit New Orleans. Joe Towers told me in an interview that the Corps biologist said it would take ten years to perform the second environmental impact study that the judge said was required. "We would have had to look at the mating habits of all the unique fin and shellfish in Lake Pontchartrain," he said.

The court ruling, Towers recalled, forced the Corps to go with "what was second-best." Since there were less legal obstacles to simply raising the levees, the Corps reluctantly abandoned the barrier and went with that plan. Tower said with sadness, "Once you crossed out the barrier [gates], the only thing you could do was to raise the levees to a level that would have given you protection. It was the only thing left."[28] The Corps might also have been mindful of what would happen if any species affected by the gates became listed under the Endangered

Species Act of 1973. The late 1970s saw two species of questionable value bring dam projects to a grinding halt.

In 1976, when doing an environmental impact study for the building of the Lincoln-Dickey dam, a federally-funded project on the St. John River in Northern Maine to bring hydroelectric power to the Northeast, researchers found a tiny weed-like plant called the Furbish lousewort. The lousewort, discovered in the 1880s, was thought to have become extinct in the 1940s. It was immediately put on the endangered species list, and the dam was put to a halt, and eventually the project was killed.[29] In one of his syndicated radio commentaries, future president Ronald Reagan would note the irony that no one even knew the lousewort was there "until humans invaded the area to build a dam."[30]

Then came the infamous snail darter. The Tellico Dam on the Little Tennessee River was 95 percent completed when anti-dam activists discovered that the dam was in the path of a three-inch fish called the snail darter. The purpose of the dam was to supplement others built by the Tennessee Valley Authority in helping to prevent flooding and providing electricity, and $116 million had been spent on the project. The snail darter was listed as endangered even though, according to the US Supreme Court, it was one of dozens of other types of darter fish in the rivers of Tennessee, and seemed to differ only in the fact that it liked to eat snails.[31] Nevertheless, the Supreme Court ruled in the 1978 case *TVA v. Hill* that the Endangered Species Act required habitat to be protected and made few exceptions. Therefore, the darter trumped the dam.

Of course, not every dam is worthwhile, and some are outright boondoggles. Neither the Lincoln-Dickey nor the Tellico were as essential as the gates project in Lake Pontchartrain. In fact, in the case of the Lincoln-Dickey Dam, there were serious questions not just about the impact on nature but on whether it would provide enough power to justify its costs. Reagan's secretary of the Interior James Watt, a man environmentalists love to hate because of his outspoken beliefs in privatization of government land and public access to public land, would ironically recommend that the Lincoln-Dickey Dam be stripped of federal funding—effectively killing it and giving enviros the result they had wanted.

The Tellico, on the other hand, would be saved by an act of Congress in 1979 specifically exempting it from the Endangered Species Act. It was passed by the narrowest of margins though: forty-eight to forty-four. In his objection to the bill, Senator Patrick Leahy (D-VT) would give an impassioned defense of the snail darter. "Ultimately we are the endangered species," he said. "Homo sapiens are perceived to stand at the top of the pyramid of life but the pinnacle is a precarious station. . . . We exist on this orbiting globe locked and joined with the environment. We share the planetary gene pool with that snail darter in the Little Tennessee River."[32]

Senator Leahy's statement transcends the Tellico Dam, and transcends it in a very bad way. It captures the zeitgeist that led directly to the levee failures at Hurricane Katrina.

Yes, lawmakers and the Corps of Engineers made mistakes. They spent money on some wasteful projects. And they miscalculated the effects of a storm. Nevertheless, they were on track to build the structures to block the surge of storms like Katrina. If it weren't for the environmentalists, those gates in Lake Pontchartrain would have been built. Sadly, when it came to flood control structures, the snail darter got *more* protection than the residents of New Orleans, since government planners didn't face a legal requirement to fend off threats of floods to the "habitat" of humans in a city like New Orleans.

The Crescent City was also enveloped by a hatred of dams brought on by the environmental movement. Because of the anti-dam philosophy that took hold in federal policy, especially in the Clinton administration with Gore, Babbitt, and other officials, the construction of needed flood-control structures has been stalled, decommissioned, or otherwise limited. This threatens to hold up flood protection for New Orleans even in Katrina's aftermath and to make disasters like Katrina more likely in the future.

FRANKLIN D. ROOSEVELT:
NO FAN OF THE "PRISTINE"

At one time, dams and the idea of humans managing the river was virtually without controversy. Even the political Left applauded dams. For instance, in President Franklin D. Roosevelt's 1935 dedication of what is now the Hoover Dam (construction was started under President Herbert Hoover and there were battles for the name among the parties until his name was permanently affixed in 1947), he said, "This morning I came, I saw, and I was conquered, as everyone would be who sees for the first time this great feat of mankind." Then, in words that would make Al Gore, Robert Redford, and even a few moderate "green" Republicans shudder, Roosevelt called the Nevada wilderness that had existed before "cactus-covered waste" and "an unpeopled, forbidding desert." He hailed the taming of the Colorado, which he called in its natural state a "turbulent, dangerous river" that added "little of value to the region this dam serves." He bragged that humans were "altering the geography of a whole region."[33]

When most people think of the Hoover today, they think of the dam that provides water and power to Las Vegas. But "Sin City" was really an aftereffect of a dam that was built for multiple purposes. Dams have three functions: they can protect a region from floods, irrigate crops, and/or provide hydroelectricity by harnessing the strength of the falling water. The primary purposes of building the Hoover were irrigation and flood control.

The areas along the Colorado River—stretching through seven states in the Southwest—were subject to a flood-and-drought cycle. Chuck D, as quoted in chapter 1, was right that the Hoover protected residents of the Southwest from the "raging Colorado." As Roosevelt noted, in the spring, "farmers awaited with dread the coming of a flood, and at the end of nearly every summer they feared a shortage of water that would destroy their crops."[34] Electricity was almost an afterthought, proposed as a method to help the dam pay for itself. Among its many other functions, the Hoover has continued to prove its worth as an effective flood barrier.

Early conservationists, such as Theodore Roosevelt, also thought of dams as a means of conserving water. Roosevelt's secretary of the Interior Gifford Pinchot successfully fought Sierra Club's John Muir to let San Francisco build a dam in Hetch Hetchy Valley for water and flood control. The Sierra Club is still trying to undam the structure. Teddy's cousin Franklin explained the conservation ethic of dams this way: "The mighty waters of the Colorado were running unused to the sea. Today we translate them into a great national possession."[35]

In his dedication speech, Roosevelt also praised public works projects such as dams on the grounds that they create jobs. As structures that have enhanced the quality of life and given people more choices of where to live, dams will stand as an enduring legacy of the New Deal. But that doesn't mean we can't privatize some of their functions, as Barry Goldwater suggested concerning the Tennessee Valley Authority to a tough crowd in his 1964 presidential campaign.

Today, much of the modern Left takes a position that would have struck many in both parties in 1964 as much more radical than what Goldwater was proposing. Considering that to the Left almost everything from the New Deal is sacrosanct—Social Security has to operate just the way it did in the 1930s—its position on dams is indeed curious. It seems that dams are the only part of the New Deal the Left now wants to dismantle. And they mean literally, physically dismantle.

Take Jacques Leslie, contributor to magazines such as *Harper's* and the liberal *Washington Monthly*. In his book, *Deep Water: The Epic Struggle over Dams, Displaced People, and the Environment*, Leslie assails all dams as "loaded weapons aimed down rivers"[36] and advocates that rivers be returned to their natural flows. Leslie inveighs against dams as "relics of the twentieth century, like Stalinism and gasoline-powered cars, symbols of the allure of technology and its transience . . . of the delusion that humans are exempt from nature's dominion."[37] Leslie even calls for the decommissioning of the Hoover Dam, consequences be damned. He wants it returned "to its virgin state: tempestuous, fickle, and in some stretches astonishing." Leslie acknowledges that if you took away Hoover and other dams along the Colorado River, you would also "take away modern Los Angeles, San Diego, and Phoenix," as well as the desert town known as Las Vegas. But it would be a fair exchange for this minor deletion from civilization as we know it, he maintains, because Americans would get a chance to marvel at a "free-flowing river" and "an unparalleled depository of marine life."[38]

Instead of pointing out the absurdity of Leslie's argument, high-minded reviews of his work seem to gaze past it. The liberal news site *Salon* heaped praise on Leslie in a September article, agreeing that "the modern dam, in short, has come to signify both the majesty and folly of our age's drive to conquer nature."[39] Coincidently, as a west coast webzine, much of *Salon*'s power to communicate these words may come from dams.

On the day that the book review ran, *Salon* also ran articles lauding protesters, who carried signs, saying, "Make Levees, Not War." The irony was that the real obstacle to making levees was the environmental movement and its influence on those in power.

BABBITT'S ANTI-DAM ANIMUS INFLUENCED BY ECO-TERRORIST TRACT

Take Bruce Babbitt. In *Cities in the Wilderness*, he admits to being "introduced to dam removal" by the picturesque band of saboteurs in Edward Abbey's eco-terrorist tract, *The Monkey Wrench Gang*. He describes fond memories of when, during his time as governor of Arizona, he witnessed what he called "Earth First! pranksters" unfurl a plastic "crack" down Glen Canyon dam, signaling the group's desire to destroy it.[40]

Dams are actually a serious target for eco-terrorists and their champions. In the influential book, *A Language Older Than Words*, eco-terrorism apologist Derrick Jensen writes, "Every morning when I wake up I ask myself if I should write or blow up a dam."[41]

Babbitt, for his part, would carry large symbolic sledgehammers for the Interior Department's "dam busters" tours that he organized. Babbitt also has grandiose visions of returning rivers to their "natural" state. Shortly after Clinton appointed him secretary in 1993, he announced to an audience that he wanted to be the first Interior secretary to tear down a large dam.

In his book, again published just before Katrina hit, Babbitt describes an interesting thought looking down at the Missouri River from an airplane shortly after he left the Interior Department. "[I]t was easy to visualize restoring the forests by simply removing the levees and allowing the river to reclaim its floodplain, letting it meander back and forth," he writes. He envisions "the three-hundred mile river length across Missouri from St. Louis to Kansas City" as a "river stretch with natural floodplain limits." When Babbitt shared this idea with the man sitting next to him on the plane, his fellow passenger asked about "the towns." Babbitt replied that "[t]hey are small towns that faded when the steamboats gave way to the railroads" and "could generate more income from being near a national park."[42]

Actually, those "towns" Babbitt thinks of as flyover country include a variety of blue and white-collar suburbs of Kansas City and St. Louis, whose residents wouldn't be too crazy about an unleveed river "meandering" into their front lawns. The river "town" of Jefferson City also happens to be the state capital.

Babbitt never got his dream of dismantling a large dam. The Clinton administration's plans to breach the dams on the Snake and Columbia River, on the Northwest met with opposition from lawmakers of both parties from those states. The plans were abandoned soon after Bush took office. But in other ways, Clinton officials were able to produce a shift in the Corps away from its basic functions of navigation and flood control and toward ecologically correct projects. Funding in the Corps was shifted from basic infrastructure and levee maintenance, to the restoration of "aquatic ecosystems." This shift may have affected the New Orleans levees and may have detrimental effects on other disaster preparations.

THE WRONG LESSONS OF THE '93 FLOOD

In many ways, it was a flood twelve years earlier that set the stage for the precarious situation of New Orleans in Hurricane Katrina. That flood was extensively studied, and many lessons were learned. Unfortunately, most of the lessons turned out to be dead wrong.

In the first year Bill Clinton was in office, flooding occurred throughout the Midwest. There was unusually heavy rain from April through August in areas around the Missouri and upper Mississippi Rivers. Although this flooding has now been overtaken as a disaster by Katrina, at the time, it was called the Great Flood of 1993. Throughout those spring and summer months, the flood did $15 billion in mostly agricultural damages and resulted in forty-seven deaths, which then seemed like a high number for a natural disaster.[43]

As a result, much of the media, with prodding from environmentalists, judged traditional flood control methods a failure. Various commentators would argue that since hundreds of levees were overtopped, these floods showed the failure of humans trying to control nature, and it was probably best just to get out of nature's way. The liberal editorial page of the *St. Louis Post Dispatch* put it this way in 1993: "Will the millions of people who live near the Mississippi and Missouri Rivers continue futile attempts to tame the water? Or will they seek a more harmonious, balanced existence that is better for both nature and human beings in the long run?"[44]

Contrary to this assertion, most attempts to "tame the water" weren't futile in the 1993 floods. The report of the respected presidential committee on the flood led by retired Corps commander Gerald Galloway—a report whose recommendations, as we will see, would be distorted and cherry-picked by enviros and the Clinton administration to fit their agendas—found that nearly all the levees that breached or were overtopped were in rural areas and constructed by communities or individual residents. By contrast, none of the urban levees or floodwalls built by the Corps of Engineers were breached or overtopped, saving cities like Kansas City and St. Louis from catastrophic flooding. They "worked essentially as designed." The Galloway committee also estimated that "reservoirs and levees built by the U.S. Army Corps of Engineers prevented more than $19 billion in potential damages."[45]

MISQUOTING MARK TWAIN ON THE MIGHTY MISSISSIPPI

In local and national media coverage, a Missourian who knew the Mississippi well was enlisted in the "you can't fight the river" cause. Mark Twain, who started his career as a steamboat pilot on the Mississippi River, made observations so witty and vivid that almost one hundred years after his death, he is still one of America's most quoted writers.

Unfortunately, he is also one of the most misquoted writers. In the Internet age, some people apparently think a quote they have heard or made up will travel much further if they attach Mark Twain's name to it in an e-mail. The urban legends Web site Snopes.com has catalogued several such witticisms wrongly attributed to Twain. Among these are: "The coldest winter I ever spent was a summer in San Francisco," "The only way for a newspaperman to look at a politician is down," and "For every problem, there is always a solution that is simple, obvious, and wrong."[46]

In the context of flood control, major media outlets have not been misquoting Twain, but they are disseminating a partial quote that greatly distorts Twain's passage from his memoir, *Life on the Mississippi*. Twain is generally quoted saying this: "Ten thousand River Commissions, with the minds of the world at their back, cannot tame that lawless stream, cannot curb it or confine it, cannot say to it, go here, or go there, and make it obey."

This quote is generally marshaled in support of the view that it's futile to tame the Mississippi River with levees and dams. Michael Grunwald, the *Washington Post* reporter who constantly propounds a "nature knows best" view on flood control issues, retrieved Twain's quote right after Katrina.[47] But quoting Twain this way greatly distorts his beliefs on the subject of river improvement. First, in many articles, including that of Grunwald, the start of Twain's sentence is omitted. Before writing "Ten thousand River Commissions," Twain began his sentence, "One who knows the Mississippi will promptly aver—not aloud but to himself—that. . . ."[48] Eliminating this phrase distorts Twain's meaning by making it seem that he was asserting his description of "Ten thousand River Commissions" as a bold pronouncement, rather than as an opinion.

Later in the paragraph, Twain casts doubt as to whether this is, in fact, his personal opinion. Praising the "West Point engineers" serving on the Mississippi River Commission, Twain contends that "since they conceive that they can fetter and handcuff that river and boss him, it is but wisdom for the unscientific man to keep still, lie low, and wait til they do it."[49] And noting that the river stretch between New Orleans and the Gulf of Mexico was much more navigable in the 1880s than when he was a pilot before the Civil War, Twain remarked that "we do not feel full confidence now to prophesy against like impossibilities."[50]

Finally, Twain features an appendix with an essay on future improvements to the river by his friend Edward Atkinson, the essayist and merchant. Atkinson writes of the latest technical innovations being discussed in the 1880s, such as narrowing and straightening the channels.[51] Twain gave his endorsement by saying that "an opinion from Mr. Edward Atkinson, upon any vast national commercial matter, comes as near ranking as authority as can the opinion of any individual in the Union."[52]

Mark Twain was cynical about many things. But not about man's ability to improve the Mississippi River through science.

CLINTON'S CORPS PRIORITIES

Politics, though, was another matter. And in the regulatory agencies of the Clinton White House, the "let the rivers flow" agenda, to which Twain's name had been unfairly attached, was triumphing. The administration was also misusing the Galloway report.

The Galloway committee has recommended that "nonstructural alternatives" be considered to prevent flood damage. This included buying up wetlands and discouraging development in rural floodplains, which are sensible enough ideas. But the report never said to neglect existing structures or put off building new ones if needed in densely populated areas. In fact, as noted above, the Galloway report argued how levees and floodwalls were essential to keeping cities from flooding in the 1993 floods.

Yet by 2000, the Corps under Clinton had a $450 to $500 million maintenance backlog on existing projects, according to *Corps Reports*, a trade publication that follows the Corps of Engineers.[53] This backlog included the levee system around New Orleans. About one-fifth of the Corps money, nearly $900 million, was being spent on environmental work in waterways, rather than traditional flood control.[54] Clinton, in a bill-signing statement in 1999, called on the Corps to "restore the environmental value of flood plains and aquatic ecosystems."[55]

Meanwhile, the Corps was getting hit with more lawsuits from environmental groups for its flood control efforts on the Mississippi River. This time the suits were not prompted by any bold new flood control devices such as the Lake Pontchartrain gates. Rather, the enviros found fault with basic levee maintenance. In the mid-1990s, the Corps announced plans to upgrade 303 miles of levees along the Mississippi River in Louisiana, Mississippi, and Arkansas. This upgrading was needed, a Corps spokesman told the Associated Press, because "a failure could wreak catastrophic consequences on Louisiana and Mississippi which the states would be decades in overcoming, if they overcame them at all."[56]

BACK TO COURT: LOUISIANA LEVEES THREATEN "ALL BIRDS"

According to another suit filed by green groups at the US District Court, the Corps had not looked at "the impact on bottomland hardwood wetlands" before performing maintenance to levees. The suit was filed by the Sierra Club, state chapters of the National Wildlife Federation, and American Rivers. American Rivers is a group that pushed numerous dam removals and has as its slogan "River Unplugged." The groups' lawsuit contended, "Bottomland hardwood forests must be protected and restored if the Louisiana black bear is to survive as a species, and if we are to ensure continued support for the source population of all birds breeding in the Lower Mississippi River valley."[57]

Note the groups' use of the words "all birds." They were not even referring to an endangered bird. The suit basically said that any bird should take precedence over life-saving projects for people. Nevertheless, the Corps settled the lawsuit in 1997 by agreeing to hold off on some of the work while doing an additional two-year environmental impact study.

Meanwhile, as basic flood-control infrastructure was deteriorating, very little headway was being made in stopping the government's encouragement of people building in floodplains. Contrary to the recommendations of the Galloway committee and others, the federal flood insurance program was not made more risk-based. Instead, it was expanded to include more and more people whom the government thought would not be flooded to cover the costs of those who were.

Now run by the infamous Federal Emergency Management Agency (FEMA), the flood insurance program began in 1969 as a means to lower the federal government's cost of disaster relief. Instead, it has encouraged development that probably would not have taken place were banks and landowners reliant on a private insurance market. Some green groups also have legitimate criticisms that it has encouraged development in environmentally sensitive areas.

The Clinton administration thought the best way to fix a fiscal shortfall was to add as many people to the program as it could. In the 1990s, a series of commercials aired saying that anyone could be a victim of a flood, and everyone should buy flood insurance from FEMA. James Lee Witt, Clinton's much-praised head of FEMA, explained the rationale behind this marketing. "The greater the coverage we can achieve, the healthier the flood insurance program will be, and there will be less of a burden on the disaster program," Witt declared in 1996. Unless, of course, cities aren't fortified, and a levee breaches leaving thousands of new enrollees with claims. As journalist James Bovard stated in 2000, "It is scant consolation for taxpayers whether they get mulcted for disaster relief directly or for payouts under an insurance program designed to reward risky behavior."[58] Government insurance has crowded out private efforts to provide insurance for floods and price for risk. The fact that private insurance companies couldn't coordinate policies for flood and wind damage is at the heart of contentious disputes that keep Katrina victims from getting more timely assistance.

BUSH'S KATRINA MISTAKE: NOT REVERSING GREEN STATUS QUO

At the heart of George W. Bush's failures in flood policy leading up to Katrina is that he didn't make substantial changes in the flood insurance program. And surprisingly, he also didn't make many changes in Clinton's "greening" of the Corps of Engineers.

As mentioned earlier, the Bush administration did stop some grandiose Clinton river policies such as the planned breaching of two large Northwest dams. Bush also put an end to Clinon-Gore's "controlled flooding" scheme of the Missouri River to make it mimic "natural" flows. But the share of spending for environmental projects remained about the same. Heritage Foundation scholar Ronald Utt found that the Corps still spent hundreds of millions of dollars on "aquatic ecosystems." And while Louisiana received more money from the Corps from 2001 to 2005 than any other state, almost $2 billion, "just 20 percent was allocated to flood control projects related to New Orleans," wrote Utt.[59]

Even now, support for a superstructure such as a floodgate seems to be fading. Instead, enviros are touting the protection of New Orleans through a $14 billion wetland boondoggle. A few months after Katrina, some environmentalists were already dismissing the idea of building stronger levees in New Orleans. Environmental Defense, the organization whose 1970s lawsuit stopped the building of the gates that could have saved New Orleans, now says more wetlands are all New Orleanians need. "We're wasting our time and money and attention contemplating large-scale levees across the entire state," Environmental Defense spokesman, attorney Tim Searchinger told the Associated Press almost a year after Katrina hit.[60]

By themselves, wetlands will not do the job. Daniel Canfield, a renowned professor of aquatic sciences at the University of Florida, says wetlands are good things to have for marine life, but are vastly overrated for flood protection. For instance, to absorb floodwater, they have to be dry when the storm begins. "If they're already wet, and filled with water, they provide no extra protection," Canfield says.[61] Even wetland advocate van Heerden at Louisiana State says that "exactly how wetlands reduce surge under a range of hurricane conditions" is still an "important research question."[62]

It's also important to realize that the use of wetlands as the primary means of flood protection has never been achieved anywhere in the world. In the Netherlands, much of which is below sea level, the Dutch built a sophisticated system of dams, walls, and canals on nearly eight hundred miles of coastal salt marshes, or "wetlands."[63] One such wall is 130 feet high and six miles long.

The Dutch and other Europeans have proved that rather than dams being seen as "dinosaurs"—as American environmentalists claim—they are the waves of the future. London, which sits below high tide of the Atlantic waterways, also experienced severe problems with flooding. So in the 1980s, the British government built the Thames River barrier with gates that can rise as high as five stories.

Both the Dutch and the British are sensitive to nature—to a point. Like the gates planned for Pontchartrain that environmentalists killed, the Dutch and British gates only activate during a storm. This gives fish plenty of room to swim, mate, and live freely. But when it comes to floods, both of these European countries put people first!

American media stories on European flood-control successes have been scattered. And most emphasize the money they spend, rather than the types of projects they spend it on. One exception is the book, *Take It Back*, written by Democratic activists James Carville and Paul Begala. In it, they discuss the details of the Dutch dams and suggest we build something similar near the Big Easy.[64] But generally there has been a silence on the Dutch achievements by usual Euro-friendly liberals. As Ann Coulter wrote with regard to European use of nuclear power, "Liberals are very picky about their admiration for Western Europe."[65]

Looked at closely, opposition to dams reveals what is darkest about today's environmental movement. Greens who are ostensibly concerned with the health effects of pollution and global warming should be applauding hydroelectric power from dams. They harness a renewable resource—water—and are, in a sense, solar, given that more power is made when the sun beats down on a dam. As a liberal but well-informed journalist, Gregg Easterbrook wrote in his book, *A Moment on the Earth*, power from a dam "burns no fossil fuel and emits no greenhouse gases, smog, or toxic or solid wastes."[66] Take away dams, and in the short run, you're stuck with other energy sources such as coal, which have their own safety and environmental concerns.

But never make the mistake in assuming that modern environmentalism's ultimate goal is to reduce pollution. Instead, it is to protect the ecosystem by limiting human action and freedom. Here is what Amory Lovins, a prominent environmental consultant, had to say in late 1977: "If you ask me, it'd be a little short of disastrous for us to discover a source of clean, cheap, abundant energy because of what we would do with it. We ought to be looking for energy sources that are adequate for our needs, but that won't give us the excesses of concentrated energy with which we could do mischief to the Earth or to each other."[67]

Unfortunately, there could be more disasters in the making if environmentalists get their way on dams. The Sierra Club has recently intensified its fight to shut down the dam in the Hetch Hetchy Valley in California that provides water and power to San Francisco. The Club has never gotten over the fight that their preservationist founder John Muir got into with conservationists of the Teddy Roosevelt type, who supported the dam. Even US senator Dianne Feinstein, a liberal Democrat from California, says that what enviros want to do to the dam is unthinkable. It would "leave the state vulnerable to both drought and blackout," she says.[68]

Environmentalists are also trying to persuade global organizations such as the Organization for Economic Cooperation and Development to block both trade and aid from third-world countries that use dams. This is, as author Paul Driessen puts it, "eco-imperialism," and would leave those countries vulnerable to both drought and flood.

A HOOVER ON THE MISSISSIPPI

In the rebuilding process after Katrina, we should construct and fortify structures that will adequately provide protection to the city should another hurricane hit New Orleans. We should build a state-of-the-art multipurpose dam on the Mississippi to both control flooding and provide energy that is often in short supply. We can debate questions as to how this should be financed, and what share of state, federal, or planned user fees should pay for such a project. As for the federal government, this does involve a multistate river and an important port. Expenditures here would certainly be more justified than a lot of proposed federal reconstruction spending, especially billion-dollar wetland boondoggles. And of course, as with Hoover, a hydroelectric dam can recoup many of its own expenses. Building a glorious man-made dam to protect New Orleans from the ravages of the seas would stand as a beacon around the world for freedom and innovation—qualities that America has always stood for.

Despite all the environmental issues, legal battles, and pains of rebuilding, New Orleans must rise again. We cannot let a great American city be claimed either by terrorists or by a crazy movement that wants to abandon a rich culture and civilization to the whims of nature. In this way, New Orleans can be seen as the first large-scale sacrifice to an ideology that is ultimately inhumane because it is anti-human.

Katrina seems to be fading in our memory. And deep down, this is because many Americans regard it as a humiliating loss—not to an armed crafty enemy, but to nature. But looks are deceiving. The devastation that occurred in New Orleans was not really a loss to nature, but instead a loss to a clever but dishonest movement that seeks an end to civilization as we know it. Let's not forget that humans, and what we do to protect ourselves, are also a part of nature!

7

Our Unhealthy Future under Environmentalism

THE GROWING THREAT OF ECO-TERRORISM, ANSWERS TO ECO-CLICHÉS, AND A FEW BUMPER STICKER SLOGANS OF OUR OWN

I t was 19 September 2001. A deeply wounded nation was still in shock and on high alert for possible follow-ups to the al Qaeda attacks on the 11th. Of particular concern were any buildings or structures that could be seen as symbols of America and the West. And certainly, hardly anything in the world is seen as a symbol of America more than McDonald's. Some restaurants had already been targets of arson by eco-terrorists.

Still, hardly anyone thought that any kind of terrorist attack would occur at a Ronald McDonald House. Although largely supported by the McDonald's Corporation and local owners of franchised McDonald's restaurants, the nondescript houses are mostly in residential areas. They also serve a noble, noncontroversial purpose: a home-like setting for the families of sick children getting treatment at nearby medical facilities.

But on that September morning at the Ronald McDonald House in Tucson, parents, children, and employees came upon a horrifying sight outside. The four-foot statue of Ronald McDonald, intended to be a welcoming face for the children who love his commercials, had been brutally attacked. Swastikas and obscenities swirled around Ronald from his face to his feet. Given the events that had gone on in New York and Washington and the arsons at McDonald's, those at the house were very frightened. "I became concerned because of the arson and the fact that we've got a full house right now," the House's executive director, Mary Kay Dinsmore, told the *Arizona Daily Star.*[1]

Close to the swastika on Ronald's face appeared sets of three letters that have become all too familiar in the past few years to investigators of domestic terrorism: ELF and ALF.

BAD ELFS

The Earth Liberation Front and its sister organization, the Animal Liberation Front, are the nation's "number-one domestic terrorism threat," according to FBI deputy assistant director John Lewis.[2] The Senate Environment and Public Works Committee estimated that ELF and ALF have caused more than $110 million in damages.[3] And the acts committed have grown more sophisticated in recent years, leaving no doubt that eco-terrorism can be as destructive as full-blown terrorism by any type of group. As the *Christian Science Monitor* reports, "somewhere along the way, vandalizing log trucks and 'liberating' lab rats escalated into firebombs, plots to blow up electrical towers and dams, code names, and anonymous communiqués boasting of destroying millions of dollars in property."[4]

Currently, members of an ELF cell called "The Family" are on trial for allegedly using "vegan jello," a napalm-like substance made of soap and petroleum, and homemade time-delayed, fire-setting devices to blow up a ski resort in Vail, Colorado, in 1998. When the eco-bomb detonated, eight buildings were left in cinders. "When the timers went off, the entire mountain would go up in smoke," reports Vanessa Grigoriadis in *Rolling Stone.*[5]

The eleven members of The Family (a twelfth committed suicide in police custody) also stand accused of destroying animal research facilities, biotech labs, forest ranger stations, a meatpacking plant, and three timber company headquarters. They have all pleaded innocent, although the US Justice Department presented mountains of evidence—including some thirty-five CDs of recorded conversations—in a sixty-five-count indictment against them.

The Family has shattered other perceptions of eco-terrorism as well. Namely, through the connection of many of its members to "mainstream" environmentalism. As Grigoriadis writes in her vivid article in *Rolling Stone*, which is a magazine not exactly known as hostile to the green movement, "It's long been assumed that those who counted themselves members of the ELF . . . were angry suburban boys in their late teens or early twenties who worked in small cells, performing one or two misdeeds and then disbanding. In fact, nearly every member of the Family was an adult committed to environmental activism."[6]

ELF, an offshoot of Earth First!, whose activity of spiking trees with metal rods was mild only by comparison to some of ELF's activities, has claimed it always makes sure people are not in the way when it commits its violent acts against property. One set of its and ALF's guidelines claimed that members "take all necessary precautions against harming any animal—human and nonhuman."[7]

But other statements made by the groups and their intermediaries indicate they are willing to countenance physical harm. The North American Animal Liberation Press Office, which acts as a spokesman for ALF, listed as an example of an appropriate activity of a "revolutionary cell" "an animal liberationist shooting a vivisector dead on his doorstep." ALF defines "vivisector" as anyone who engages in medical research. The Press Office lauded what it called "extensional self-defense," a term, it explained, that means "humans who stand up for animals and stop their suffering, using, in the words of Malcolm X, 'any means necessary.'"[8]

Similarly, ELF said in a press release taking credit for setting fire to a Pennsylvania laboratory in 2002: "[W]here it is necessary we will no longer hesitate to pick up the gun to implement justice and provide the needed protection for our planet that decades of legal battles, pleading, protest and economic sabotage have failed so drastically to achieve. The diverse efforts of this revolutionary force cannot be contained, and will only continue to intensify as we are brought face to face with the oppressor in inevitable, violent confrontation."[9]

So far, no one has been killed in the attacks ALF and ELF have claimed credit for. Not, as the FBI seems to realize, for lack of trying. And Tom Randall, a conservative environmental consultant, thinks they may have more direct casualties on their hands than they let on: "My suspicion is if they did kill someone, they wouldn't take credit for it."[10] So while there may have been fatal fires set by ELF members, the national leaders wouldn't take credit for them, leading the public to think the groups are nonviolent.

But that couldn't be further from the truth. ALF and ELF know full well when they set timing devices that research scientists can work anytime during the day, Randall says. And he knows of research scientists who have received life-threatening phone calls.

EXTREMISM IN THE DEFENSE OF TUFTED TITMICE IS NO VICE

Indirectly, eco-terrorists are killing thousands of people, the most vulnerable members of our society. People with debilitating diseases depend on research conducted with animals or with techniques of biotechnology such as gene-splicing, which environmentalists criticize as "unnatural." In the third world, food derived from biotechnology can be fortified with special ingredients to make sure poor children are getting the nutrients they need. When life-saving research is delayed or shut down because of terrorist acts or terrorist threats, the real casualties are the sick and the poor who depend on the ability of scientists to do their work.

Susan Paris, president of Americans for Medical Progress, which represents scientific researchers, detailed the human costs of this type of terrorism: "Because of terrorist acts by animal activists . . . crucial research projects have been delayed or scrapped. More and more of the scarce dollars available to research are spent on heightened security and higher insurance rates. Promising young scientists are rejecting careers in research. Top-notch researchers are getting out of the field."[11]

The good news is that people from diverse fields—fields vital to public health and our standard of living—have recognized the threat of eco-terrorism and are coming together to fight it. In Pennsylvania, the state legislature passed a bill toughening penalties for the use or threat of force against facilities involved with animals, plants, and natural resources.

According to the regional Ottaway News Service, "The coalition supporting the legislation includes industries, academic institutions and professional associations that ordinarily have little in common." Supporters included the Pennsylvania Farm Bureau, the Pennsylvania Forestry Association, pharmaceutical firms, biotech entrepreneurs, and the academic institutions of Pennsylvania State University, the University of Pittsburgh, and the University of Pennsylvania.[12]

The bill was passed in April 2006 by both houses of the Republican-controlled Pennsylvania legislature and signed by Democratic governor Ed Rendell. "Destroying property, intimidating Pennsylvania residents, or illegally confiscating animals as a way of political protest will not be tolerated in Pennsylvania," Governor Rendell said upon signing the bill.

Rendell emphasized that he and the legislature worked hard to see to it that the bill did not infringe on the right to protest or even punish civil disobedience per se, such as trespassing. "If this legislation imposed additional penalties on persons who were only engaged in peaceful protest that did not involve property damage, I would have vetoed the bill," he remarked. Instead, he noted, the bill only targets acts "against property with the specific intent to intimidate." Rendell concluded that this "type of conduct cannot be countenance in any free society," and—in an encouraging example of bipartisanship for the common good—put his signature to the bill.[13]

ECO-TIES THAT BIND

Unfortunately, the eco-terrorists have a lot of people in their corner too, even if they're not direct supporters. One would think, for instance, that mainline environmental groups would be the first to want to throw the book at those committing violent acts in the name of protecting the environment, for fear that the whole environmental movement would be tarnished. Yet the state chapter of the Pennsylvania Sierra Club has staunchly opposed any bill that would more harshly punish eco-terrorism. Ottaway News Service paraphrased one of the group's lobbyists as saying, "The Sierra Club bars its own members from engaging in civil disobedience and blockading or trespassing on property, but there is concern about the bill's impact on other environmental groups."[14] Concern over its impact on groups that resort to violence and destruction of property?

Indeed, some mainline environmental leaders have publicly said that eco-terrorism enables the green movement to pursue a good-cop, bad-cop approach to getting what it wants. The late David Brower, longtime head of the Sierra Club and founder of other groups, put it this way to the radical green magazine *E* in 1990: "The Sierra Club made the Nature Conservancy look reasonable. Then I founded Friends of the Earth to make the Sierra Club look reasonable. Then I founded Earth Island Institute to make Friends of the Earth look reasonable. Earth First! now makes us look reasonable. We're still waiting for someone to come along and make Earth First! look reasonable."[15]

The close links between Earth First! founder Dave Foreman and prominent greens gives a chilling look at the place of eco-terrorism in the environmental movement. Foreman has in fact glided back and forth from top-level environmental policy making to "monkeywrenching" and eco-terrorism with relative ease. Foreman had taken a job at a regional chapter of Wilderness Society in the early 1970s, and by the end of the decade was its Washington representative.

But he lost his patience with politics and decided direct force would be more effective. In the early 1980s, Foreman cofounded Earth First!, which carried as its slogan "No compromise in defense of Mother Earth." In 1985, Foreman published a 350-page how-to guide to eco-sabotage. Entitled *Ecodefense: A Field Guide to Monkeywrenching*, Foreman's book gave its readers useful instructions on how to down power lines, disable heavy equipment, vandalize billboards, and most infamously, "spike" trees. Tree-spiking involves driving a metal rod as deeply as possible into trees that might be logged. "Spike a few trees now and then whenever you enter an area," reads the book's dust jacket.

And readers did.

One man who found out all about tree-spiking was George Alexander. He was a twenty-three-year-old sawmill worker for the Louisiana Pacific paper company. In 1987, Alexander was cutting a section of a redwood log with a saw when all of a sudden the saw hit a metal rod that had been placed there. According to the *San Francisco Chronicle*, Alexander then "incurred severe face lacerations, cuts on both jugular veins and the loss of upper and lower front teeth." As Neal Hrab would later write in a report for the Capital Research Center, "Dave Foreman's response was chilling." Foreman told the *Chronicle*, "It is unfortunate this worker was injured and I wish him the best. But the real destruction and injury is being perpetrated by Louisiana-Pacific and the forest service in liquidating old-growth forests."[16]

As consultant Randall pointed out, it is hard to know how many have been physically harmed or killed by eco-terrorism, because groups will never take credit for incidents in which those injuries occur. In his 1991 memoir, *Confessions of an Eco-Warrior*, Foreman tried to further distance Earth First! and ultimately himself from Alexander's injury. He said it didn't look like an Earth First! sabotage because the "spiked tree was not an old-growth redwood from a sale in a pristine area." He then tried to blame Louisiana-Pacific, because the company may not have put its wood through a metal detector to check for spikes![17]

Foreman said tree-spikers should minimize the chances for harm to workers by warning companies through various methods. Yet he still defended the practice of spiking, even while acknowledging it could lead to more injuries like those of Alexander. "Safety is a relative concept; nothing in life is entirely safe," Foreman wrote. "The record shows, however, that tree spiking is one of the least dangers a logger faces."[18]

If Foreman's was a lone voice on the fringe of the environmental movement—shunned by movement leaders—there would be less cause for concern. Instead, what is most alarming about Foreman's book is its back cover. There, even after the injuries of George Alexander had been widely reported, Foreman is warmly embraced by some of the nation's leading environmental thinkers.

Bill McKibben calls Foreman "[o]ne of the towering figures, the mighty sequoias of American conservation." James Lovelock, developer of the "Gaia hypothesis" widely cited by greens, writes that "Dave Foreman is one who truly understands that the Earth must come first." And Kirkpatrick Sale, author of many influential environmental tracts, gushes that "if anything is to save this imperiled Earth, it is the kind of biocentric ecological vision he [Foreman] here puts so clearly and forcefully."[19]

No, in their statements, the authors do not expressly support tree-spiking and Foreman's other recommended "monkeywrenching" activities. But their words of praise do countenance Foreman and, in turn, the activities he recommends. And showing just how few links separate eco-terrorism from environmentalism's "mainstream," McKibben, Sale, and Lovelock—the writers who praised Foreman—are themselves regularly praised by Al Gore.

Foreman has gone back to a role in formulating environmental policy. He was a founder of the Wildlands Project, which proposes vast swaths of interconnecting land inhabited by wild animals, with human "islands" in-between. It also advocates repopulating many areas with large predators such as wolves, mountain lions, and grizzly bears. Foreman's project lists many academic advisers and claims success in community land-use planning. In fact, the next time you see a cougar in your yard, Foreman may be the guy you want to thank. He has since left the Wildlands Project and is promoting the same ideas at the Rewilding Institute.

Reinforcing the notion that the radical and the mainstream are too close for comfort, Foreman was also elected to the board of the Sierra Club in the mid-1990s and stayed there until 1997.

During his Earth First! days, Foreman also had another fan. Theodore Kaczynski, also known as the Unabomber, mailed dozens of letter bombs. He killed three people and wounded twenty-eight before he was arrested in the late 1990s and was sentenced to life in prison after a guilty plea. But even though Kaczynski led a solitary existence in a cabin, he was never exactly alone. FBI agents discovered several volumes of the *Earth First! Journal* when they raided his cabin. Also found was an issue of the publication *Live Wild or Die,* which was financed by an Earth First! cofounder and featured a "hit list" of individuals and corporations it considered most destructive to the environment.[20] Yet one searches in vain in the mainstream media for articles noting the connection of Earth First! to the Unabomber's actions. In fact, there is precious little media asking the question if the harsh rhetoric of mainline environmental groups has anything to do with the spike in eco-terrorism.

A different media situation occurred, however, in another act of domestic terrorism. When Timothy McVeigh blew up the federal Murrah building in Oklahoma City in 1995, pundits rushed in to blame any radio talk show host who had harsh words for big government. Richard Lacayo of *Time* magazine infamously called conservative talk radio hosts "an unindicted co-conspirator" in McVeigh's bombing.[21] This, despite the fact that McVeigh appeared to be more influenced by the white supremacy movement than any arguments about limited government. Nevertheless, conservatives did examine their rhetoric against the government and, in some cases, moderated their tone.

We should always be careful about drawing links between strong words and violent deeds, no matter who the speakers in question are. Those who use violence are solely responsible for their actions. I am a strong believer in the First Amendment and oppose any restrictions on expression, with limited exceptions such as Justice Holmes' example of falsely shouting "fire" in a theater, and speech that directly incites to riot. Strong debate is essential to a free society.

Nevertheless, actions are always preceded by beliefs, and no belief exists in a vacuum. If overstated rhetoric and false information is encouraging violence and terrorism, then society—again, not government—has an obligation to examine that rhetoric and discourage its use. And conservative rhetoric against the government around the time of the bombing in Oklahoma pales in comparison to the attacks on and vilification of those who disagree with environmentalists. And it paints apocalyptic end-of-the-world rhetoric if opponents get their way. Here is a sampling:

In fund-raising material for the Natural Resources Defense Council, Robert F. Kennedy Jr. proclaims, "The Bush Administration is quietly putting radical new policies in place that will let its corporate allies poison our air, foul our water and devastate our wildlands for decades to come."[22] Casting his opponents as "evil," Defenders of Wildlife president Rodger Schlickeisen writes, "The evil special interests are still actively trying to cut major loopholes in the Endangered Species Act."[23] Al Gore said in April 2006, "We have been blind to the fact that the human species is now having a crushing impact on the ecological system of the planet."[24]

Anti-human statements like Gore's are actually the most poisonous kind of environmental rhetoric. Statements about the evil of humanity in general are ultimately more destructive than any verbal attacks on individual humans, such as George W. Bush and Dick Cheney. And this is what binds terrorism advocates like Foreman together with "mainstream" environmentalists like Paul Ehrlich.

In *Confessions of an Eco-Warrior*, Foreman repeatedly refers to what he calls the "humanpox" plague of too many people. He praises the views of Thomas Malthus, whose 1798 treatise that overpopulation would exhaust resources influenced the modern population control movement. But Foreman writes that even if Malthus were wrong about humans running out of resources to sustain themselves, there are still too many darn humans: "Even if inequitable distribution could be solved, six billion human beings converting the natural world to material goods and human food would devastate natural diversity.[25]

Population control guru Ehrlich says much the same thing on the Web site of the Wildlands Project, which, as we have noted, was founded by Foreman. After so many of his doomsaying predictions about humans have been proven wrong, he now speaks of limiting human population and development to solve "the only realistic strategy for enduring the extinction crisis."[26]

Foreman and Ehrlich are Malthusians with a twist. They may no longer believe that humans will starve themselves by exhausting all resources, but that's not really important to them. To them, and to most environmental leaders, population will always be a problem because humans roam on too much habitat that they think belongs exclusively to cougars, wolves, and plants and should be left almost completely undisturbed. That's why environmental groups continue to push population control measures, even as economists and demographers insist that we have an *underpopulation* problem. For environmentalists, there will always be too many people and too few species! All statements coming from environmentalists must be evaluated by looking through the anti-human lens that much of them hold.

ECO-CLICHÉS AND BERLAU'S BUMPER STICKERS

Unfortunately, there are sayings and bumper sticker slogans that many good people who don't share environmentalists' anti-human premises will repeat without further examination. Also as unfortunate, these statements shape public policy in ways that are detrimental, as we have seen, to the health of humans and even wildlife. Let's look at a few, view the problem of their implications, and see if we can come up with our own simple slogans for better ways to conserve resources and solve public health problems.

SUSTAINABLE DEVELOPMENT

This is a term that has been used for coercive population control policies, blocking development in the name of stopping urban sprawl, and managing forest and fisheries. Jared Diamond uses the term a lot in his popular doomsaying volume *Collapse*. We can buy products that are certified they are made in a "sustainable" way.

But what does the term really mean? For many environmentalists, it means limiting the impact of humans on the planet, and all human impacts are necessarily bad. Not every method of producing things labeled "sustainable" is necessarily bad. But the vagueness of the term and the anti-human implications of it mean that both products and policies labeled "sustainable" merit closer scrutiny.

PRECAUTIONARY PRINCIPLE

Some amount of precaution is certainly good. We never want to rush into things. And environmentalists point to the common sense aphorism, "Look before you leap."

But, as one commentator has pointed out, there is an equally powerful common sense saying, "He who hesitates is lost."[27] If the Precautionary Principle had been used when DDT was developed, and World War II soldiers were not allowed to spray it on themselves, many could have died from typhus. So, too, would probably thousands more Holocaust victims if the Allied forces had not immediately cleansed them with it upon liberation from the concentration camps. Unfortunately, the Precautionary Principle did prevent floodgates from being built that probably would have saved New Orleans from Hurricane Katrina.

But let's also apply the Precautionary Principle consistently. Let's use precaution before we ban some chemical or technology, as well as before we introduce it. Let's ask ourselves, is there a greater hazard to public health that will occur if we ban this product than the unknown risk that may occur if we continue using it. So, in the name of the Precautionary Principle, I propose bringing back DDT and other pesticides that were banned, to help us deal with the emerging problems of insect-borne West Nile virus and Lyme disease.

The real problem with the Precautionary Principle is its inconsistent application by environmentalists. They want precaution only against risks created by humans. They're not as concerned about minimizing "natural" risks such as diseases.

The Environment

I've talked a lot in this book about environmentalists, and some readers may be left wondering if we can care about clean water and clean air and special animals and trees without subscribing to all the crazy notions of environmentalists? Yes, we can. But one of the most important things is to stop using vague words like "the environment" and "the planet."

It's important to do what we can to protect the *inhabitants* of the environment or the planet. I would say humans first, then animals, and then plant life. If there is a specific pollutant, man-made or natural, affecting human health, we should figure out a way to deal with it. The same goes for feasible solutions for threats to wildlife and plants. But we shouldn't look at these problems from the standpoint that more human impact is necessarily bad. All too frequently these days, a dam or a road is prevented from being built not because it will even reduce the number of the species, but because environmentalists say it will affect that species' ecosystem.

The difference lies in conservation vs. preservation. Teddy Roosevelt was a conservationist. He believed in conserving, as well as using, natural resources and outdoor spots. But unlike John Muir and his disciples at the Sierra Club, Roosevelt was not a preservationist. He knew it was folly to freeze in place the land as it always was. And in truth, we don't know how the land always was. As we discussed in chapter 6, contrary to myths, Native Americans made great changes to the American landscape. We shouldn't be afraid to do the same.

One thing that has changed since Roosevelt's day is that the folly of government management of natural resources has clearly been shown. When the Soviet Union opened up, scholars were appalled at the rotten treatment of its land.[28] In the United States, by contrast, many private landowners go out of their way to create habitats for animals, and the stiff mandates of the Endangered Species Act actually acts as a disincentive to conservation. The Center for Private

Conservation, affiliated with the Competitive Enterprise Institute and run by skilled outdoorsman Robert J. Smith, offers plenty of excellent examples of the private preservation of habitat.[29]

HUMANS SHOULDN'T STAND APART FROM OR CONTROL NATURE

Environmentalists often assert that humans arrogantly try to bend nature to their ways, and that they should be more humble. Humans aren't any more special than other parts of nature and should stop acting like they are.

This belief directly conflicts, of course, with many of our religious traditions of Judaism and Christianity. The book of Genesis clearly tells us that God intended us to have "dominion" over and to "subdue" the earth to our needs. We should be wise stewards, but the earth is here for us and for future generations to use.

The ironic thing here is that environmentalists are actually the ones asking us to stand apart from nature. They're asking us not to do the same things as other animals. It's perfectly fine with greens when elephants knock down trees with their trunks and when beavers build dams. It's all right with animal rights proponents when wolves and lions eat other animals, just not when humans do it.

We're animals too. The difference is that we're animals with intelligent minds, capable of restraining our desires. And, of course, we should restrain ourselves sometimes. But we shouldn't argue that doing the things we need and want to do for comfort and survival are in any way "unnatural."

THE ENVIRONMENT ISN'T A CONSERVATIVE OR LIBERAL ISSUE

This saying I agree with. But not for the reasons it's usually stated. I think both conservatives *and liberals* should reject the tenets of modern environmentalism.

The merging of liberalism with environmentalism is actually a rather new political phenomenon, not quite forty years old. Recall

Franklin D. Roosevelt's speech in dedicating the Hoover Dam in which he bragged about "altering" the geography of a region and called the area that had existed before "cactus-covered waste."

Karl Marx and the early communists and socialists were not against factories. In fact many saw them as liberating to farm drudgery. They just wanted the factories to be owned by "the people," a.k.a. the government. Marx himself attacked what he called the "Malthusian population fantasy" as "swaggering, sham-scientific, bombastic ignorance."[30] His colleague Friedrich Engels, sounding so much like Ehrlich's nemesis Julian Simon, said that "it is ridiculous to speak of overpopulation" because the progress of "science . . . is just as limitless and at least as rapid as that of population."[31]

Those liberals who really care about humanity, and I believe there are more than a few, should be the first in line to advocate spraying DDT to combat malaria outbreaks in Africa, even if some birds get killed (which, as I show in chapter 2, they most likely won't). It might also help liberals win some of their arguments. It's hard to argue that you're for government-run health care and against Social Security private accounts because you care so much about people when you then turn around and say that people's needs should take second place to those of the snail darter.

There are both liberals and conservatives who care about people and public health. And if we could put aside our differences to fight environmentalists, the world would be a lot better off.

And that leads me to my final eco-cliché.

DON'T LEAVE A FOOTPRINT

The idea here is that humans should leave no lasting trace in nature, that we should have no impact in the ecosystems in which we live. I say, "Leave a Footprint." In fact, leave many footprints. I'd like to put that on a bumper sticker.

The Native Americans left footprints when through their burnings of nature they created the Great Plains. Another who left a big footprint was John Chapman, better known as Johnny Appleseed, when he planted apple trees all over nineteenth-century America.

And leave behind human "footprints" like those that comprise much of the "natural" beauty of Hawaii, as the eminent microbiologist and essayist Renè Dubos points out in his book, *The Wooing of Earth*. Before European settlers arrived, he writes, "the Hawaiian biota was relatively simple and disharmonic. . . . It had no pine trees, no oaks, no maples, no willows, no fig trees, no mangroves [aka wetlands], one single species of palm, and only a few insignificant orchids." The introduced plant species, Dubos writes, "have prospered even better than in their native habitats."[32]

Dubos, the recipient of many awards for his scientific contributions to germ-fighting, concludes his 1980 book with some wise words. There was a character in Voltaire's eighteenth-century novel, *Candide*, called Dr. Pangloss, who always said that whatever situation occurred was "the best of all worlds." To Dubos, "'[n]ature knows best' is the twentieth century equivalent to Pangloss's affirmation." And to Dubos, "[t]he interplay between humankind and the Earth has often generated ecosystems that, from many points of view, are more interesting and more creative than those occurring in the state of wilderness."[33]

So be wise, but don't be afraid to change the landscape and make it better for future generations. The other animals will probably thank you as well. And let's have another homesteading act to privatize the one-third of the land the federal government owns, so that there can be many unique footprints on this land of ours.

Everybody say it loud. We're humans and we're proud!

Acknowledgments

I have known Fred Smith, president and founder of the Competitive Enterprise Institute (CEI) think tank, for more than a decade. Fred and his wife, Fran—who was my first DC boss, at the policy group Consumer Alert—have always shown incredible kindness to me. Fred was a great source for me at *Investor's Business Daily* and *Insight*, as he was always brimming with ideas and looked at issues in an unconventional way.

I came to CEI in late 2004. I was first the Warren T. Brookes Journalism Fellow and then a Fellow in Economic Policy. Fred and Wayne Crews, CEI's vice president for policy, both gave me guidance. More than that, they also gave me an incredible amount of freedom to pursue researching and reporting on my interests—such as barriers to entrepreneurship caused by securities laws like Sarbanes-Oxley or destructive and counterproductive environmental rules. Fred and Fran have New Orleans roots, and the devastation caused by Hurricane Katrina affected them deeply. When I wrote in September 2005 about the environmentalists' role in scuttling and delaying effective flood control for New Orleans, Fred and Wayne supported me as I faced harsh attack. They were also encouraging and helpful when I came to them with the idea of writing this book that describes Katrina and other instances in which environmentalism has increased hazards and reduced public health.

I owe a huge amount of thanks to Joel Miller, Associate Publisher at Nelson Current, who guided my proposal through its infancy and has taught me so much about writing a good book. I also thank Nelson Current editor Alice Sullivan for her patience and for helping to format my manuscript into attractive book form.

At CEI, an army of experts—including Sam Kazman, Angela

Logomasini, Greg Conko, Myron Ebell, Iain Murray, Marlo Lewis, R.J. Smith, and Chris Horner—patiently answered my queries and educated me about many environmental issues. In addition, I thank all the CEI staff for their support and encouragement.

I should note, however, that though the CEI staff did provide me with many ideas on issues covered in this book, the opinions expressed in the previous pages are mine and do not necessarily represent the viewpoints or policy positions of the Competitive Enterprise Institute.

The same opinion qualifier goes for a great group of friends from all over the world who gave me encouragement and helpful advice. Thanks to Dennis Avery, Paul Driessen, Adrienne Freda, Nina Graybill, Tom and Janet Grow, Christopher Hitchens, Richard Levine, Ben Lieberman, Tom Lutz, Jennifer Marohasy, Kay McClanahan, Sean Paige, Wes Seaton, Norman Singleton, David Skinner, Scott Stanley, Ken Timmerman, and Richard Tren.

Two interns were of great help in gathering research materials and giving their analyses. Nicole Kurokawa spent hours collecting a forest of information on trees and other subjects. Kate DeSorrento peered through the small type of old newspapers and magazines in library microfilm machines, looking at articles on asbestos from the eras before Google and LexisNexis.

Of course, I could not have accomplished this book and many other things in my life without the strong love and support of my parents, Marcia and Harry Berlau. They are my constant providers of wisdom and friendship. And Dad, this book should show you that your frequent corrections of the miseducation I received as a child about paper wasting trees did indeed get through to me.

I'm also lucky to have the friendship of my wonderful sister, Nancy, and her husband, Eric Batdorf.

Finally, I would like to thank my ninth-grade English teacher and good friend, Nancy "Debe" Bramley. She showed me that I had writing potential and helped me develop that talent. Ms. Bramley, this is what you've wrought, for better or for worse!

Notes

Chapter One: What I Learned about Environmentalism from Chuck D

1. Felicia R. Lee, "Laurie David Raises Awareness of Global Warming," *New York Times*, 22 April 2006, http://www.nytimes.com/2006/04/22/arts/television/ 22hot. html?ex=1303358400&en=855a359ed196676f&ei=5088&partner= rssnyt&emc=rss.
2. James Trefil, *Human Nature: A Blueprint for Managing the Earth—by People, for People* (Times Books, 2004), 11–12.
3. Ibid., xii.
4. Ronald Reagan, Radio speeches on "Pollution," August 1975, in Kiron K. Skinner, Annelise Anderson, and Martin Anderson, eds., *Reagan's Path to Victory: The Shaping of Ronald Reagan's Vision: Selected Writings* (Free Press, 2004), 44–46.
5. Franklin D. Roosevelt, Speech dedicating the Boulder (Hoover) Dam, 30 September 1935, http://xroads.virginia.edu/~1930s/DISPLAY/hoover/fdr.html.
6. *The Situation*, MSNBC, Telecast 15 September 2005.
7. Roosevelt, Speech dedicating the Boulder (Hoover) Dam.
8. Paul Driessen, *Eco-Imperialism: Green Power, Black Death* (Free Enterprise Press, 2004), 40.
9. Mary Douglas and Aaron Wildavsky, *Risk and Culture: An Essay on the Selection of Technological and Environmental Dangers* (University of California Press, 1982), 10.
10. Will Dana, "Al Gore 3.0," *Rolling Stone*, 13–27 July 2006, 45, http://www. rollingstone.com/news/story/10688399/al_gore_30.
11. Ross Gelbspan, "Katrina's Real Name," *Boston Globe*, 30 August 2005, http://www.boston.com/news/globe/editorial_opinion/oped/articles/2005/08/ 30/katrinas_real_name? mode=PF.
12. R.A. Scotti, *Sudden Sea: The Great Hurricane of 1938* (Little, Brown and Company, 2003), 216.
13. Erik Larson, *Isaac's Storm: A Man, a Time, and the Deadliest Hurricane in History* (Crown, 1999), 272.

Chapter Two: Rachel Carson Kills Birds

1. US Geological Survey, National Wildlife Health Center, "Frequently Asked Questions about West Nile Virus and Wildlife," http://www.nwhc.usgs.gov/disease_ information/west_nile_virus/frequently_asked_questions.jsp.
2. Maria Burke, "Don't Worry, It's Organic," *Chemistry World*, June 2004, http://www. rsc.org/chemistryworld/Issues/2004/June/organic.asp; Dixy Lee Ray and Lou Guzzo, *Environmental Overkill: Whatever Happened to Common Sense?* (Regnery Gateway, 1993), 75–76.
3. Emma Wilcox and William M. Giuliano, "Red Imported Fire Ants and Their Impacts on Wildlife," University of Florida Institute of Food and Agricultural Sciences, April 2006, http://edis.ifas.ufl.edu/UW242.

4. Quoted in Michael Fumento, "How to Save Endangered Species: As Costs Soar, Markets May Be the Best Tool," Investor's Business Daily, 8 January 1993, available at http://fumento. com/endangered.html.
5. Tina Rosenberg, "What the World Needs Now Is DDT," New York Times (magazine), 11 April 2004.
6. Al Gore, Introduction to Silent Spring (Houghton Mifflin, 1994), xviii.
7. Ibid., xv.
8. Ibid., xix.
9. Carson, Silent Spring, 16.
10. Ibid.
11. Malcolm Gladwell, "The Mosquito Killer," New Yorker, 2 July 2001, 42, available at http://www.gladwell.com/2001/2001_07_02_a_ddt.htm.
12. See Jared Diamond, Guns, Germ, and Steel: The Fates of Human Societies (W.W. Norton, 1999); and his follow-up, Collapse: How Societies Choose to Fail or Succeed (Viking, 2004).
13. O.T. Zimmerman and Irvin Lavine, DDT: Killer of Killers (Industrial Research Service, 1946), 1–29.
14. Ibid.
15. Gladwell, "The Mosquito Killer," 42.
16. Joseph J. Jacobs, The Anatomy of an Entrepreneur: Family, Culture, and Ethics (ICS Press, 1991), 85–86.
17. Associated Press, "Joseph J. Jacobs, Engineer, at 88," Boston Globe, 31 October 2004, http:// www.boston.com/news/globe/obituaries/articles/2004/10/31/joseph_j_jacobs_engineer_at_88/.
18. John Berlau, "The Author of Bush's Favorite Phrase Details Compassionate Conservatism," Investor's Business Daily, 20 June 2000, A26.
19. See Kasem endorsement in Joseph J. Jacobs, The Anatomy of an Entrepreneur: Family, Culture, and Ethics, back cover.
20. Joseph J. Jacobs, The Compassionate Conservative: Assuming Responsibility and Respecting Human Dignity (ICS Press, 1996), 99.
21. Gladwell, "The Mosquito Killer," 44.
22. Zimmerman and Lavine, DDT: Killer of Killers, 1–29.
23. Gladwell, "The Mosquito Killer," 44.
24. Edmund Russell, War and Nature: Fighting Humans and Insects with Chemicals from World War I to Silent Spring (Cambridge University Press, 2001), 127.
25. Gladwell, "The Mosquito Killer," 42–44.
26. Raymond Phillips, ed., Trial of Josef Kramer and 44 Others: The Belsen Trial (William Hodge, 1949), 31–34.
27. "The 11th Armoured Division (Great Britain)," United States Holocaust Memorial Museum Holocaust Encyclopedia, http://www.ushmm.org/wlc/article.php?lang=en& ModuleId=10006188.
28. Paul Kemp, "The British Army and the Liberation of Bergen-Belsen, April 1945," in Jo Reilly, ed., Belsen in History and Memory (Frank Cass, 1997), 139–40.
29. Jon Bridgman, The End of the Holocaust: The Liberation of the Camps (Areopagitica Press, 1990), 67.
30. Telephone interview with Gloria Hollander Lyon, 3 March 2006.
31. Ronald Bailey, "Precautionary Tale," Reason, April 1999, http://reason.com/9904/fe.rb.precautionary.shtml.

32. Frank B. Cross, "Paradoxical Perils of the Precautionary Principle," *Washington and Lee Law Review*, vol. 53, no. 851 (1996), 924–25.
33. Jacobs, *The Compassionate Conservative: Assuming Responsibility and Respecting Human Dignity*, 99.
34. Carson, *Silent Spring*, 21.
35. Alexander Gourevitch, "Better Living through Chemistry," *Washington Monthly*, March 2003, http://www.washingtonmonthly.com/features/2003/0303.gourevitch.html.
36. D.P. Morgan and C.C. Roan, "Adsorption, Storage, and Metabolic Conversion of Ingested DDT and DDT Metabolites in Man," *Archives of Environmental Health*, vol. 22 (1971), 301–308.
37. Gladwell, "The Mosquito Killer," 48.
38. "Damage from Tree-Killing Beetle Reaches Far," CNN.com, 31 December 2003, http://www.cnn.com/2003/US/Midwest/12/31/tree.beetles.ap/index.html.
39. Telephone Interview with Frank Knight, 1 March 2006.
40. Virginia Wright, "Champion of Trees," *American Profile*, 16–22 February 2003, https://www.americanprofile.com/issues/20030216/20030216_2820.asp.
41. Interview with Knight.
42. Ibid.
43. Jack Mounts, "1974 Douglas-Fir Tussock Moth Control Project," *Journal of Forestry*, vol. 74, no. 2 (1976), 82–86, abstract and (for purchase) full study available at http://www. ingentaconnect.com/content/saf/jof/1976/00000074/00000002/art00010;jsessionid=2nkoic16c7103.alice. "Almost total insect mortality occurred immediately after treatments were applied. Defoliation ceased almost completely, and a high proportion of foliage was saved."
44. H. Patricia Hynes, *The Recurring Silent Spring* (Pergamon Press, 1989), 154–55.
45. "Sudden Oak Death," *Brooklyn Botanic Garden Pest Alerts*, http://www.bbg.org/gar2/pestalerts/diseases/2003_suddenoak.html.
46. Interview with Knight.
47. Vivian Baulch, "How Detroit Lost Its Stately Elms," *Detroit News*, no date given, http:// info.detnews.com/history/story/index.cfm?id=9&category=life.
48. Ibid.
49. Chicago Park District, "City Fights Dutch Elm Disease in Grant Park," News Release, 17 August 2005, http://www.chicagoparkdistrict.com/index.cfm/fuseaction/news.detail/ object_id/6f67f75a-8387-4cb8-89d4-440f74092311.cfm.
50. Al Gore, *An Inconvenient Truth* (Rodale, 2006), 154–57.
51. Carson, *Silent Spring*, 114.
52. Ibid., 105.
53. Ibid., 114–15.
54. Baulch, "How Detroit Lost Its Stately Elms."
55. Carson, *Silent Spring*, 116.
56. Ibid., 105.
57. J. Gordon Edwards, "The Lies of Rachel Carson," *21st Century Science & Technology*, Summer 1992, http://www.21stcenturysciencetech.com/articles/summ02/Carson.html.
58. Ibid.
59. Ibid.

60. Ronald Bailey, "DDT, Eggshells, and Me," *Reason Online*, 7 January 2003, http://www.reason.com/rb/rb010704.shtml.

61. Edwards, "The Lies of Rachel Carson."

62. Zimmerman and Lavine, *DDT: Killer of Killers*.

63. Stevan D. Stellman et al., "Breast Cancer Risk in Relation to Adipose Concentrations of Organochlorine Pesticides and Polychlorinated Biphenyls in Long Island, New York," *Cancer Epidemiology Biomarkers and Prevention*, vol. 9 (2000), 1241–49, http://cebp. aacrjournals.org/cgi/content/full/9/11/1241. "The present analysis for the Long Island population is consistent with numerous studies that have shown little association between OCC [organochlorine compounds, including DDT] body burden and breast cancer risk."

64. Carson, *Silent Spring*, 116.

65. Roger E. Meiners and Andrew P. Morriss, "DDT: An Issue of Property Rights," *PERC Reports*, http://www.perc.org/perc.php?id=315.

66. Article in *Seattle Times*, 5 October 1969; cited in J. Gordon Edwards and Steven Milloy, "100 Things You Should Know about DDT," JunkScience.com, 1999, http://www. junkscience.com/ddtfaq.htm.

67. E.M. Sweeney, "EPA Hearing Examiner's Recommendations and Findings Concerning DDT Hearings," 25 April 1972 (40 CFR 164.32); cited in Edwards and Milloy, "100 Things You Should Know about DDT."

68. Roger Bate, "The Worst Thing Nixon Ever Did," *Tech Central Station*, 15 April 2004, http://www.tcsdaily.com/Article.aspx?id=041504I.

69. Elizabeth Whelan, *Toxic Terror* (Jameson Books, 1985), 85. I attempted to give Ruckelshaus the opportunity to elaborate on the reasons for his DDT decision, but received no response to my e-mail and telephone queries.

70. Question of US Rep. John Rarick (D-LA) at Hearing of House Agriculture Committee, Serial No. 92–A, 1971, 266–267.

71. Jim Norton, "Unquote," Info-Pollution, http://info-pollution.com/unquote.htm.

72. Telephone interview with Victor Yannacone, 29 August 2006.

73. Gladwell, "The Mosquito Killer," 48.

74. National Academy of Sciences, *The Life Sciences: Recent Progress and Application to Human Affairs, the World of Biological Research, Requirements for the Future* (NAS Press, 1970), 432; cited in Edwards and Milloy, "100 Things You Should Know about DDT."

75. Ray and Guzzo, *Environmental Overkill: Whatever Happened to Common Sense?*, 76.

76. Robert S. Desowitz, *The Malaria Capers* (W.W. Norton & Company, 1991), 217.

77. J. Gordon Edwards, "Malaria: The Killer That Could Have Been Conquered," *21st Century Science and Technology*, Summer 1993. This is the earliest reference I have seen to this quote. Edwards writes that McCloskey said this in February 1971, but does not cite a source. The quote has been referenced several times since then in published articles. Edwards, as noted, has since passed away. On 31 August 2006, McCloskey told me over the phone that he didn't recall the quote, but added, "I'm not saying I didn't say it, necessarily."

78. Alexander King, *The Discipline of Curiosity: Science in the World* (Elsevier Science, 1990), 43; cited in Tom Bethell, *The Politically Incorrect Guide to Science* (Regnery, 2005), 76.

79. Jeff Hoffman, "Is There an Environmentalist out There?," *Grist*, Blog post on 12 January 2005, http://gristmill.grist.org/comments/2005/1/9/173940/4293/5#5.

80. "Gristmill," Grist, Blog thread beginning 9 January 2005, http://gristmill.grist. org/story/ 2005/1/9/173940/4293?source=daily.

81. George M. Woodwell and Paul R. Ehrlich, "Using DDT: Pro and Con," *New York Times*, 13 January 2005, A34.

82. Paul R. Ehrlich, *The Population Bomb* (Buccaneer Books, 1971), 132.

83. Ibid., 130–31.

84. Ibid., 151–52.

85. Ibid., 147–48.

86. Ibid., 146–48.

87. Fred L. Smith Jr., "Jared Diamond and the Terrible Too's," *Energy & Environment*, vol. 16, no. 3&4 (2005), 428.

88. See Ed Regis, "The Doomslayer," *Wired*, February 1997, http://www.wired.com/ wired/ archive/5.02/ffsimon_pr.html.

89. Michael Crichton, "Let's Stop Scaring Ourselves," *Parade*, 5 December 2004, http:// www.parade.com/articles/editions/2004/edition_12-05-2004/featured_0.

90. Gladwell, "The Mosquito Killer," 48–49; Whelan, *Toxic Terror*, 68–70.

91. World Health Organization, "Sri Lanka: Overview of Malaria Control Activities and Programme Progress," *World Malaria Report 2005*, http://www.rbm.who.int/ wmr2005/profiles/srilanka.pdf.

92. World Health Organization, "Situation Report 5," *Health Action in Crises*, http:// www.who.int/hac/crises/international/asia_tsunami/sitrep/05/en/. "Millions of people are now under serious threat of disease outbreaks as a result of damaged water sanitation systems, sea water contamination and the congested and crowded conditions of the displaced."

93. "Yes, Roll It Back," *Addis Tribune*, 19 September 2003.

94. "Over 6 Million People, Mostly Children, at Risk of Looming Malaria Epidemic," *UNICEF Humanitarian Action: Ethiopia Donor Update*, 20 September 2005, http:// www.reliefweb.int/rw/RWB.NSF/db900SID/KHII-6GF9YQ?OpenDocument.

95. Personal interview with Mesfin Mekonen, 13 April 2006.

96. Africa Fighting Malaria, "Kill Malarial Mosquitoes Now! A Declaration of the Informed and Concerned," 22 January 2006, http://www.fightingmalaria.org/ pdfs/KMMN_Decl_ Feb06.pdf.

97. Angela Logomasini, "Six Tsunamis," *Tech Central Station*, 20 January 2005, http://www. tcsdaily.com/article.aspx?id=012005A.

98. Gore, *An Inconvenient Truth*, 173.

99. R.W. Snow et al., "The History of Malaria Epidemics in Kenya: Their Political Significance and Control," *The Epidemiology, Politics, and Control of Malaria Epidemics in Kenya: 1900–1998*, July 1999, Report prepared for Roll Back Malaria, Resource Network on Epidemics, World Health Organization, http:// www.who.int/malaria/docs/ek_report3.htm.

100. East African Institute of Malaria & Vector Borne Diseases, *Annual Report 1961/62*; cited in Snow et al., "The History of Malaria Epidemics in Kenya: Their Political Significance and Control."

101. Personal interview with Marlo Lewis, March 2006. See also Marlo Lewis, "A Skeptic's Guide to *An Inconvenient Truth*," Policy report of the Competitive Enterprise Institute, 61–63, http://www.cei.org/pdf/5478.pdf.

102. Desowitz, *The Malaria Capers*, 63.

103. Ibid., 145.

104. Ray and Guzzo, *Environmental Overkill: Whatever Happened to Common Sense?*, 104.

105. Ibid., 103.

106. Centers for Disease Control, "Epidemiologic Notes and Reports Mosquito-Transmitted Malaria, California and Florida, 1990, *Morbidity and Mortality Weekly Report*, 15 February 1991, 106–108, http://iier.isciii.es/mmwr/preview/mmwrhtml/00001911.htm; and "Transmission of Plasmodium Vivax Malaria, San Diego County, California, 1998 and 1989, *Morbidity and Mortality Weekly Report*, 16 February 1990, 91–94, http://iier.isciii.es/mmwr/preview/mmwrhtml/00001559.htm.

107. Bethell, *The Politically Incorrect Guide to Science*, 85.

108. No Spray Coalition, "WNV-Mosquito Bite Odds," http://www.nospray.org/WNVodds.shtml.

109. Ibid.

110. New York City Green Party, "Stop Spraying NY City with Pesticides," circa 2000, http:// www.greens.org/ny/tohtml.cgi?stop-spraying/home.htm (no longer available at this address); cited in Angela Logomasini, "Pesticides and the West Nile Virus," Policy report of the Competitive Enterprise Institute, March 2004, 17, http://www.cei.org/pdf/3893.pdf.

111. Ted Williams, "Out of Control," *Audubon*, September 2001, http://magazine.audubon.org/ incite/incite0109.html.

112. Curtis L. Taylor and Dan Janison, "City Nixes Malathion Spraying," *Newsday*, 14 April 2000, A03.

113. Angela Logomasini, "West Nile Virus: A Public Health Crisis," *USA Today* (magazine), July 2003, 53.

114. Logomasini, "Pesticides and the West Nile Virus," 19.

115. No Spray Nashville/ BURNT Coalition, "Frequently Asked Questions," http://www.burnt-tn.org.moses.com/sprayfaq.htm.

116. Byron Hensley, "Resident First West Nile Death in State This Year," *Daily News Journal*, 1 September 2006, http://dnj.com/apps/pbcs.dll/article?AID=/20060901/NEWS01/609010322/1002.

117. Angela Logomasini, "Side Effect of the War on Pesticides," *Washington Times*, 21 August 2002.

118. National Academy of Sciences, *Carcinogens and Anticarcinogens in the Human Diet* (NAS Press, 1996), 5.

119. US Geological Survey, National Wildlife Health Center, "Frequently Asked Questions about West Nile Virus and Wildlife," http://www.nwhc.usgs.gov/disease_information/west_nile_virus/frequently_asked_questions.jsp.

120. "West Nile Virus Found in Dead Bird from WH Lawn," CNN, 29 July 2002, http://cnnstudentnews.cnn.com/2002/ALLPOLITICS/07/29/wh.west.nile.bird/.

121. Donna Tommelleo, "Robin, Not Crow, May Be West Nile Culprit," Associated Press, 29 July 2005, http://abcnews.go.com/Technology/Science/wire Story?id=990605.

122. Frank D. Roylance, "Raptors' Die-off Spread Fear of West Nile Virus," *Baltimore Sun*, 30 September 2002, http://www.baltimoresun.com/news/health/bal-te.raptors30sep30,0,2140982.story?coll=bal-health-utility.

123. Jeff Cole, "West Nile Devastating Wild Birds," *Milwaukee Journal Sentinel*, 29 October 2002.

124. "Virginia Becomes Hot Spot for West Nile in Wildlife," Associated Press, 28 August 2003, http://www.wset.com/news/stories/0803/100393.html.

125. Telephone interview with Henry Miller, 1 March 2006.

126. Ibid.

127. Rosenberg, "What the World Needs Now Is DDT."

128. Tim Lambert, "Facts on DDT and Malaria," *Deltoid*, 27 June 2005, http://tim-lambert.org/ 2005/06/ddt10.

129. Carson, *Silent Spring*, 264.

130. Ibid., 266.

131. Ibid., 270.

132. Todd Seavey, "The DDT Ban Turns 30," *ACSH Health Issues*, 1 June 2002, http://www. acsh.org/healthissues/newsID.442/healthissue_detail.asp, ("Greece saw malaria cases drop from 1–2 million cases a year to close to zero, also thanks to DDT."); Dave D. Chadee and Uriel Kitron, "Spatial and Temporal Patterns of Imported Malaria Cases and Local Transmission in Trinidad," *American Journal of Tropical Medicine and Hygiene*, vol. 61, no. 4 (1999), 513, http://www.ajtmh.org/ cgi/reprint/61/4/513.pdf, ("Trinidad and Tobago was declared free of malaria in 1965.").

133. Interview with Miller.

134. Telephone interview with Donald Roberts, 16 March 2006.

135. Richard Tren et al., "Is DDT Safe? Considering Its Use for Malaria Control in Uganda," *Health Policy and Development*, vol. 2. no. 2 (2004), 107, http://www.fightingmalaria.org/ pdfs/hpd_DDT_uganda.pdf.

136. David Wert, "Ribbon-Cutting Marks Dedication of Hospital," *Press-Enterprise*, 20 March 1999, http://www.press-enterprise.com/newsarchive/1999/03/20/ 921911195.html.

137. See the group's joint report, "Delhi Sands Flower Loving Fly Fact Sheet," http:// www. xerces.org/Endangered/Delhi_Sands_Flower_Loving_Fly_Fact_Sheet.PDF.

138. Al Gore, "The Time to Act Is Now," *Salon*, 5 November 2004, http://dir.salon. com/story/ opinion/feature/2005/11/04/gore/index.html.

139. Stephen S. Morse, "Factors in the Emergence of Infectious Diseases," *CDC Emerging Infectious Diseases*, vol. 1, no. 1 (1995), http://www.cdc.gov/ncidod/EID/vol1no1/ morse.htm.

140. Ronald Bailey, "Global Warming Disease Hype," *Reason Online Hit & Run*, 5 May 2006, http://www.reason.com/hitandrun/2006/05/global_warming_disease_ hype_.shtml#013764.

141. Occupational Safety and Health Administration, "Lyme Disease," *Hazard Information Bulletin*, 20 April 2000, http://www.osha.gov/dts/hib/hib_data/hib 20000420.pdf.

142. Dan Cappiello, "Spitzer Calls on EPA to Ban Pesticide," *Albany Times Union*, 23 February 2000, B5.

143. Environmental Protection Agency, "Clinton-Gore Administration Acts to Eliminate Major Uses of the Pesticide Dursban to Protect Children and Public Health," News release, 8 June 2000, http://yosemite.epa.gov/opa/admpress.nsf/ b1ac27bf9339f1c28525701c005e2edf/880b35adc877c301852568f8005399ed! OpenDocument.

144. Michael Fumento, "Let Us Spray," *Forbes*, 21 August 2000, http://www.forbes. com/forbes/ 2000/0821/6605069a.html.

145. Environmental Protection Agency, "EPA Announces Elimination of All Indoor Uses of Widely Used Pesticide Diazinon; Begins Phase-Out of Lawn and Garden Uses," 5 December 2000, http://yosemite.epa.gov/opa/admpress.nsf/b1ac27bf9339f1c28525701c005e2edf/c8cdc9ea7d5ff585852569ac0077bd31!OpenDocument.

146. National Academy of Sciences, "Need Still Exists for Chemical Pesticides While Alternatives Are Sought," News release, 18 July 2000, http://www8.nationalacademies.org/onpinews/newsitem. aspx?RecordID=9598.

147. Angela Logomasini, "Eroding U.S. Sovereignty," *CEI Monthly Planet*, December 2003, 8, https://www.cei.org/pdf/3894.pdf. (Emphasis added.)

148. Personal interview with Richard Tren, April 2006.

149. Frank Ackerman and Rachel Massey, *The True Costs of REACH* (Tufts University Global Development and Environmental Institute, 2004), 17; cited in Angela Logomasini, "Europe's Global REACH: Costly for the World; Suicidal for Europe," Policy report of the Hayek Institute, November 2005, 23, https://www.cei.org/pdf/4951.pdf.

150. Daniel J. Mitchell, "The OECD's Dishonest Campaign Against Tax Competition: A Regress Report," *CF&P Foundation Prosperitas*, January 2006, http://www.freedomandprosperity.org/Papers/oecd-dishonest/oecd-dishonest.shtml.

151. Paul Driessen, "Uganda Fighting for Right to Eradicate Malaria," *Environment News*, 1 November 2005, http://www.heartland.org/Article.cfm?artId=17983.

152. Testimony of Roger Bate and Richard Tren before the Senate Environment and Public Works Committee, 28 September 2005, available at http://www.fightingmalaria.org/EPW_testimony_TrenBate.doc.

153. D. Rutledge Taylor, "A Doctor and Documentarian Against the DDT Ban," *ACSH Health Facts and Fears*, 10 April 2006, http://www.acsh.org/factsfears/newsID.725/news_detail.asp.

154. Ibid.

155. Sarah Randolph, "The Changing Incidence of Tickborne Encephalitis in Europe," *Eurosurveillance Weekly*, 6 June 2002, http://www.eurosurveillance.org/ew/2002/020606.asp.

156. "Rocky Mountain Spotted Fever: Essential Data," CBWInfo.com, http://www.cbwinfo.com/Biological/Pathogens/RR.html.

157. Alicia Chang, "LA Woman Hospitalized with Bubonic Plague," *Boston Globe*, 18 April 2006, http://www.boston.com/yourlife/health/other/articles/2006/04/18/la_woman_hospitalized_with_bubonic_plague/.

158. Robert Traub, "Advances in Our Knowledge of Military Medical Importance Fleas Due to Postwar Experiences in the Pacific Area," *Recent Advances in Medicine and Surgery Based on Professional Medical Experiences in Japan and Korea 1950–1953*, Report of conference held by US Army Medical Service Graduate School, Walter Reed Army Medical Center, 19–30 April 1954, available at http://history.amedd.army.mil/booksdocs/korea/recad2/ ch6-3.htm.

159. "Japan Says Found Bird Flu in Flies from 2004 Outbreak," Reuters, 22 February 2005, available at http://in.news.yahoo.com/050222/137/2jrr1.html.

160. Carson, *Silent Spring*, 277.

CHAPTER THREE: The Anti-Asbestos Inferno

1. Testimony of Donald J. Trump before the Senate Homeland Security and Government Affairs Committee Subcommittee on Federal Financial Management, Government Information, and International Security, 21 July 2005, http://hsgac.senate.gov/_files/072105Trump.pdf.
2. Telephone interview with Rachel Maines, 19 May 2006.
3. "Profiles of Osama bin Laden, Ayman Al-Zawahiri," *CNN People in the News*, CNN, 20 March 2004, transcript available at http://transcripts.cnn.com/TRANSCRIPTS/0305/10/pitn.00.html.
4. Rachel Maines, *Asbestos and Fire: Technological Trade-offs and the Body at Risk* (Rutgers, 2005), 18.
5. Ibid., 8–9.
6. Ibid., 6–7.
7. Interview with Maines.
8. Maines, *Asbestos and Fire: Technological Trade-offs and the Body at Risk*, 8–9, 96.
9. Cassandra Chrones Moore, *Haunted Housing: How Toxic Scare Stories Are Spooking the Public Out of House and Home* (Cato Institute, 1997), 161.
10. Moore, *Haunted Housing: How Toxic Scare Stories Are Spooking the Public Out of House and Home*, 162–63.
11. Maines, *Asbestos and Fire: Technological Trade-offs and the Body at Risk*, 7.
12. Ibid., 40.
13. Interview with Maines.
14. Ibid.
15. Jane E. Brody, "Scientist at Work: Bruce N. Ames; Strong Views on Origins of Cancer," *New York Times*, 5 July 1994, http://query.nytimes.com/gst/fullpage.html?sec=health&res=9902E3DA1E3CF936A35754C0A962958260.
16. Tom Bethell, *The Politically Incorrect Guide to Science* (Regnery, 2005), 61.
17. Walter K. Olson, *The Rule of Lawyers* (St. Martin's Press, 2003), 185.
18. *Schenk v. United States*, 249 US 47, 1919.
19. Maines, *Asbestos and Fire: Technological Trade-offs and the Body at Risk*, 57.
20. Ibid., 57–58. The theater owners had claimed that the curtain was made from fireproof asbestos. Subsequent investigations proved that to be a falsehood.
21. Moore, *Haunted Housing: How Toxic Scare Stories Are Spooking the Public Out of House and Home*, 163.
22. Maines, *Asbestos and Fire: Technological Trade-offs and the Body at Risk*, 59–66.
23. Ibid., 61–66.
24. Quoted in Michael Fumento, "The Asbestos Rip-Off," *American Spectator*, October 1989.
25. Maines, *Asbestos and Fire: Technological Trade-offs and the Body at Risk*, 125.
26. Interview with Maines.
27. Maines, *Asbestos and Fire: Technological Trade-offs and the Body at Risk*, 131.
28. Interview with Maines.
29. Maines, *Asbestos and Fire: Technological Trade-offs and the Body at Risk*, 74–77.
30. Ibid., 92.
31. "Roosevelt Urges Fireproof Vessels," *New York Times*, 13 September 1934, 1, 17.
32. Maines, *Asbestos and Fire: Technological Trade-offs and the Body at Risk*, 89–90.
33. Telephone interview with Arthur M. Langer, 7 June 2006. See also Arthur M.

Langer and Roger G. Morse, "The World Trade Center Catastrophe: Was the Type of Spray Fire Proofing a Factor in the Collapse of the Twin Towers?", *Indoor and Built Environment*, vol. 10 (2001), 350–60.

34. Will Knight, "Fireproofing Key to Twin Towers' Collapse," *New Scientist*, 6 April 2005, http://www.newscientist.com/article.ns?id=dn7236.

35. Interview with Langer.

36. Steven Milloy, "Asbestos Could Have Saved WTC Lives," FoxNews.com, 14 September 2001, http://www.foxnews.com/story/0,2933,34342,00.html; and "Asbestos Column Raised Awareness," FoxNews.com, 20 September 2001, http://www.foxnews.com/story/0,2933,34756,00.html.

37. Colby Cosh, "Four Hours They Didn't Get," *Alberta Report*, 19 November 2001.

38. Jana J. Madsen, "Concrete vs. Steel," *Buildings*, June 2005, http://www.build-ings. com/Articles/detailBuildings.asp?ArticleID=2511.

39. Jim Dukelow, "Flogging a Hobby Horse," *RadSafe*, 27 September 2001, http://www.vanderbilt.edu/radsafe/0109/msg00468.html.

40. P.W.J. Bartrip, "Irving John Selikoff and the Strange Case of the Missing Medical Degrees," *Journal of the History of Medicine and Allied Sciences*, vol. 58 (2003), 3–33.

41. I.J. Selikoff and E.C. Hammond, "Asbestos and Smoking," *Journal of the American Medical Association*, vol. 242 (1979), 458–59; cited in Moore, *Haunted Housing: How Toxic Scare Stories Are Spooking the Public Out of House and Home*, 168.

42. Olson, *The Rule of Lawyers*, 192–93.

43. B.T. Mossman et al., "Asbestos: Scientific Developments and Implications for Public Policy," *Science*, vol. 47, no. 4940 (1990), 296; cited in Moore, *Haunted Housing: How Toxic Scare Stories Are Spooking the Public Out of House and Home*, 162.

44. Interview with Langer.

45. Andrew Schneider and David McCumber, *An Air that Kills: How the Asbestos Poisoning of Libby, Montana, Uncovered a National Scandal* (Putnam Adult, 2004), 333.

46. Morse, "The World Trade Center Catastrophe: Was the Type of Spray Fire Proofing a Factor in the Collapse of the Twin Towers?", 354.

47. Nicholas J. Carino et al., "Passive Fire Protection, Federal Building and Fire Safety Investigation of the World Trade Center Disaster," in National Institute of Standards and Technology, *Final Report on the Collapse of the World Trade Center Towers* (Government Printing Office, 2005), section 1–6A, 168–73, http://wtc.nist.gov/NISTN CSTAR1-6A.pdf.

48. Interview with Langer.

49. Carino et al., "Passive Fire Protection," section 1–6A, 170.

50. Ibid., 174.

51. Carino et al., "Passive Fire Protection," section 1–6A, 167.

52. Interview with Langer.

53. Interview with Maines.

54. "Trade Center Hit By 6-Floor Fire," *New York Times*, 14 February 1975, 41.

55. W. Robert Powers, "One World Trade Center Fire," Report of the New York Board of Fire Underwriters, 1975, 3–5.

56. Mary Breasted, "Sprinklers Urged For Trade Center," *New York Times*, 15 February 1975, 45.

57. Interview with Maines.
58. Nicholas J. Carino et al., "Passive Fire Protection," section 1–6A, 175–79.
59. Ronald Hamburger et al., "WTC 1 and WTC 2," in Federal Emergency Management Agency, *World Trade Center Building Performance Study: Data Collection, Preliminary Observations, and Recommendations* (FEMA, 2002), chapter 2, 15–16, http://www.fema.gov/pdf/library/fema403_ch2.pdf.
60. Ibid., 21.
61. National Institute of Standards and Technology, "Answers to Frequently Asked Questions," 30 August 2006, http://wtc.nist.gov/pubs/factsheets/faqs_8_2006.htm.
62. Ibid.
63. Thomas W. Eagar and Christopher Musso, "Why Did the World Trade Center Collapse? Science, Engineering, and Speculation," *JOM*, vol. 53, no. 12 (2001), 8–11, http://www.tms.org/pubs/journals/JOM/0112/Eagar/Eagar-0112.html.
64. "9/11: Debunking the Myths," *Popular Mechanics*, March 2005, http://www.popularmechanics.com/science/defense/1227842.html?page=1.
65. "Federal Building and Fire Safety Investigation of the World Trade Center Disaster," in NIST, *Report*, section 1, 185, http://wtc.nist.gov/NISTNCSTAR1 CollapseofTowers.pdf.
66. Carino et al., "Passive Fire Protection, section 1–6A, 67–68. All temperature measurements in this and the following references are converted from Celsius to Fahrenheit.
67. Interview with Langer.
68. "Federal Building and Fire Safety Investigation of the World Trade Center Disaster," section 1, 185.
69. Carino et al., "Passive Fire Protection," section 1–6A, 99.
70. Interview with Maines.
71. Interview with Langer.
72. Art Robinson, "Terrorists 1,000 and Enviros 5,000," *Access to Energy*, September 2001.
73. "9/11: Debunking the Myths."
74. Fumento, "The Asbestos Rip-Off."
75. Occupational Safety and Health Administration, "Asbestos," 29 CFR 1910.1001, 62.
76. Reed Irvine, Foreword, in Michael J. Bennett, *The Asbestos Racket* (Free Enterprise Press, 1991), ix.
77. James Surowiecki, "Asbestos, Inc.," *New Yorker*, 3 March 2006, http://www.newyorker.com/talk/content/articles/060306ta_talk_surowiecki.
78. Maines, *Asbestos and Fire: Technological Trade-offs and the Body at Risk*, 157.
79. Surowiecki, "Asbestos, Inc."
80. Maines, *Asbestos and Fire: Technological Trade-offs and the Body at Risk*, 156–57.
81. Olson, *The Rule of Lawyers*, 205–06.
82. Moore, *Haunted Housing: How Toxic Scare Stories Are Spooking the Public Out of House and Home*, 188.
83. Ibid., 187.
84. "Nightclub Inferno," *People Specials*, 26 June 2006, 86–88.
85. Interview with Maines.
86. State of Rhode Island, "An Act Relating to Health and Safety, Fire Safety Code,"

Rhode Island Public Laws, chapter 107, http://www.rilin.state.ri.us/PublicLaws/
law03/law 03107.htm.

87. Richard Wilson, "Combating Terrorism: An Event Tree Approach," transcript
of speech at Sandia National Laboratory, 20 March 2003.

88. Maines, *Asbestos and Fire: Technological Trade-offs and the Body at Risk*, 97.

89. W. Keith C. Morgan and J. Bernard L. Gee, "Asbestos-Related Diseases," in
Occupational Lung Diseases, ed. W. Keith C. Morgan and Anthony Seaton
(Saunders, 1994), 308–73.

90. Maines, *Asbestos and Fire: Technological Trade-offs and the Body at Risk*, 97–98.

CHAPTER FOUR: Smashing the Engine of Public Health

1. Randal O'Toole, "Lack of Automobility Key to New Orleans Tragedy,"
Vanishing Automobile Update, 4 September 2005, http://ti.org/vaupdate55.
html.

2. Jason DeParle, What Happens to a Race Deferred," *New York Times*, 4
September 2005, http://www.nytimes.com/glogin?URI=http://www.nytimes.com/
2005/09/04/weekinreview/04depa.html.

3. Ibid.

4. Randal O'Toole, "Mobility Counted Most in Fleeing New Orleans," *Seattle Times*,
14 September 2005, http://seattletimes.nwsource.com/html/opinion/2002492931_
randal14. html.

5. Blanco expressed gratitude to Barbour in testimony before the US Senate. See
Testimony of Kathleen Blanco, US Senate Committee on Homeland Security
and Government Affairs, 2 February 2006, http://www.gov.state.la.us/index.
cfm?md=newsroom&tmp=detail&articleID=1640.

6. "Now What," *Popular Mechanics*, March 2006, http://www.popularmechanics.
com/science/earth/2315076.html?page=1&c=y.

7. "Poll: Fewer Than Half of Evacuees in Houston Want to Return Home," Associated
Press, 16 September 2005.

8. John Renne, "Car-less in the Eye of Katrina," Planetizen.com, 6 September 2005,
http://www.planetizen.com/node/17255.

9. Ibid.

10. O'Toole, "Lack of Automobility Key to New Orleans Tragedy."

11. John Berlau, "Not a Normal Morning," InsightMag.com, 11 September 2001. I
also contributed to the *Washington Times* coverage that appeared the next day.
See Dave Boyer and Audrey Hudson, "Capitol Clears Soon After Initial Attacks,"
Washington Times, 12 September 2001, A14.

12. Margy Waller, "Auto-Mobility," *Washington Monthly*, October/November 2005, http://
www.washingtonmonthly.com/features/2005/0510.waller.html.

13. Metro, *Regional Transportation Plan Update* (Metro, 1996), 1–20; quoted in
Randal O'Toole, *The Vanishing Automobile and Other Urban Myths* (Thoreau
Institute, 2001), 348.

14. James D. Johnston, *Driving America: Your Car, Your Government, Your Choice*
(AEI Press, 1997), 193–97.

15. Earl Blumenauer, "Portland: Ground Zero in the Livable Communities
Debate," Speech to the Congress for New Urbanism, 16 June 2000, http://www.
cnu.org/cnu_reports/Blumenauer2000.pdf#search='earl%20blumenauer%
20and%20congestion.

16. Steve Inskeep, "Commuting IV," *All Things Considered*, 30 May 1997, http://www.npr.org/ramfiles/970539.atc.04.ram; quoted in O'Toole, *The Vanishing Automobile and Other Urban Myths*, 349.
17. O'Toole, *The Vanishing Automobile and Other Urban Myths*, 352.
18. Al Gore, *Earth in the Balance: Ecology and the Human Spirit* (Houghton Mifflin, 1992), 325–26.
19. Phil Kent, "Vice President Gore, We Hardly Knew Ye," *Augusta Chronicle*, 4 April 1999, http://chronicle.augusta.com/stories/040499/opi_087-4828.shtml.
20. Dan Gainor, "Media Declare Warming Debate Ended . . . Again," Business & Media Institute, 29 March 2006, http://www.freemarketproject.org/commentary/2006/com20060329.asp.
21. See Monica Harvey, "Converting the Masses," *Environmental Protection*, undated, http:// www.stevenspublishing.com/Stevens/EPPub.nsf/frame?open& redirect=http://www. stevenspublishing.com/stevens/epPub.nsf/d3d5b4f938b22 b6e8625670c006dbc58/a277a052eaeb4313862567740074fd1b?OpenDocument. Offers a good explanation of how a catalytic converter works.
22. The White House, "Bush Will Not Require Power Plants to Reduce Carbon Emissions," press release, 13 March 2001, http://usinfo.state.gov/gi/Archive/2003/Dec/02-50965.html.
23. Seth Borenstein, "Bush Administration Says It Won't Regulate Carbon Dioxide," *Guardian Online*, 10 September 2003, http://www.theguardianonline.com/media/storage/paper373/ news/2003/09/10/News/Bush-Administration.Says.It. Wont.Regulate.Carbon.Dioxide-461717.shtml?norewrite20060724 0734&sourcedomain=www.theguardianonline.com.
24. Bill McKibben, *Maybe One: A Personal and Environmental Argument for Single-Child Families* (Simon & Schuster, 1998), 94.
25. Peter Gwynne, "The Cooling World," *Newsweek*, 28 April 2006, 64.
26. See Stephen Moore and Julian L. Simon, *It's Getting Better All the Time: 100 Greatest Trends of the Last 100 Years* (Cato Institute, 2000).
27. Mayo Clinic, "Good Roads and the Mayos," http://www.mayoclinic.org/tradition-heritage/good-roads.html.
28. O'Toole, *The Vanishing Automobile and Other Urban Myths*, 85–86.
29. Johnston, *Driving America: Your Car, Your Government, Your Choice*, 137.
30. Joseph E. Persico, "The Great Swine Flu Epidemic of 1918," *American Heritage*, June 1976 (Vol. 27, No. 4), http://www.americanheritage.com/articles/magazine/ah/1976/4/1976_4_ 28.shtml.
31. James J. Flink, *The Automobile Age*, (MIT Press, 1988), 169–187.
32. Ibid., 179.
33. Barbara Mikkelson, "Nobody's Fuel," *Urban Legends Reference Pages*, 28 April 2002, http://www.snopes.com/autos/business/carburetor.asp.
34. Judy Villa, "Firefighters Are Wary of Gas-Electric Cars," *Arizona Republic*, 13 June 2004, http://www.azcentral.com/specials/special21/articles/0613hybrid13.html. An expert at a center that promotes electric vehicles is quoted in the article as saying: "They're very safe, but I can't say they're as safe as a gasoline car. . . . [Y]ou've got a car going down the road with a tank of gas and a high-voltage battery."
35. Telephone interview with Leonard Evans, 13 and 31 July 2006.
36. Science and Environmental Policy Project, "SEPP Comments to New York Times

Catalytic Converter Story," 29 May 1998, http://www.junkscience.com/news2/singer39.htm.

37. Leonard Evans, "Casual Influence of Car Mass and Size on Driver Fatality Risk," *American Journal of Public Health*, vol. 91, no. 7 (2001), 1076–81.

38. Johnston, *Driving America: Your Car, Your Government, Your Choice*, 19–21.

39. Paul E. Godek, "The Regulation of Fuel Economy and the Demand For 'Light Trucks,'" *Journal of Law and Economics*, vol. 40, no. 2, 495–509.

40. R.W. Crandall and J.D. Graham, "The Effect of Fuel Economy Standards on Automobile Safety," *Journal of Law and Economics*, vol. 32, no. 1 (1989), 97–118.

41. Keith Bradsher, *High and Mighty: SUVs—The World's Most Dangerous Vehicles and How They Got That Way* (PublicAffairs, 2002), 38–39.

42. Johnston, *Driving America: Your Car, Your Government, Your Choice*, 15.

43. Crandall and Graham, "The Effect of Fuel Economy Standards on Automobile Safety," 97–118.

44. CEI v. NHTSA, 956 F.2d. 321 (D.C. Cir. 1992). Excerpts available at http://www.heartland. org/pdf/72126a.pdf.

45. National Research Council, *Effectiveness and Impact of Corporate Average Fuel Economy Standards* (National Academy Press, 2002), 77, http://darwin.nap.edu/books/0309076013/ html/R1.html.

46. James R. Healey, "Death By the Gallon" *USA TODAY*, 2 July 1999, 01B–02B.

47. Crandall and Graham, "The Effect of Fuel Economy Standards on Automobile Safety," 110.

48. Charli E. Coon, "Why the Government's CAFE Standards for Fuel Efficiency Should Be Repealed, Not Increased," *Heritage Foundation Backgrounder*, 11 July 2001, http://www.heritage.org/Research/EnergyandEnvironment/BG1458.cfm.

49. Center for Auto Safety, *Small on Safety: The Designed-in Dangers of the Volkswagen* (Grossman Publishers, 1972), 87.

50. "Be Safer in the 90s: New Warnings from Ralph Nader," *Woman's Day*, 24 October 1989, 32; cited in Sam Kazman,, "Flip-Flopping on Small Car Safety, Report of the Competitive Enterprise Institute, http://www.cei.org/pdf/2353.pdf.

51. Testimony of Clarence M. Ditlow before the Senate Commerce, Science and Transportation Committee, 6 December 2001, http://commerce.senate.gov/hearings/120601Ditlow.pdf.

52. Quoted in Patrick Bedard, "SUVs Face Charge: Hit Someone and You'll Kill 'Em," *Car and Driver*, March 2001, http://www.caranddriver.com/columns/3469/patrick-bedard.html.

53. Cited in Coon, "Why the Government's CAFE Standards for Fuel Efficiency Should Be Repealed, Not Increased."

54. Testimony of Ditlow.

55. Michelle Malkin, "This Is One Highway CAFE Motorists Should Avoid," *Seattle Times*, 18 June 1996, B4.

56. Johnston, *Driving America: Your Car, Your Government, Your Choice*, 23.

57. John Berlau, "Safety Takes a Back Seat," *Insight*, 13 August 2001, 18–19.

58. "Earth Liberation Claims Responsibility for SUV Firebombing," WJETTV.com, 3 January 2003.

59. Bradsher, *High and Mighty: SUVs—The World's Most Dangerous Vehicles and How They Got That Way*, 101.

60. Patricia Gallagher Newberry, "Feuding Kids Might Need Hummer to be Happy,"

Enquirer, 2 December 2005, http://news.enquirer.com/apps/pbcs.dll/article?AID=/20051202/LIFE/ 512020358/1079/rss04.

61. Department of Transportation, "Children and Air Bags," http://www.nhtsa.dot.gov/people/injury/airbags/Airbags.html.

62. See Associated Press photo at http://www.airbagonoff.com/images/20000207 pr01.jpg.

63. Testimony of Adrian K. Lund before the Senate Commerce, Science and Transportation Committee, Subcommittee on Consumer Affairs, Foreign Commerce and Tourism, 24 April 2001, http://www.iihs.org/laws/testimony/pdf/testimony_akl_042401.pdf.

64. Alas (a blog), "Top Ten Reasons Americans Like Our Cars So Darn Big," http://www.amptoons.com/blog/archives/2006/01/17/top-ten-reasons-americans-like-our-cars-so-darn-big/.

65. Amanda Griscom, "Rebel with a Cause," *Grist*, 21 May 2003, http://www.grist.org/news/maindish/2003/05/21/cause/index.html.

66. Alas (a blog), "Top Ten Reason Why Americans Like Our Cars So Darn Big."

67. Paul R. Ehrlich, *The Population Bomb* (Buccaneer Books, 1971), 132, 163–64.

68. Quoted in Christopher C. Horner, "In Gaia We Trust," *National Review Online*, 16 January 2003, http://www.nationalreview.com/comment/comment-horner011 603.asp.

69. Geoffrey T. Holtz, *Welcome to the Jungle: The Why Behind "Generation X"* (St. Martin's Griffin, 1995), 15–16, 48.

70. Walter Truett, "Environmentalist Rift as Everyone Joins, 'Movement' Splits into Factions," *Rocky Mountain News,* 23 December 1989, 53.

71. Telephone interview with Allan Carlson, 14 July 2006.

72. Ibid.

73. Sierra Club, "Sierra Club Population Policies," http://www.sierraclub.org/policy/ conservation/population.asp.

74. Linda Hirshman, "Homeward Bound," *American Prospect*, December 2005, http://www.prospect.org/web/page.ww?section=root&name=ViewWeb&articleId=10659.

75. The Huffington Post, "This Is Why So Many People Hate Feminists," Thread of responses to blog post by Kirsten Powers, 19 June 2006, http://www.huffingtonpost.com/kirsten-powers/this-is-why-so-many-peopl_b_23328.html.

76. "America Addicted to Oil?," News release of Competitive Enterprise Institute, 1 February 2006, http://www.cei.org/gencon/003,05121.cfm.

77. "Study: Ethanol Production Consumes Six Units of Energy to Produce Just One," *Science Daily*, 1 April 2005, http://www.sciencedaily.com/releases/2005/03/05032 9132436.htm.

78. Dennis Avery, "Farming For Ethanol Would Have Serious Consequences For Forests, Food Production," *Environment News*, 1 July 2006, http://www.heartland.org/Article.cfm?artId =19333.

79. Institute for the Analysis of Global Security, "National Security Experts Call to Reduce Dependence on Oil," 11 November 2004, http://www.iags.org/n111 104a.htm.

80. Jeff Jacoby, "Dying for Better Mileage," *Jewish World Review*, 20 July 2001, http:// jewishworldreview.com/jeff/jacoby072001.asp.

81. Bradsher, *High and Mighty: SUVs—The World's Most Dangerous Vehicles and How They Got That Way*, 149.

82. Ibid., 151. "[E]ven though rollovers were rare."
83. Berlau, "Safety Takes a Back Seat," 18–19.
84. Ralph Hoar, "The Real Root Cause of the Ford/ Firestone Tragedy: Why the Public Is Still at Risk," Report of Public Citizen and SafetyForum.com, April 2001, 18, http://www. citizen.org/documents/rootcause.pdf.
85. Berlau, "Safety Takes a Back Seat," 18–19.
86. Ibid.
87. Bradsher, *High and Mighty: SUVs—The World's Most Dangerous Vehicles and How They Got That Way*, 445, note 10.
88. Thomas Sowell, *The Vision of the Anointed: Self-Congratulation As a Basis for Social Policy* (Basic Books, 1995).
89. Ed Regis, "The Doomslayer," *Wired*, February 1997, http://www.wired.com/wired/archive/5.02/ffsimon_pr.html.
90. Paul Ehrlich, "An Ecologist's Perspective on Nuclear Power," *Federation of American Scientists Public Issue Report*, May-June 1978.

CHAPTER FIVE: **Reagan Was Right: Forests Cause Pollution**

1. Gillian Shepherd and Marian Betancourt, *What's in the Air?: The Complete Guide to Seasonal and Year-Round Airborne Allergens* (Pocket Books, 2002), 39–40, 59.
2. Ibid., 39.
3. Ibid., 36–37.
4. Ibid, 28–30.
5. "The Mendacity Index," *Washington Monthly*, September 2003, http://www.washington monthly.com/features/2003/0309.mendacity-index.
6. Warren T. Brookes, "Clean Air: Killer Trees vs. Family Cars," *Detroit News*, 29 January 1990; also available in Thomas J. Bray, ed., *Unconventional Wisdom: The Best of Warren Brookes* (Pacific Research Institute, 1997), 216–18.
7. Ronald Reagan, "Pollution," Radio broadcasts of August 1975, in Kiron K. Skinner, Annelise Anderson, and Martin Anderson, eds., *Reagan's Path to Victory: The Shaping of Ronald Reagan's Vision* (Free Press, 2004), 44–49.
8. Ronald Reagan, "Interview with Jerry Rankin of the Santa Barbara News-Press," in John Woolley and Gerhard Peters, *The American Presidency Project* (online), http:/www. presidency.ucsb.edu/ws/inex.php?pid=38232.
9. Reagan, "Redwoods," Radio broadcast of 13 April 1977, in Skinner, Anderson, and Anderson, eds., *Reagan's Path to Victory: The Shaping of Ronald Reagan's Vision*, 140–41.
10. Cannon, *Governor Reagan: His Rise to Power* (PublicAffairs, 2003), 177.
11. Reagan, "Redwoods," 140–41.
12. Cannon, *Governor Reagan: His Rise to Power*, 301.
13. Ibid.
14. Larry Tye, "Trees Called Factor in Urban Pollution," *Boston Globe*, 16 September 1988, 10.
15. Ibid.
16. Brookes, "Clean Air: Killer Trees vs. Family Cars."
17. The Geological Society of London, "Trees Cause Pollution After All—Reagan Vindicated," 11 January 2001, http://www.geolsoc.org.uk/template.cfm?name=Reaganright.

18. Andrew Bridges, "Here We Go Again!", CBSNews.com, 17 March 2003, http://www.cbsnews.com/stories/2003/03/17/tech/main544188.shtml.
19. Anna Gosline, "New Trees Cancel out Air Pollution Cuts," *NewScientist*, 17 October 2004, http://www.newscientist.com/article.ns?id=dn6526.
20. "Trees Have a Part in Big-City Smog, EPA Confirms," *San Jose Mercury News*, 12 May 1989, 2A.
21. Telephone interview with Joel Schwartz, 8 August 2006.
22. James Bovard, *Feeling Your Pain: The Explosion and Abuse of Government Power in the Clinton-Gore Years* (St. Martin's Press, 2000), 230.
23. "Clinton Backs Gore, Browner, Approves Air Rule Proposals," *Livestock Weekly*, 10 July 1997, http://www.livestockweekly.com/papers/97/07/10/10airrule.html.
24. Bovard, *Feeling Your Pain: The Explosion and Abuse of Government Power in the Clinton-Gore Years*, 230.
25. Interview with Schwartz.
26. Ibid.
27. Hillary Rodham Clinton, "Time to Take the Next Step to Clean the Air We Breathe," *Staten Island Advance*, 25 May 2001, available at http://clinton.senate.gov/speeches/010525_oped.html.
28. Princeton University, "Study: Emission of Smog Ingredients from Trees Is Increasing Rapidly," News release, 27 September 2004, http://www.princeton.edu/pr/news/04/q3/0927-trees.htm.
29. "Wily Coyote Captured in Central Park," CBSNews.com, 22 March 2006, http://www.cbsnews.com/stories/2006/03/22/ap/national/mainD8GGSVC00.shtml.
30. John Jahoda, "The Return of the Wild," *Bridgewater Review*, December 1999, http:// www.bridgew.edu/NewsEvnt/BridRev/Archives/99Dec/wild.htm.
31. Samuel R. Staley, "The 'Vanishing Farmland' Myth and the Smart-Growth Agenda," *Reason Public Policy Institute Policy Brief*, January 2000, http://www.reason.org/pb12.pdf.
32. Jane S. Shaw, "Nature in the Suburbs," in Jane S. Shaw and Ronald D. Utt, eds., *A Guide to Smart Growth: Shattering Myths, Providing Solutions* (Heritage Foundation, 2000), 32.
33. Pacific Research Institute, 2005 Index of Leading Environmental Indicators, http://www. pacificresearch.org/pub/sab/enviro/05_enviroindex/35_forests.html.
34. John Roach, "Studies Measure Capacity of 'Carbon Sinks,'" *National Geographic*, 21 June 2001 http://news.nationalgeographic.com/news/2001/06/0621_carbonsinks.html.
35. Jeff Wheelwright, "Captive Wilderness," *Discover*, August 2006, 42.
36. Jay Baird Callicott, "Contemporary Criticisms of the Received Wilderness Idea," Paper submitted to US Forest Service, 2000, available at http://www.wilderness.net/library/documents/Callicott_1-4.pdf#search='wilderness%20and%20ethnocentric'.
37. Alston Chase, *Playing God in Yellowstone: The Destruction of America's First National Park* (Atlantic Monthly Press, 1986), 95.
38. Ibid., 111.
39. Matthew Klingle and Joseph E. Taylor III, "Caste from the Past," *Grist*, 8 March 2006, http://www.grist.org/comments/soapbox/2006/03/08/klingle/.
40. Sierra Club, "John Muir Exhibit," http://www.sierraclub.org/john%5Fmuir%5Fexhibit/.

41. Carl Pope and Paul Rauber, *Strategic Ignorance: Why the Bush Administration Is Recklessly Destroying a Century of Environmental Progress* (Sierra Club, 2004), 12–13.
42. Carl P. Russell, "Coordination of Conservation Programs," *Regional Review*, January-February 1941, available at http://www.cr.nps.gov/history/online_books/regional_review/vol6-1-2e.htm.
43. Robert H. Nelson, *Public Lands and Private Rights: The Failure of Scientific Management* (Rowan & Littlefield, 1995), 48.
44. Pope and Rauber, *Strategic Ignorance: Why the Bush Administration Is Recklessly Destroying a Century of Environmental Progress*, 38.
45. Joan Barron, "Judge Declares 'Roadless Rule' Illegal," *Casper Star-Tribune*, 16 July 2003, http://www.casperstartribune.net/articles/2003/07/16/news/wyoming/8eae0898c8b88a7868121d4ce9dd3a9b.txt.
46. Natural Resources Defense Council, "The National Forest 'Roadless Area' Rule," http:// www.nrdc.org/land/forests/qroadless.asp.
47. Bill Clinton, "Our Forests May Be on a Road to Ruin," *Los Angeles Times*, 8 August 2004, available at http://www.cincypost.com/2004/08/09/clint080904.html.
48. "Clinton Preserves Pristine Roadless National Forests," Environment News Service, 5 January 2001, http://forests.org/archive/america/prrdnatf.htm.
49. Montanans for Multiple Use, "Public Access Issues," http://www.mtmultipleuse.org/public_access/public_lands_issues.htm.
50. Bonner R. Cohen, *The Green Wave: Environmentalism and its Consequences* (Capital Research Center, 2006), 94–95.
51. Ibid.
52. Ibid., 84.
53. Kimberley Strassel, "Owls of Protest," *Wall Street Journal*, 19 October 2005, A12.
54. Cohen, *The Green Wave: Environmentalism and its Consequences*, 85.
55. Ibid., 99
56. Robert H. Nelson, "Forest Fires Scorch Seven Million Acres," *Environment and Climate News*, November 2000, http://www.heartland.org/archives/environment/nov00/ fires.htm.
57. Government Accountability Office, Wildland Fires: Forest Service and BLM Need Better Information and a Systemic Approach for Assessing the Risks of Environmental Effects," No. 04–705, June 2004, http://www.gao.gov/htext/d04705.html.
58. John N. Maclean, *Fire and Ashes: On the Front Lines of American Wildfire* (Henry Holt, 2003), 211–12.
59. Pope and Rauber, *Strategic Ignorance: Why the Bush Administration Is Recklessly Destroying a Century of Environmental Progress*, 89.
60. Robert H. Nelson, "Fires By Design," *Washington Post*, 9 August 2000, A25.
61. Cohen, *The Green Wave: Environmentalism and its Consequences*, 113.
62. Cathy Nikkel, "Deer Collisions Cost Millions," AutoMedia.com, available at http://www. advanceautoparts.com/english/youcan/html/dsm/dsm20030101dc.html.
63. Ibid.
64. James A. Swan, "It's Raining Deer," *National Review Online*, 13 January 2001, http://www.nationalreview.com/weekend/outdoors/outdoors-swan011301.shtml.

65. Joel Gay, "First Wolves Killed in Largest Effort Since Alaska Statehood," *Anchorage Daily News*, 30 November 2004, http://www.shns.com/shns/g_index2.cfm?action=detail&pk=WOLFKILL-11-30-04.

66. James R. Dunn, "Wildlife in the Suburbs," *PERC Reports*, September 1999, http://www. perc.org/publications/percreports/sept1999/suburbs.php.

67. Andrew C. Revkin, "Out of Control: Deer Send Ecosystem into Chaos," *New York Times*, 12 November 2002.

68. John J. Ozoga, "Should We Save the Green Barns . . . Or Manage Them," *Deer & Deer Hunting*, March 2006, 31–32.

69. Joel Fawcett, "Don't Curse the Lumberjacks!", *Deer & Deer Hunting*, March 2006, 68.

70. Doug Rose, "Timber Company Blacktail Hunts," *Washington-Oregon Game & Fish,* http://www.wogameandfish.com/hunting/mule-deer-blacktail-deer-hunting/wo_aa075603a/. "Intensively managed private timberlands hold the highest concentrations of blacktailed deer in western Washington."

71. Cohen, *The Green Wave: Environmentalism and Its Consequences*, 96.

72. Samuel A. MacDonald, *The Agony of an American Wilderness: Loggers, Environmentalists, and the Struggle For Control of a Forgotten Forest* (Rowan & Littlefield, 2005).

73. Nelson, *Public Lands and Private Rights: The Failure of Scientific Management*, 75–76.

CHAPTER SIX: Hurricane Katrina: Blame It on Dam Environmentalists

1. Congressional Research Service, "The Impact of Hurricane Katrina on Biological Resources," *CRS Report for Congress*, 18 October 2005.

2. Timothy Dwyer, Jaqueline L. Salmon, and Dan Eggen, Katrina Take Environmental Toll," *Washington Post*, 7 September 2005, A01.

3. Michael Fumento, "Toss Out the New Orleans 'Toxic Soup' Myth," *Human Events*, 3 February 2006, http://www.fumento.com/pollution/toxic.html.

4. Al Gore, Speech at the Sierra Summit, 9 September 2005, http://www.sierra-club.org/ pressroom/speeches/2005-09-09algore.asp.

5. "NOAA Reviews Record-Setting 2005 Atlantic Hurricane Season," *NOAA News*, 13 April 2006, http://www.noaanews.noaa.gov/stories2005/s2540.htm.

6. Al Gore, Speech at the Sierra Summit.

7. Testimony of William Gray, US Senate Committee on Environment and Public Works, 28 September 2005, http://epw.senate.gov/hearing_statements.cfm?id=246768.

8. "Now What," *Popular Mechanics*, March 2006, http://www.popularmechanics.com/science/earth/2315076.html?page=&c=y.

9. Robert Kunzig, "Hurricanes Intensify Global-Warming Debate," *Discover*, January 2006, 20.

10. Hillary Rodham Clinton, E-mail and web posting, 20 April 2006, http://www.hillaryclinton.com/email/20060420/.

11. Robert Kunzig, "Hurricanes Intensify Global-Warming Debate," *Discover*, 20.

12. Barack Obama, Speech at Robert F. Kennedy Human Rights Award ceremony, 16 November 2005, http://obama.senate.gov/speech/051116-remarks_of_senator_barack_ obama_at_the_robert_f_kennedy_human_rights_award_ceremony/index.html.

13. Bruce Babbitt, *Cities in the Wilderness: A New Vision of Land Use in America* (Island Press, 2005), 48.

14. Ibid.

15. Robert Stokes, "Environmentalist Deal that Cannot Be Refused: Greenmail," *Wheat Life*, August-September 2005, http://www.wheatlifemagazine.com/08_905/pg08_0805.pdf.

16. *Gibbons v. Ogden*, 22 US 1, http://www.tourolaw.edu/patch/Gibbons/.

17. Statement of Joseph A. Towers, Hearing of the US House of Representatives Committee on Resources NEPA Task Force, November 10, 2005, available at http://www.washingtonwatchdog.org/rtk/documents/cong_hearings/house/109/househearing109_24546.html.

18. Ralph Vartabedian and Peter Pae, "A Barrier That Could Have Been," *Los Angeles Times*, 9 September 2005.

19. Ivor van Heerden and Mike Bryan: *The Storm: What Went Wrong and Why During Hurricane Katrina—the Inside Story from One Louisiana Scientist* (Viking, 2006), 272.

20. Save Our Wetlands, "The Creation of Save Our Wetlands and its Early Legal Battles," http://www.saveourwetlands.org/edenislehistory.htm.

21. Statement of Towers.

22. Michael Tremoglie, "New Orleans: A Green Genocide," FrontPageMag, 8 September 2005, http://www.frontpagemag.com/Articles/ReadArticle.asp?ID=19418.

23. John Berlau, "Greens vs. Levees," *National Review Online*, 8 September 2005, http:// www.nationalreview.com/comment/berlau200509080824.asp.

24. Save Our Wetlands, http://www.saveourwetlands.org/hbpnotsaved.html; Center for Progressive Reform, "Broken Levees: Why They Failed," 12, http://www.progressivereform.org/articles/CPR_Special_Levee_Report.pdf.

25. Vartabedian and Pae, "A Barrier That Could Have Been."

26. Van Heerden and Bryan: *The Storm: What Went Wrong and Why During Hurricane Katrina—the Inside Story from One Louisiana Scientist*, 273. (Emphasis added.)

27. Sierra Club, "Blaming Environmentalists for Katrina: What You Should Know!", News Release, 22 September 2005, http://www.sierraclub.org/pressroom/releases/pr2005-09-13a.asp.

28. Telephone interview with Joe Towers, 17 August 2006.

29. Beurmond Banville, "St. John River's Rare Furbish Lousewort under Review by Feds," *Bangor Daily News*, 13 August 2005, C1.

30. Ronald Reagan, "Endangered Species," Radio broadcast of 6 July 1977, in Kiron K. Skinner, Annelise Anderson, and Martin Anderson, eds., *Reagan, in His Own Hand* (Touchstone, 2002), 330.

31. *TVA v. Hill*, 437 US 153, Footnote 7 in majority opinion.

32. Renè Dubos, *The Wooing of Earth* (Charles Scribner's Sons, 1980), 77.

33. Franklin D. Roosevelt, Speech dedicating the Boulder (Hoover) Dam, 30 September 1935, http://xroads.virginia.edu/~1930s/DISPLAY/hoover/fdr.html.

34. Ibid.

35. Ibid.

36. Jacques Leslie, *Deep Water: The Epic Struggle Over Dams, Displaced People, and the Environment* (Farrar, Strauss, and Giraux, 2005), 345.

37. Ibid., 347.

38. Ibid., 3–5.
39. Ira Boudway, "Earth Be Dammed," *Salon*, 23 September 2005, http://archive. salon.com/books/int/2005/09/23/leslie/index_np.html.
40. Babbitt, *Cities in the Wilderness: A New Vision of Land Use in America*, 133–34.
41. Derrick Jensen, *A Language Older than Words* (Context Books, 2000), 50.
42. Babbitt, *Cities in the Wilderness: A New Vision of Land Use in America*, 52–53.
43. US Army Corps of Engineers, "Upper Mississippi River Comprehensive Plan," http://www.mvp.usace.army.mil/fl%5Fdamage%5Freduct/?pageid=586.
44. "Lessons from the Flood," *St. Louis Post-Dispatch*, 18 July 1993, 2B.
45. Gerald E. Galloway Jr., "Floodplain Management: A Present and a 21st Century Imperative," *Journal of Contemporary Water Research and Education*, vol. 97, 5–6, http://www.ucowr.siu.edu/updates/pdf/V97_A2.pdf.
46. "And Never the Twain Shall Tweet," *Urban Legends Reference Pages*, 5 October 2002, http://www.snopes.com/quotes/twain.asp.
47. Michael Grunwald and Susan B. Glasser, "The Slow Drowning of New Orleans," 9 October 2005, A01, http://www.washingtonpost.com/wp-dyn/content/article/2005/10/08/AR2005100801458_pf.html.
48. Mark Twain, *Life on the Mississippi* (Bantam Books, 1990), 138.
49. Ibid.
50. Ibid., 139.
51. Ibid., Appendix B, 295–99.
52. Ibid., 142.
53. "Corps Proposes $4.1B Budget in 2001, Plans to Upgrade Recreation Facilities," *Corps Report*, 9 February 2000.
54. Ibid.
55. Bill Clinton, "Statement on Water Resources Development Act," The White House, 17 August 1999.
56. "Groups Sue to Halt Wetlands Levee Project," *Biloxi Sun Herald*, 5 October 1996, C5.
57. Bob Anderson, "Groups Sue to Stop Levee-Raising Program," *Advocate* (Baton Rouge), 3 October 1996, 1A.
58. James Bovard, *Feeling Your Pain: The Explosion and Abuse of Government Power in the Clinton-Gore Years* (St. Martin's Press, 2000), 75–76.
59. Ronald D. Utt, "The Army Corps of Engineers: Reallocating Its Spending to Offset Reconstruction Costs in New Orleans," *Heritage Foundation Backgrounder*, 4 November 2005, http://www.heritage.org/Research/Budget/bg1892.cfm.
60. Matt Crenson, Government Fulfills Few Katrina Promises," *Yahoo News*, 19 August 2006, http://news.yahoo.com/s/ap/20060819/ap_on_go_pr_wh/katrina_promises.
61. Telephone interview with Daniel Canfield, December 2005; quoted in John Berlau, "Dam Environmentalists," *Weekly Standard*, 16 January 2006, 16–18.
62. Van Heerden and Bryan, *The Storm: What Went Wrong and Why During Hurricane Katrina—the Inside Story from One Louisiana Scientist*, 169.
63. Dubos, *The Wooing of Earth*, 96.
64. James Carville and Paul Begala, *Take It Back: Our Party, Our Country, Our Future* (Simon & Schuster, 2006), 301.

65. Ann Coulter, *Godless: The Church of Liberalism* (Crown Forum, 2006), 6.
66. Gregg Easterbrook, *A Moment on the Earth: The Coming Age of Environmental Optimism* (Viking, 1995), 335.
67. "The Plowboy Interview," *Mother Earth News*, November-December 1977, http:// www. motherearthnews.com/library/1977_November_December/Plowboy_Interview.
68. Dianne Feinstein, "Statement on Proposals to Tear Down O'Shaughnessy Dam," 18 May 2005, feinstein.senate.gov/05releases/r-hetchhetch2.pdf.

CHAPTER SEVEN: Our Unhealthy Future under Environmentalism

1. M. Scot Skinner, "McDonald House Statue Is Vandalized with Graffiti," *Arizona Daily Star*, 20 September 2001, 1.
2. Vanessa Grigoriadis, "The Rise & Fall of the Eco-Radical Underground," *Rolling Stone*, 28 July 2006, http://www.rollingstone.com/politics/story/110 35255/the_rise_fall_of_the_ecoradical_underground/1.
3. Ibid.
4. Brad Knickerbocker, "Backstory: Eco-vigilantes: All in 'The Family?'", *Christian Science Monitor*, 30 January 2006, http://www.csmonitor.com/2006/ 0130/p20s01-sten.html.
5. Grigoriadis, "The Rise & Fall of the Eco-Radical Underground."
6. Ibid.
7. North American Animal Liberation Press Office, "Frequently Asked Questions about the North American Animal Liberation Press Office, http://www.ani-malliberationpressoffice. org/faq.htm.
8. Ibid.
9. Randall Sullivan, "Hunting America's Most Wanted Eco-Terrorist," *Rolling Stone*, 12 December 2002, http://www.rollingstone.com/politics/story/11034035/ hunting_americas_most_wanted_ecoterrorist.
10. Telephone Interview with Tom Randall, 23 August 2006.
11. Steven Best, "Behind the Mask: Uncovering the Animal Liberation Front," http://www.drstevebest.org/papers/exerpts/TOFF/Behind_The_Mask_p2.php.
12. Robert B. Swift, "Unusual Coalition Backs Ecoterrorism Legislation," *Pocono Record*, 12 April 2006, http://www.poconorecord.com/apps/pbcs.dll/ article?AID=/20060412/ NEWS/604120341/-1/NEWS.
13. "Governor Signs Ecoterrorism Bill into Law," Office of the Governor of Pennsylvania, News Release, 14 April 2006, http://www.state.pa.us/papower/ cwp/view.asp?Q=4517 90&A=11.
14. Swift, "Unusual Coalition Backs Ecoterrorism Legislation."
15. Quoted in David Almasi, "The Radical Spectrum: Environmentalists Push the Envelope to Push Their Cause," *National Policy Analysis*, April 2002, http://www. nationalcenter. org/NPA403.html.
16. Neil Hrab, "Greenpeace, Earth First!, PETA," *Organization Trends*, March 2004, 4, http://www.capitalresearch.org/pubs/pdf/03_04_OT.pdf.
17. Dave Foreman, *Confessions of an Eco-Warrior* (Harmony Books, 1991), 151–52.
18. Ibid., 153.
19. Ibid., back cover.
20. Profile of Earth First!, DiscoverTheNetworks.org. http://www.discoverthenet-work.org/ groupProfile.asp?grpid=7229.

21. Richard Lacayo, "A Moment of Silence," *Time*, 8 May 1995, 42.
22. Robert F. Kennedy Jr., Natural Resources Defense Council fund-raising mail solicitation, circa spring 2006.
23. Rodger Schlickeisen, "Heroes, Villains and the Endangered Species Act," *Defenders*, winter 2006, http://www.defenders.org/defendersmag/issues/winter06/view.html.
24. Ian Hoffman, "Gore: Will We Destroy Earth? It's a Moral Issue," *Oakland Tribune*, 7 April 2006.
25. Foreman, *Confessions of an Eco-Warrior*, 28.
26. Wildands Project, "What We Do," http://www.twp.org/cms/page1090.cfm.
27. Ronald Baily, "Precautionary Tale," *Reason*, April 1999, http://www.reason.com/9904/fe.rb.precautionary.shtml.
28. "Health and the Environment in the Former Soviet Union Part I," *Environmental Review*, September 1995, http://www.environmentalreview.org/vol02/feschba.html.
29. See description at http://prfamerica.org/CEI-CPC.html.
30. Karl Marx, "Malthusianism and the 'Struggle for Existence,'" Letter of 27 June 1870, in Ronald L. Meek, ed., *Marx and Engels on the Population Bomb* (Ramparts Press, 1971), 196.
31. Friedrich Engels, "The Myth of Overpopulation," Essay of 1844, in Ibid., 63.
32. Renè Dubos, *The Wooing of Earth* (Charles Scribner's Sons, 1980), 86.
33. Ibid., 81.

Index